YOUR EX-FACTOR

YOUR EX-FACTOR
overcome heartbreak & build a better life

Stephan B. Poulter PhD

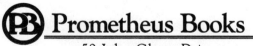 Prometheus Books

59 John Glenn Drive
Amherst, New York 14228-2119

Published 2009 by Prometheus Books

Inquiries should be addressed to
Prometheus Books
59 John Glenn Drive
Amherst, New York 14228–2119
VOICE: 716–691–0133, ext. 210
FAX: 716–691–0137
WWW.PROMETHEUSBOOKS.COM

13 12 11 10 09   5 4 3 2 1

Library of Congress Cataloging-in-Publication Data

Your ex-factor : overcome heartbreak and build a better life / by Stephan B. Poulter
   p. cm.
Includes bibliographical references and index.
ISBN 978–1–59102–724–9 (pbk. : alk. paper)
   1. Divorce. 2. Divorce—Psychological aspects. 3. Divorced people—Psychology.
4. Man-woman relationships. I. Title.

HQ814.P677—2009
155.6/43—dc22

2009013241

Printed in the United States on acid-free paper

To:

Madison, Jonathan, and Lisa, who always have found a way to encourage me when I needed it the most.

My parents, Peter Brett and Charlotte Elizabeth, whose marriage shaped and changed my life.

I want to thank all the couples who have gone through divorce, heartbreak, and shattering endings and have generously shared their love stories. There isn't enough space here to acknowledge all the people—professionally and personally—who helped me create this book over the last five decades. I started writing this book when I was a child, and it is an ongoing process.

OTHER BOOKS BY THE AUTHOR

The Mother Factor:
How Your Mother's Emotional Legacy Impacts Your Life

The Father Factor:
How Your Father's Legacy Impacts Your Career

Father Your Son:
How to Become the Father You've Always Wanted to Be

Mending the Broken Bough:
Restoring the Promise of the Mother-Daughter Relationship

AUTHOR'S NOTE

All the stories, examples, and voices in this book are derived in part from more than forty-five years of personal, family, professional, research, law enforcement, and life experience. However, the names, places, and other details contained in this book have been altered to protect the privacy and anonymity of the individuals to whom they refer. Therefore, any similarities between the names and stories of the individuals and families described in this book and those individuals known to readers are inadvertent and purely coincidental.

ACKNOWLEDGMENTS

I could write another two volumes for all the people—past and present—who have contributed to the creation of this book. The amount of love, pain, and despair that has been shared with me concerning the topic of "your ex-factor" is stunning and overwhelming. I have never heard such deeply moving stories of marriage, divorce, remarriage, and blended families—and the process of overcoming the disappointment, "heartbreak," and emotional pain of a lost love. Special recognition goes to those souls who have braved the pathway of hope and overcome their despair.

I want to acknowledge my ex-wife, who has taught me many constructive things. I needed every lesson—whether or not I knew it—in order to change and expand my life to become more empathetic, loving, and self-accepting. The never-ending lessons of intimate emotional pain are priceless and life changing for all of us. I also want to thank Linda Greenspan Regan for giving me another invaluable opportunity to create a book that I hope is meaningful. I would have never been able to do it without her excitement, support, and enthusiasm. I also want to thank Julia Wolfe, Lisa Jacobson, and Dr. Barry Weichman for giving freely of their verbal and nonverbal support, wisdom, and insight. I needed every word and idea they shared, and their encouragement to be creative was vital. I want to extend my gratitude to James Myerson for his loving contribution of endorsing and writing the foreword to this book. I want to sincerely thank and acknowledge Madison Wendy and Jonathan Brett for their patience in trying to understand what this book is all about and how it (love) "all" works in our lives.

Your Ex-Factor has a long list of contributors, past and present: George Morales, Charis Ray, Kye and Kathleen Hellmers, Bill and

Mary Klem, Ed Vanderflet, and many others whom I can't mention by name (but you know who you are) and who have had a tremendous impact on this entire process—and on me.

CONTENTS

SECTION III: CHANGING YOUR "EX-FACTOR"

ENDNOTES   279

BIBLIOGRAPHY   285

INDEX   291

FOREWORD

If you are reading this, you are poised to step before a very special looking glass. Instead of showing your physical exterior, the reflection will pass through your skin to places deep inside your heart and soul. You will see some familiar places, some unfamiliar places, and, considering the topic, some uncomfortable and scary places too. Yet these are the places we all must go if we are ever going to heal and create a different today and tomorrow.

The need to feel love and acceptance is fundamental to human happiness. If we feel loved, we have a nearly inexhaustible source of fuel to burn against the intricate and unpredictable maze of challenges and fears that make up our daily lives. An equally powerful *loss* of fuel accompanies the dissolution of an intimate relationship. Making the trip from "running on empty" to "all systems go" is an individual journey. Everyone's itinerary is different, but one of the first things packed in nearly everyone's suitcase is the ex-factor. *We all have an ex-factor.* How did yours happen? Who was he or she? How long ago did you last speak to him or her? Do you still love him or her? The ex-factor isn't based on sexual orientation or preference. All relationships are between two adults consisting of many facets that build an intimate bond. Relationships are challenging, and experiencing a major breakup is never easy.

As adults, how often do we mourn the loss of our dreams? Emotional heartbreak, psychological suffering, and the loss of our childhood dream of enduring love and marriage have a way of wiping out all the remnants of youthful innocence we still hold dear as adults. The world around us, it seems, continues to grow more complicated and, at times, more emotionally painful. In our own lives, the frenetic period between graduation and retirement—when we hope things will be finally simple again—oscillates like a light wave. Work, marriage, children, and, for many, divorce present an ongoing wave of increasing complexity and relentless challenges. The questions that never stop nagging me are: What happened to my marriage? Where did the love of my life go? How did this happen? What could I have done differently? Will I ever feel good again? These questions challenge anyone who has lost or left a love relationship. The emotional waves of life seem to bring us back to this place of introspection.

"It's hard to be simple" is a favorite phrase of one of my mentors. I've come to believe that this is so because of that pesky organ, the brain. With its inherent feature of enabling us to think—and often to overthink—the brain complicates things. When speaking of intimate love relationships, it is even *harder* to be simple and to escape pain. Into the arena with the brain steps the heart, creating a clash of Titans. At the end of the day, my heart aches and my brain obsesses. Who won? My brain says "never" and my heart says "keep going."

When I read the manuscript for *Your Ex-Factor*, I was a newly minted divorcé from a twenty-four-year marriage and the father of two wonderful teenage boys. A recurring thought resonated as I read chapter after chapter: *Yes!* As I read, my own experience of surviving a divorce jumped out at me from the text. I found empathy and clarity of thought on each page, and from that common ground, where the emotion of the heart and the protests of the overthinking brain could coexist. Two and half years into the journey of resolving my ex-factor, I was in a place of greater calm and objectivity than I might have been without this guide.

Wherever you find yourself in your journey when you begin this book, you will find much of yourself and your own experience throughout these pages. Moreover, this book will take you to places you may have yet to visit. You know you need to heal, to find understanding, and to move in the direction of your romantic future. Know simply that you are not the first to feel deep despair, nor will you be the last to make the trip out of the valley of disappointment and pain.

The need to love and the hope *to be loved* are simple, fundamental human drives. Choose to love again, and allow your ex-factor to be just one step along your path to completeness. After you have turned the last page of *Your Ex-Factor*, I feel certain that the eyes looking back in the mirror will seem clearer, brighter, and happier.

Fight on!

James Myerson, father, divorced and single
Fall 2008

SECTION 1

THE BREAKUP—
IN SLOW MOTION

Your power is in your thoughts, and actions, so stay aware. In other words—remember to remember.
—Rhonda Byrne

Chapter 1

HOW DID THIS EVER HAPPEN?

The Process of Breaking Up

We had had problems for years. She threatened to divorce me on a regular basis. This time Tamara wrote me a letter and demanded I move out. I could have prevented this, but this pattern of coming and going had been our style since we dated. I don't want to lose my family or be a failure.
—Matt, age fifty-six,
married for twenty-eight years, divorced

We dated for seven years. We were engaged for three years and lived together for two, and he left me. I knew we had issues but I always thought we would work them out. We went to therapy and I thought we were making progress. Then I found out Brad had an affair with his personal trainer at the gym. I am still devastated—six months later!
—Tracy, age thirty-nine, single and dating again

THE ENDING

Picking up this book will be the beginning of a great journey. The trip will require of you things that you might not expect but that you truly need. It will start with your complete honesty and end with finding within yourself your own personal truth and courage. You picked up this book because you have had an intense relationship crisis, a traumatic breakup, an unforeseen loss, and/or a great disappointment in your adult romantic life. But regardless of how devastated, emotionally betrayed, bitter, angry, hateful of the opposite sex, and hopeless you feel, deep down in your heart you still believe in relationships and their curative nature and power.

Intimate relationships are the gold standard by which we measure success or disappointment in our lives. Business and careers will come and go, but nothing is more timeless than the experience of a solid marriage, a lifelong partner, and a loving relationship. A scholar once said that your life is the summation of all your relationships. I would also like to add it is the ongoing summation of all your intimate love relationships. Regardless of the despair, fear, and disappointment that you have experienced, you can recover your sense of well-being and build a new relationship life that better fits who and what you are today.

Despite the disappointment, embarrassment, and heartbreaking pain, we cannot get away from the fact that *love relationships matter.* We all know it, and that truth never changes. We never truly stop attempting to re-create deep emotional attachments when relationships end. Ironically, it is in trying to recover and overcome the heartbreak that we often set up the roadblocks that will damage our future love relationships. *The underlying problem and crisis in not resolving your ex-factor issues is the "pain" will continue to persist in your life.* The key is not to take the prior disappointments and bitterness wrapped up in your relationship with your ex-husband/wife/lover with you into your next intimate relationship. You can't bring your ex-husband on your honeymoon. It will never work. Again, you know this—but how do you stop recycling your pain and disappointment? This question will be repeatedly addressed, examined from all possible perspectives, and answered and explained thoroughly throughout this book. The short answer is that you can stop making the same self-defeating choices; creating the same painful attachments; and getting caught up in the same old patterns of abuse and loveless, codependent romantic connections.

Never before has the concept of the "ex" been so significant to families, children, new marriages, and future partners. According to a November 2007 article appearing in *Time* magazine, approximately 66 to 70 percent of all American families are some type of blended family combination.[1] Blended families are those in which children live with one biological parent part of the time. Being a blended family has nothing to with marital status but rather the birth parents not living together with their biological or adopted children. Second marriages, two adults cohabituating, stepchildren, no new children, new wives, new husbands, and in-laws are all impacted by this growing social family phenomenon. Overcoming your heartbreak is essential to the possibility of creating future intimate relationships. Divorce or emotional rejection by a lover isn't the death sentence it once was to future intimate relationship potential. Now, emotional despair and disappointment can be catalysts for a more fulfilling relationship future and for creating the type of family that you desire. The emotional and psychological ability to move forward in your life after heartbreak is as important as your physical health. The ending of a relationship isn't the final stop in your romantic adult life, but rather a fork in the road of your life. In today's world, you have romantic choices and new opportunities that once were not even considered possible.

EX-FACTOR FACTS

An article in the January 24, 2008, edition of *Time* magazine states, "Married people live longer and are healthier throughout those extra (over 62) years; Studies have linked marriage to lower rates of cardiovascular disease, cancer, respiratory disease and mental illness; Marriage helps both spouses cope better with stress, though men benefit more than women."[2] There is no doubt—medically, psychologically, or biologically—that we are wired for emotional attachment and intimate loving relationships. Men typically report the highest levels of satisfaction in long-term relationships. Women report being more emotionally content and less anxious in marriage-type love relationships than women who aren't in such relationships. It doesn't take a federal grant or a university research project to know that the opposite holds true for men and women when their love relationships end. The end of any type of romantic relationship is emotionally, mentally, and physically devastating for all parties concerned. No one is spared the rod of emotional pain when a relationship ends in divorce or in broken engagement.

One of the major premises of the ex-factor is that *there is no such thing as a relationship failure.* The fact that your marriage ended doesn't mean you failed as a wife, mother, woman, husband, father, or man. It means that the relationship ran out its natural time line and is now over. Every relationship has a timetable. You will have to draw on tremendous courage and weather severe emotional pain (unfortunate, but it is always present) to process the relationship and move forward with your life. *Endings don't equal failure!* Failure is the inability to realize that your prior belief system about relationships and how you operated in them needs to be expanded, changed, and reevaluated. Relationships change, and this is a natural process, like all things in life.

Endings are endings—nothing more or less—and it is what you ascribe to them that is paramount. The amount of shame and guilt you feel, as well as your prior relationship history, play a very large role in your present-day struggles and grief. Your current breakup can reactivate feelings of loss and rejection you've felt your whole life. Remember the heartbreak from your first romantic crush? It was a big event then, and heartbreaks today are no different. In fact, relationship endings are *cumulative* when we ignore them and carry them with us into our next intimate relationship. Do you *really* know what you have accumulated along your romantic path? The potential of your future relationships hinges on your ability, insight, courage, and desire to separate your past from your present. Your emotional, psychological, and physical health are greatly impacted by your ability to keep the past from recurring.[3] You are the only one who can determine whether your ex-factor will be a positive legacy or an ongoing drama/tension–filled soap opera. You *don't* want to be the star in your own soap. You don't want the emotional drama, arguing, and raging conversations with your ex in front of the kids or in front of your new partner. If this type of drama is happening, you are bringing old behaviors from your past relationship endings and disappointments into your current romantic experience.

Relationships can end abruptly, slowly, suddenly, or traumatically—for reasons that husbands, wives, and lovers often ignore, deny, or avoid until the relationship has dissolved or "blown up." It is the emotional and psychological damage caused by these tragic endings that is so problematic and so difficult for adults to fathom. The goal of this entire discussion is to help you learn to resolve your traumatic relationship endings and move your current or future relationship forward in the direction that you desire. Recycling old relationship material every time you meet someone of significant romantic interest is self-defeating and pointless. It is extremely problematic, emotionally frustrating, and nauseating to continually repeat your personal history of romantic encounters. Unfortunately, replaying old relationship patterns is very common.

EMOTIONAL SEVERITY

It is the severe emotional toll of a marriage (any type of romantic relationship) ending combined with a three-year bloodbath divorce that leaves all the participants psychologically reeling for years. The couple ends up spending thousands of dollars arguing over who gets the rosebushes, the airline miles, and the kids on Christmas and Thanksgiving. This type of divorce only exacerbates the deep emotional heartbreak of the parties involved. The ending can also be one of a long-term relationship that ends prior to marriage; the ex-lover might be a forty-two-year-old woman who wants children—and feels like that prospect ended when her partner walked out the door with his new girlfriend. The loss of both a dream and a partner creates an immediate sense of hopelessness and profound disappointment. Yet the unresolved residual effect of such an enormous disappointment is generally dismissed and/or minimized (we will expand on this topic throughout the book). This unresolved disappointment then becomes the primary cause of frustration and pain in future relationships.

The actual ending of a relationship is usually shocking for all parties involved. Yet there are very clear patterns, unresolved issues, and "clues" that occur over time to undermine a relationship and contribute to its tragic ending. These elements of the relationship breakup create a deep sense of disappointment in both partners. The loss of the relationship, the dreams, and the partnership become the fabric of your disappointment.

WHAT IS THE EX-FACTOR?

Now that we have discussed how relationship endings create your ex-factor, it is important to clearly identify what the ex-factor is. *The accumulation of lost dreams, broken promises, disillusionment, regret, emotional setbacks, disenchantment with past romantic partners, and unrealistic expectations all make up your ex-factor.* All these elements—acting singly or together—are impairments to future satisfaction and fulfillment in relationships.

The length of the love relationship isn't an issue when coping with the immense power of your ex-factor and the residual effects and myriad feelings it creates. The sheer horror of losing the "love of your life"—whether through divorce, a broken engagement, or the termination of an exclusive long-term dating relationship—is all the same: It is *devastating*. Breakups have no regard for sexual orientation, race, education, socioeconomic status, gender, or age. No one is exempt from the cycle of despair, hopelessness, and anger created by a romantic breakup. It is for good reason that divorce is considered one of the most important events that an adult will ever encounter.[4] In fact, the only thing considered more psychologically traumatic than divorce (or a divorce-like breakup) is the loss of a child. You don't need to experience death to know that after the breakup of a romantic relationship, you are living through your own emotional funeral. When you look in the mirror and don't recognize yourself, that is one of the signs that you are in the process of a major life trauma and change. This recognition is a key to becoming aware that your personal, intimate, family, and social life is in the process of transformation.

WHY SO MUCH PAIN?

The emotional roller coaster of despair and loss of stability is so traumatic that those experiencing it often become extremely depressed and anxious, emotionally numb, or physically sick. The sense of abandonment, rejection, and despair from a broken heart is so profound that some people foolishly consider the option of suicide. The psychology behind suicidal thinking is the hope of escaping the extreme emotional grief and hopelessness that seems never ending. But that pain will end. *However, in the meantime, many people underestimate the powerful impact of a breakup on both partners.* For instance, the birth of a child is usually the result of the powerful bond of romantic love consummated in the special connection of creating a life. It is in the context of an intimate love relationship that all personal insecurities, fears, emotional strength, weaknesses, positive and negative feelings, wishes, and conscious and unconscious hopes are played out. Your entire life is transformed in the romantic bond and the context of a supportive, loving relationship.

But many times the relationship you were involved in—once it is over—seems like it wasn't anything other than a huge disappointment and a lie. That loss, which touches your heart, is palpable.

Life is a collection of different relationships—professional, social, familial, and intimate. The intimate connection is the ultimate relationship that we all crave and desire. It is the only place that we can be completely, totally, and fully ourselves, without fear of judgment. Intimate relationships are the emotional foundation for how we function in the outside world. When these significant bonds end, the psychological fallout can be severe. This helps to explain why we have such powerful emotional responses when these relationships end.

There is nothing in your life that isn't affected by your adult romantic relationships, marriages, and/or emotionally significant bonds (i.e., long-term friendships). On a personal level, nearly everything is enmeshed in that experience. The birth of your children, your career, your choice of pets, your accomplishments together—all of these were shared by that person who is now *gone.*

The desire for a loving, supportive life partner in an enduring relationship is as natural as breathing. The problem is that the disappointment created by this quest leaves millions of adults isolated, lonely, and feeling like "damaged goods." One question that my clients, friends, and colleagues repeatedly ask is: *Will I ever feel good again?* The short answer is yes—and the long answer is also yes. After a relationship fails, the people involved want to feel better and move forward with their lives—but that is almost impossible if they are emotionally wounded and ignoring all the extenuating factors that are involved (i.e., loss of open communication, anger, loss of sexual intimacy, resentment, loss of respect for your partner). Denial, avoidance, and placing blame only create more problems and complicate issues that make things worse. Throughout this book, we will discuss different ways to stop compounding these problems.

It is in the pursuit of a new love where our exes can become constant roadblocks to our future fulfillment. No one wants his or her ex to be any more of a negative factor than he or she already is. But the residual fallout from such severe disappointment leaves men and women of all ages, circumstances, and education levels emotionally staggered. No one can step over disappointment, betrayal, and hopelessness and pretend it didn't happen. Starting a new relationship in the wake of a divorce or a serious breakup is a guaranteed formula for more emotional pain and suffering. Relationship jumping (going from one love relationship to another with no time in between) is an emotional defense mechanism against feelings of rejection, abandonment, and disappointment. This defensive style of avoidance is commonly referred to as a "rebound" relationship. Men tend to fall into this relationship jumping dynamic more often than women. In fact, women often withdraw from the relationship scene for too long. Neither style is particularly productive or curative to emotional heartbreak and creating a different relationship future.

THE ENDING

The horror of losing our dreams, our lover, and our support system is actually the opportunity for a big change. It is in the process of reviewing, learning, questioning, and taking responsibility for our role in these monumental breakups that we find our way out of the valley of despair. It takes time, support, insight, and courage to move forward. It is important to remember that in every intimate relationship—or, for that matter, any relationship—that we are responsible for 100 percent of our 50 percent of the relationship. *You own 100 percent of your 50.* No one is responsible for the other person's actions or feelings, regardless of what has been said, done, or misunderstood. You can have an influence, impact, and effect—but you aren't responsible for all of the problems in your love relationship. *You just aren't. It is simply impossible.* There is a beginning and ending point for our responsibility, but many times we become so emotionally desperate and scared that we will try to fix or do anything to keep our potential ex-partner around. We all naturally hate this sense of desperation and panic within ourselves, but it is understandable and very common in most breakups and divorces.

Everyone knows that the inner quality of life is directly related to how well our personal relationships are functioning. When you experience a major breakup, it is as if the foundation of your life has been torn out. The loss of companionship, your best friend, lover, partner, and all the other nouns that can best convey your emotional connection are no longer part of your everyday life. It is these losses that cause us to start feeling desperate, disappointed, depressed, and angry. Many times, to survive the breakup, we drink the drink of anger. This is a short-term solution to a long-term problem. People who get accustomed to being angry, raging, and hostile toward nearly everyone aren't able to process their range of feelings and emotions about relationships. *Holding on to anger is like drinking rat poison and hoping it will kill your ex.* Ultimately, anger only kills—or severely damages—its primary source: *you.*

Previously high-functioning professionals; career-minded men and women; intelligent adults; mothers, fathers, and grandparents suddenly find themselves thinking, saying, doing things, and acting in ways that they normally never would. Take as an example the two vignettes at the beginning of this chapter. Matt lost twenty-five pounds in one month and stopped eating for days at a time. He decided that he wouldn't eat until Tamara returned. Matt ultimately had to be hospitalized for an eating/starvation disorder. And one night after having a few glasses of wine, Tracy decided to drive over to her ex's house and confront him at 3 o'clock in the morning (nothing very good happens after alcohol or mind-altering drugs are involved in this type of discussion). Unfortunately, Tracy drove her car through his garage door when she arrived at his house and was arrested for drunk driving. Neither Matt nor Tracy was behaving in the positive, emotionally mature, stable manner they normally did—though they eventually behaved that way again. They both told me they thought they were losing their minds and couldn't believe how "awful" they felt. The sense of panic and sudden emotional emptiness was almost unbearable for both of them. These types of feelings, experiences, and behaviors are the foundation of your ex-factor.

The emotional pain from the loss of a partner is in most cases mind-boggling and, in some, horrific. No one needs to tell you that your ex-lover, partner, husband, wife, or significant other wasn't right or good for you. All you want to know is will you ever feel happy again? Will your world ever stop feeling emotionally bare, cold, and overwhelming? When will the pain stop? The idea of living and thriving— feeling excitement, joy, love, hope, and contentment—seems like a lost chapter in your life. Gone is your life's dream, never to return again. You feel you are too old, too hurt, to date or to fall in love again. In many cases the idea of feeling good or normal or romantically fulfilled seems impossible.

You have experienced the empty, hollow feeling of seeing your significant love relationship blow up and disintegrate before your eyes. Because of this, you may have lost or gained weight, moved, changed jobs, and considered changing your approach to—and belief in—personal intimate relationships. Though many acknowledge the intense emotional pain, panic, despair, and hopelessness that can be engendered by a romantic breakup, living through it is something else entirely. And you don't have to be formally married to know and experience the despair as described above. For the sake of this discussion, "marriage" and "divorce" are not used as literal terms. You can be emotionally married to someone for fifteen years and never have a formal marriage ceremony. It is all about the emotional connection and partnership: having children, living together, building a home, sleeping next to each other every night for years, taking vacations, celebrating birthdays, mourning at funerals—in short, sharing a life with someone. This is the stuff and material that makes up a marriage—whether or not on paper—that binds us together.

The word "divorce" is so commonly used that its true impact is many times dismissed or trivialized. Just because divorce is more socially acceptable and unfortunately occurs more frequently than it did thirty-five years ago doesn't diminish its true destructive effect on us. Divorce is a private emotional hell that both partners feel when embarking on the long process of creating separate lives. The time leading up to the breakup (see below for the warning signs), all the relationship issues, and the people (children, relatives, friends, parents) involved are as varied as the people involved in the heart-breaking stories of partners, formerly a unit, now doing painful and destructive things to each other. It is important to remember that no two divorce stories are the same, although some of the common emotional problems, mental distress, and other issues that occur are often similar.

MISREADING THE ROAD SIGNS— DANGER AHEAD

Matt is typical of many of us. He knew that his marriage with Tamara was always on the verge of disaster. He was aware that their problems were ever-present, cyclical, and ongoing, but he didn't know how to adequately address them. When Matt came to therapy to discuss his feelings of heartbreak and hopelessness about the impending divorce, he related the following story:

> I know she is gone and on to another guy. I have had this pressure from Tamara to be perfect. She resents my career [as a lawyer] and all the hours and time I put into it. I felt that I couldn't do enough to make her happy and feel safe. I knew it was only a matter of time before she would leave. Ever since we met at NYU, I was always trying to make her happy. I will never forget our second date in New York City on a beautiful fall afternoon. Tamara jumped out of the cab and started walking down the street because she was furious with me about some minor misunderstanding. I had a thought that day as I watched her walk away, that she would even-tually leave me over some minor infraction or issue. I ran after her and took her to a small café and bought a bottle of Dom Perignon champagne. I fully ignored that thought and married her anyway.

We had a good sex life, but it was never enough. Now she is dating some guy fifteen years younger. I don't want to lose my family [two teenage boys] and I am not going to file for the divorce.

Matt was served divorce papers three months after our initial meeting. During the next eighteen months he came to terms with his despair, rage, and codependence (wanting to excessively please Tamara and "fix" all her problems and worries). It is natural and very appropriate to want to "take care" of your partner/lover. Problems develop in a relationship when the "care-taking" becomes the sole purpose and only source of value to your partner and to yourself. Matt began to take all the responsibility for issues in their relationship that he had passionately ignored, denied, and avoided. In the final analysis, he possibly could have moved his marriage in a different direction had he earlier attempted to address the underlying relationship concerns with Tamara. His growing sense of well-being and positive feelings and actions about his future were the result of his taking full emotional responsibility for his role in his marriage and despair. Matt stopped blaming Tamara and stopped trying to rescue or "save" her. His relationship with his two teenage boys dramatically improved after the divorce. He spent quality time with them when they stayed at his house four nights a week, and he wasn't distracted by the relationship tension with Tamara. We will discuss Matt's recovery and the excellent prognosis for his future intimate relationships throughout the book. Matt's situation represents an increasing number of families in the United States today that have children living with one parent, though not all by divorce. Matt's emotional recovery in overcoming his heartbreak was valuable not only to him but to Tamara and their two sons as well.

Tracy represents another large percentage of adult Americans: those who are unmarried, either divorced or never married, who do not have children but would like to. Prior to her relationship with Brad, Tracy dated another man for four years; he didn't want children either. Brad was in the process of changing careers and didn't feel it was the right time to marry or start a family. Tracy came to therapy to resolve her sense of disappointment and despair over turning forty without children. She related the following:

> I have always believed I wanted children. My last two significant relationships have been with men who don't want kids. Hmmmm. I have blamed them for being selfish and insensitive to me. I guess I don't know if I really wanted kids, or I would probably be with that kind of man. I feel so disappointed about my life. I never expected to be forty, unmarried, and childless. Several of my girlfriends feel the same way and they are divorced. I feel like I have been divorced twice, I just never got to have the wedding, the party, and the gifts. I just never expected to be in this place in my life. It is hard for me to believe that I will meet a man at this point in my life and have what I have always really wanted. I don't believe that there are any good men out there.

Tracy continued to attend regular therapy sessions, resolving her disappointment with her life and her different self-defeating choices. She began to realize that she had unconsciously been ambivalent about having children, and because of this she never developed an intimate relationship with a man who wanted children. She developed insight into her own contribution to her current life circumstances and she stopped blaming her two past lovers for her current situation. She started doing the things that are necessary to change the direction of her relationships and heal her feelings of emotional betrayal, resentment, and ambivalence. (See section III for more on this issue.) Tracy ultimately took full responsibility for her status, recognizing that being single and not having children were her choices, not "bad luck" or a lack of available "good guys."

THE BREAKUP PROCESS QUESTION-AND-ANSWER LIST

The following items are designed to help you to start seeing where your role begins and ends in an intimate relationship. This is a free-flowing discussion and inventory of the real issues behind your breakup. This isn't about saving your public reputation or blaming your partner, but learning the truth about you. Our primary goal here is to help you begin to develop some emotional clarity and insight into how your relationship ended. This list is very neutral because it is about your assuming responsibility and gaining understanding into your contribution to the end of your relationship. How you got to this point isn't a matter of right or wrong, good or bad, or any judgment about emotional weaknesses. Instead, this is an opportunity to fully understand your relationship in a more complete and nonreactive mode. Once you understand your role in the breakup of your relationship, you can redirect your future intimate relationships in a very powerful, courageous, and positive way. No behavioral change or emotional relief is possible until you are able to gain two things: a nonreactive emotional perspective and a clearer picture of your contribution to and participation in what your prior relationship was.

Consider the following questions.

- Did you ignore the obvious signs that your relationship was dying?
- Was communication very strained for months or years, or was it never good at all?
- Did the kids monopolize your life?
- Did you secretly resent your partner for not paying attention to you?
- Did you use the kids as an excuse to maintain emotional distance from your partner?

- Did you resent your partner for his or her unpredictable behavior?
- Did you feel that you couldn't be your "real" self with your partner?
- Do you feel that you emotionally and mentally outgrew your partner?
- Did you not want to remain in a loveless and/or sexless marriage?
- Did you not want a relationship like that of your parents?
- Did your husband leave you for a younger woman?
- Did your wife or husband leave you for someone completely different than you? For instance, the contractor remodeling your house or the personal trainer at the gym?
- Was your partner emotionally abusive?
- Was your partner physically and mentally abusive?
- Did you find yourself romantically attracted to a coworker, the yoga instructor, or your child's elementary school teacher?
- Did you fantasize about being with other partners—romantically and physically?
- Did you stay at work late to avoid your partner?
- Can you remember the last time you had sex with your partner?
- Did you stay in the marriage for the kids?
- Did you stay in an abusive marriage because you never wanted to be divorced?
- Did you want to avoid feeling like a three-time loser with a third divorce?
- Did you marry your partner so you could have kids, rather than for love or for an emotional partnership?
- Did you and your partner take separate vacations rather than together?
- Did you resent your partner's ex for the emotional bond created by their kids?
- Have you ever been really happy or excited about your partner?

- Did you feel comfortable in your relationship, but not in love with your partner?
- Did you believe your partner was never emotionally available for you?
- Have you secretly thought about ending the relationship for a long time?
- Did you never expect your partner would leave you?
- Do you hate not having control of the relationship anymore?
- Do you dislike your stepchildren?
- Do you want children while your partner wants a new house?
- Do you resent your partner's ex because of the alimony payments?
- Do you hate being single?
- Do you fear being alone?
- Do you not want to be like your mother: divorced with two young children?
- Did you think you could wait until the kids went to college before you got divorced?
- Did you never think your partner was as unhappy as you were?

This list is deliberately designed to help you find your emotional center of gravity again and realize that the breakup of your relationship didn't occur in a vacuum. In fact, it likely was a long time in coming before it finally did land, but the landing was unexpected because the problems were around as long as the relationship. Please feel free to add to this list of items, ideas, fears, wishes, and unspoken feelings that you have about your divorce—and your ex-partner. Please add your own questions and thoughts that would best describe your divorce/breakup. Again, it is important to note that when I use the word "divorce" I am referring to the end of all kinds of love relationships, whether or not a legal marriage took place. An emotional heartbreak is an emotional heartbreak; how you got here is your path and your own personal story.

One of the purposes of these questions is to clarify how we all tend to ignore some of the most obvious, painful, and very telling signs of a relationship in crisis. This book will focus on how to pick up the pieces of your life, reinvent yourself, and never ignore your concerns about you and your partner. One of the essential elements of resolving your relationship disappointment is to become abundantly honest and clear with yourself about the issues/tensions that existed in your romantic relationship. Your romantic future directly hinges on your ability and insight to recognize what is transpiring in your life and love relationship. Nothing that has occurred in your past romantic relationships has to ever be repeated in the future. Avoiding this is a matter of taking this time in your life to fully understand your past relationship patterns and to realize your desires for you and your next partner. To start the process of healing and of overcoming the major emotional setback of a divorce, we should first discuss and clarify some very common relationship myths.

REALITIES AND MISPERCEPTIONS ABOUT HEARTBREAK

Please mark each statement either true or false based on your honest opinion and current belief system about relationships. No one else needs to know what you really think and feel about yourself, your ex-partner, or your previous lovers. It is normal and very common to want to keep a certain degree of confidentiality about your marriage/relationship ending. Your emotional, psychological, and personal healing isn't based on disclosing to your entire "world" all the elements of your marriage or intimate relationship. It is difficult and emotionally draining to keep retelling your "story" to everyone you know. Your personal opinion on the breakup is of paramount importance (it is the only one that truly matters) and is necessary to see more clearly and to be less emotionally reactive, without shame, guilt, or anger. There is a wealth of personal information in your answers to each of these ten statements.

1. It is all my fault.
2. There is something wrong with me.
3. I will never get over this heartbreak/betrayal.
4. I will never find anyone to love again.
5. I can live without an intimate relationship.
6. Men suck.
7. Women are cold.
8. Anger is useful in getting over an ex-lover.
9. Divorce is a failure; the children, my family, and I are emotionally scarred for life.
10. Marriages never work.

Answers

1. False. You can be responsible for only your portion/half of the relationship. It is impossible for you to explain why he/she left or for you to take care of what your partner wouldn't or couldn't. *Relationships are like playing tennis.* You can only be responsible for 100 percent of your side of the tennis court. You can hit or return the ball only when it is hit to you; you can't run to the other side of the court and hit the ball for your partner. Your partner has to use his or her own racket and return the serve—or not. The tennis analogy describes a codependent relationship: *You do it all and wonder why you never get what you want in a relationship.* The reason is that you are playing alone. Both tennis and relationships require two participants, not one.

2. False. The ending of a relationship has a way of dredging up every unresolved personal issue in your past. Second, relationship endings have a way of clouding any clear picture or hope of your romantic future. The shame, guilt, and grief of disconnecting from your ex can be very confusing and emotionally disorientating. It is easy to think that your "issues" screwed up the relationship or caused its demise, but the truth is that every relationship is a com-

posite of both people's histories, issues, concerns, values, and desires. You can become more aware of your own emotional concerns and desires to do things differently in the future. Feeling like "damaged goods" is a common reaction after a breakup. Blaming the other person for all your pain and suffering is an emotional defense mechanism to help you feel better about yourself and to offset your overwhelming "bad" feelings. But the truth is that things were not working in the relationship, and you can learn from them—if you chose to. Your goal is to learn the valuable lessons buried inside the pain and misery of your marriage/love relationship.

3. False. One thing is certain in this life: *Everything changes, even your sadness, heartbreak, and sense of betrayal.* Time doesn't heal; it creates emotional amnesia, and the intense throbbing pain in your heart begins to fade. Time creates emotional distance until we see or are reminded of our "ex." Thankfully, we are genetically wired over time to forget the staggering memories of our breakup. It is a mechanism of self-preservation that we all have. Over time the pain will diminish, and you will find that closure can be possible and eventually accomplished with your ex. Your deeper insight, new relationship awareness, and clarity will be the keys to processing your emotional pain and moving forward in your life. The sooner you stop blaming your partner and begin looking at your role in the relationship, the faster your emotional pain and hopelessness will decrease.

4. False. The biggest relationship myth is that everyone has a soul mate—one person who is "right" for us for our entire life. *The truth is that there are perfect relationships for us at different times in our life.* To expect that a given relationship must last longer than it can is where we fall into despair and anger. Some relationships last six weeks, some last six months, some last sixteen years, and some last sixty-six years. It is impossible to predict the longevity of any relationship. This relationship "time" concept may sound very cold but it is really a powerful insight. The key is to appreciate the time

you had with your ex and to know that your future contains more—and greater—relationship possibilities. Every relationship has a beginning, a middle, and an end. Endings don't have to mean terminal loneliness and isolation or perpetual heartbreak. We will discuss in chapter 9 in greater detail the "soul mate" syndrome and its positive and negative effect on you.

5. True. You can live without an intimate relationship. Your life will not collapse or be ruined if you don't have an intimate partner. It is critical to your emotional recovery to remember that *intimate relationships are a choice.* If you want to open up your heart, life, and emotions to another person, it is your choice to do so. The choice of being emotionally connected to another person is worth the effort. We all have the potential to thrive in our love relationships. For that dynamic to happen to a greater degree is one of the primary focuses of section II. It is a natural emotional drive and a psychological fact that almost all of us crave intimate connections and bonds with other people. In fact, the need to completely isolate oneself from others is considered a mental/personality disorder. The desire to isolate is an emotional defense mechanism from feeling "vulnerable" or "rejected" with another person. Our quality of life and mental health are equated with our ability to create all types of fulfilling relationships (i.e., personal, intimate, professional, family, social). Humans are designed to be with partners, form relationships, and create safe and secure emotional bonds with the people in their lives. No matter what circumstances surrounded your breakup, it is possible to create a new relationship template for your future intimate partner.

6. False. Male bashing is almost an Olympic sport. When you have been emotionally wounded, rejected, and/or abandoned by the man in your life, it is essential not to globalize your pain to all men. Resenting men is like digging two ditches, one for your ex and the other for you. Neither of you benefits. When you project your resent-

ment onto all men or develop a pattern of distrusting, resenting, or hating men, it can result in the very thing that you don't want: *more heartbreak and disappointment*. You can stop the cycle of disappointment with men. The first place to start is to explore your own father-daughter relationship. Remember that the first man you ever loved was your father, regardless of his relationship with your mother. Learning about your father can be a source of invaluable information about the men you form relationships with as an adult. The wants, longings, likes, and dislikes about your father-daughter relationship can be a wealth of new insight for how you choose a future intimate partner and develop a relationship with him. Second, the more you know about what you wanted and needed from your father can be valuable for what you will want and need from your intimate partner. Third, you will be able to explain to your partner what you want from him. Last, not wanting anything more to do with your ex may be very sound judgment, but resenting *all* men is something else. If you have had long-standing resentment and mistrust toward all men, it likely began with your father-daughter relationship. The more you understand the relationship between your father and you, the more insight it will lend to your relationship with men in general. Your father-daughter relationship is the first model of how you related to men in your world growing up. In this case of romance, the secret to your healing and to letting go of the past will involve your father and that first love relationship. All men aren't bad, and you deserve to have a wonderful intimate relationship with a quality man.

7. False. Woman bashing is like sticking a fork in your eye and wondering why it hurts. The man who rejects women and bashes, demeans, and devalues them is almost always a son (remember we are all sons regardless of age) carrying a load of unfinished emotional baggage with his mother. Men's adult relationships are usually an emotional continuation of the mother-son relationship. The key for men is to develop meaningful and significant intimate relation-

ships in order to avoid the "mother replacement" syndrome, which will be discussed in length in section II. In short, it involves men developing relationships with the same emotional problems, issues, and tensions that they had with their mother. This isn't classic Freudian psychology, but rather insight-orientated, problem-solving action. The unfinished business of your mother-son emotional bond, the process by which you separated yourself from her, and your style of communication based on that relationship, constitutes a gold mine of useful information about you. For instance, if you find yourself not trusting women, consider the root of your problem started in your childhood mother-son bond.

8. False. The misunderstanding of emotional pain is to use it to consistently blame your ex for all of your suffering. People argue all the time about not having to resolve their anger, bitterness, resentment, betrayal, and rage toward their ex. They feel very "entitled" and "justified" with their powerful feelings of disappointment. The short-term comfort of feeling "powerful" compared to feeling devastated or despairing is useful and purposeful. However, anger is a generalized feeling that covers up much deeper emotional wounds, relationship violations, disappointments, and heartbreaks. Anger is only the symptom of your feelings, it isn't the cause. Underneath the thin veil of anger lie your emotional devastation, genuine loss, disillusionment, and feelings of betrayal that can become toxic if they are not resolved. Many people who go through a divorce or breakup never truly recover—emotionally, relationally, or psychologically—from the loss or heartbreak. These types of deep emotional wounds can be resolved and overcome through psychological clarity and new insight. Your ex-factor doesn't need to be your "angry love factor." You can move beyond the emotional wreckage of your former relationship and not feel as though ten thousand volts of rage were vibrating through your body every time you hear your ex's name or see him or her at your child's Little League game, at the school parent-teacher conference, or driving down the street. Anger can be

very informative about the depth of your pain and loss you are experiencing. Try to understand your anger. Your anger can be very informative about your personal feelings about love and what you want and expect in a relationship.

9. False. Marital tension is an ongoing problem in dysfunctional marriages, antagonistic divorces, and hostile breakups. It isn't the status of your marriage or having an intact family that guarantees emotional health for you and your children; what is critical to your emotional health and well-being is *not* to live or raise your children in an emotionally, physically, and psychologically hostile home. Relationship conflict between parents is the number one problem for a child's psychological development and growth. Studies have repeatedly shown that children from conflicted and hostile families suffer more emotional problems and distress than children from less conflicted homes.[5] Many times, divorced parents have a "good divorce," where there is no tension and animosity, and the children don't show the signs of emotional distress. It is the ongoing fighting between parents—whether or not they remain together—that is problematic for all the parties involved. Children, parents, lovers, and other family members suffer when divorce issues become an ongoing family theme and the emotional glue that binds them together. Divorce, breakups, or relationship disillusionment aren't necessarily catastrophic for children, but when two parents unconsciously, reactively use their kids as allies against the other parent, the problems can be overwhelming. These unresolved behaviors can cause lifelong problems for children in their future love relationships. Last, divorce isn't a death sentence to your life, happiness, or future. Your ability to resolve this major relationship heartbreak *will be your choice*. It is well worth your time and energy to resolve your heartbreak so that you and your children don't have to carry it into the future.

10. False. The pessimistic view that love/marriage relationships don't work says more about the person who believes it than about

the relationships themselves. All types of relationships are "risky," whether they are business or social ones. Just because heartbreak can occur, that doesn't necessarily mean that you shouldn't strive for connections and attachments. Marriages and intimate relationships work only as well as the people involved in them. So, for example, if your significant other hates women and you are a woman, it is a fair assumption that trust and intimacy will be problematic. But these types of relationship problems have nothing to do with marriage, per se, but rather with the combination of individuals involved in a given relationship. Anything in your life can work when you make good choices, apply yourself, and understand how you function in that particular context with an emotionally available partner. Your relationship desires, expectations, needs, and emotional attachments impact your career, stepparenting, second marriage, parenting, and love relationships. There is no magic or wishing involved in forming and maintaining a long-term romantic relationship or marriage. The better you understand your relationship history and style, emotional bonds, your parents, and yourself, the greater likelihood that your love relationships will be very satisfying and fulfilling.

It is my hope that after reading and responding to these statements, you will begin to see some of your relationship blind spots and biases. Awareness of your beliefs about relationships is critical to your future relationships. Whatever you have experienced or believed up to now, you need not automatically continue in those beliefs. Change is in the air, and you are ready for it. In the following chapters, we will discuss, elaborate, and expand upon how you can move forward—emotionally, mentally, spiritually, and psychologically—in your love relationships. Overcoming the betrayal and heartbreak of a failed relationship is one of the biggest challenges that any adult faces. Dealing with the complexities stemming from divorce—including remarriage, stepchildren, new children with a new partner, your ex-partner's remarriage, or your children resenting you for the divorce—*all starts and ends with you.* To the degree that you resolve these major emotional challenges, your relationship future will flourish and become everything you desire and want.

As you read the chapters that follow, bear in mind this wonderful quote about the journey you are embarking on:

> *He who loses wealth loses much; he who loses a friend loses more; but he that loses his courage loses all.*
>
> —Miguel de Cervantes

Chapter 2

EMOTIONAL WHIPLASH— FIVE STAGES

The Pain of Being Left

I will never forget that Sunday afternoon when Karen came home from her yoga retreat and announced to me while eating a bag of chips in the kitchen that she wanted a divorce. I seriously thought I was going to die. Maybe it might have been easier if I had died; it felt like my life ended. I never saw the divorce coming.

—Eric, age fifty-four, married for twenty-four years, divorced three years

We had a ring picked out, [had] been dating for seven years, and I was ready for the next step in our relationship: marriage and babies. My birthday came and went, Christmas came and went, and there was no proposal, engagement, or ring. Two days after Christmas, Ron came over and broke up with me. I stayed in bed for the rest of the year and didn't stop crying. I always thought Ron would be a man and take that step.

—Linda, age thirty-seven, single and not dating

STAGE ONE: WHIPLASH

You don't have to be married for twenty-four years or have dated the "love" of your life to know the unbelievable pain of hearing the dreaded death sentence of: *"I want a divorce!"* or *"I want to break up!"* There is absolutely nothing you can do to change the course of your romantic life with your partner from that moment on. The intimate relationship between you and your partner will never be the same again. The door between you and your partner has closed, and you are on the outside looking in. The natural knee-jerk response— *"I will fix this and make this work"*—is usually too little, too late. Your partner has decided that your relationship is no longer viable and doesn't want to be involved in it anymore. It might have taken years—or not very long at all—for this moment to occur. The length of a relationship isn't the best indicator of the degree of emotional devastation that both partners will feel or experience; rather, it is the strength and depth of the emotional bond between them that is the real barometer of how deep the emotional pain will be. Regardless of the circumstances and tensions leading up to the breakup, there is always that excruciating reality check of undeniable truth: *The relationship is over*.

There are very few things in our lives for which we have picture-perfect recall and memory. The "death sentence" moment for the receiver of those life-changing words will live eternally in the receiver's memory. Many of us can remember our first kiss, our high school graduation, our first car—but nothing measures up to the ending of a significant relationship. These moments are timeless. However, the passage of time usually reduces the pain and softens the memory, reducing the life-changing impact of that day. The passage of time will bury your pain—that is, until it happens again. The pain, terror, and despair will immediately surface when your old wounds are cut open again by another breakup.

The memory of the breakup event never totally disappears. It can be forgotten until another breakup or divorce triggers the dormant pain of your unresolved past (your ex-factor). For some, the automatic emotional defensive response is to immediately move on and find another partner before the dust has settled. But there are no shortcuts or means of denial that will ease the pain or loss of an intimate relationship. In fact, many psychologically high-functioning adults do everything in their personal power to keep such a moment from ever taking place. People generally have an inkling when the end of their relationship is near. For instance, new patterns may emerge: a sudden work crisis is not really a crisis but a convenient excuse to avoid spending time with the partner, a new hobby that doesn't include you, taking trips without you or extending the invitation, increased drug or alcohol use, self-created distractions (a hyperactive social/work schedule), sudden health issues or concerns with family and children, unusual spending habits, and buying a new house are all distractions from the relationship issues and tensions. These new patterns develop to "buy" more time in the relationship or to clarify that the relationship is "dead" are very common. Many of these patterns are unconsciously motivated and sometimes consciously designed to see if the relationship can be "saved." In some cases, the new pattern or sudden new interest in the other partner can, in fact, resolve long-term issues and re-create a new and deeper intimate connection. But in most cases, it is just another attempt to avoid the inevitable end. In these cases, the timetable of the relationship has played itself out, and that is a very difficult thing to accept.

Most of us—in spite of whatever education, career success, and emotional maturity we may have achieved—aren't psychologically equipped to handle endings on an intimate level. The reason we fall into personal crisis is that all the hidden negative personal beliefs about ourselves—our childhood issues regarding love and deepseated fears of rejection, shame, failing, abandonment—are all instantly activated. Relationship endings have the power to instantly bring back every negative thought or feeling we have ever felt or had about ourselves. Our sense of rejection is a timeless feeling going back to our first love, childhood disappointments, and all our romantic relationships up to this point in our lives. This is one of the major reasons these endings are such life-changing events for the receiver. Being told your partner wants to end the relationship can be likened to a missile being fired into your house and then wondering why there is so much damage. Your life might feel like an "emotional rubble" pile after hearing this devastating news. Everything in your life feels like it is now open to change and examination.

Regardless of how the moment arrives; the amount of energy spent avoiding, postponing, or accepting it; or the hundreds of hours and dollars spent in couples counseling, if your relationship has run its course, it's over. *Your life is instantaneously altered* and will be suddenly going a million miles an hour in another direction. Regardless of how you got there, the relationship is over. For example, in the vignettes that open this chapter, neither Eric nor Linda truly believed their intimate relationships were in trouble or on the verge of ending. Their sense of shock and surprised is more the norm than both partners mutually agreed on the divorce or breakup. The harsh reality of the end of a relationship is as serious as anything that you will encounter in your adult life. A symbolic death is, in many ways, as difficult an experience as an actual death of a loved one. The death of the relationship dream is heartbreaking and many times very confusing. It might have taken years, numerous affairs, financial crisis, broken engagements, marriage therapy, chronic arguing, and the eventual loss of passion between you and your partner, but it is completely over! This harsh emotional, mental, psychological, and physical reality creates a "whiplash" effect.

The emotional whiplash is serious and extremely painful beyond description when you are on the receiving end of a relationship breakup. All of us have either been the recipient of such a breakup, known a friend going through it, or watched a parent agonize over it. From any perspective or position, it is painful and heartbreaking to watch and experience. In the next chapter we will discuss the heartbreak associated with the giver of the "death sentence" speech. It is important to remember that it takes two people to build a relationship—and those same two people to disassemble it. Neither party walks away from the ending unscathed, emotionally neutral, or feeling good about the breakup/divorce. Regardless of the circumstances, the whiplash is powerful and life changing. It takes a lot of emotional maturity and insight to understand each side of the relationship and each person's perspective. Yet you *must* completely understand your role in the ending, so you can allow your intimate relationship life to move forward with as much insight and hope as possible.

STAGE TWO: DENIAL

When a love life is thrown around like a baseball during a Little League game, multiple emotional injuries occur. We have trouble enduring the emotional trauma we must undergo before we can psychologically accept that our relationship is over. It may take years for the relationship to fully end as we fight it every step of the way, or it might take all of one hour for one partner or the other to move out. At both ends of the spectrum, physically separating is painful and difficult. *The primary purpose of denial is to avoid the prospect of having to emotionally, mentally, physically, and sexually disconnect from your ex.* The disconnection process is the most problematic and traumatic part of relationship endings. The discussion that ends the relationship might take five minutes or five hours, but the emotional, psychological, and physical disconnection process from your ex can take years. Disconnecting from your former lover is never a fast, one-time event. *Separating is a process that takes time and understanding.*

No Preparation—Denial's Friend

The one who does the breaking up has a huge emotional lead on the receiver of the news. The "giver" might have emotionally started disconnecting weeks, months, or years before taking the final action of terminating the intimate partnership. The lead time experienced by the person ending the relationship is critical. It isn't unusual or odd for adults who are being left to do almost anything to avoid the long emotional and psychological process of separating from a partner. But once it happens, there is little that can be done. Upon hearing that you will be served actual divorce papers (no longer threatening to end the relationship with divorce), you are likely emotionally unprepared for the surprise or shock. Even if there have been prior discussions and agreements about ending the relationship, it is still a blow to the heart. The reality of feeling the full emotional force of the breakup is beyond words. In fact, it is considered second in terms of emotional severity only to the death of a child.[1]

Most people don't see any warning signs about the approaching dramatic change of direction in their relationships. Neither Eric nor Linda did. They both told me in therapy that they knew their relationships were having problems, but those problems didn't seem fatal. Eric asked, "Dr. Poulter, don't all couples go through highs and lows?" The answer is yes—and many of these issues don't signal the end, but rather indicate that change is needed in order to strengthen the emotional bond between the partners. Nonetheless, there *are* signs that signal the end of a relationship is near. (These are discussed in the list below.) When you are the receiver of the breakup, all your personal power, emotional strength, and courage are immediately neutralized. The impact to the heart of the sledgehammer of rejection is indescribable. It doesn't matter if you have also wanted to end the relationship; the fact remains that you didn't and your ex did. The receiver of the breakup news often believes that there is still hope for the partnership; otherwise he or she would have initiated the separation. The powerlessness of being on the receiving end of a breakup is difficult at best and traumatizing at worst, particularly when you don't want the relationship to terminate. It is the belief regardless of all the problems, hope, and desire for the relationship to continue that becomes the tremendous tension point between the husband/

wife, girlfriend/boyfriend. Wanting the relationship to continue while your partner has resigned from it is the starting point for your despair and your journey into a new chapter in your life.

No one consciously pursues or invites the end of a relationship. No one falls in love in order to plan a future termination date. When these very painful endings occur, they must be understood. No one is immune from being left, disappointed, or feeling "dumped" or abandoned. It is important to view your breakup/divorce as an abstract emotional process (i.e., feeling disappointment, anger, rejection, relief, or hopelessness), while simultaneously it is a linear event (i.e., moving out, separated households, filing for divorce, custody of the children). Feelings of rejection are unavoidable when you are handed your walking papers, and many people choose to live for years in isolation from any romantic connections as a result of a devastating intimate breakup. It is important to remember that romantic and intimate emotional isolation has nothing to do with your daily activities or career. Your emotional connections to your family, friends, and people closest to you are different from the connection to an intimate partner. Functioning in your career or in your familial and social relationships and functioning in your love life require very different talents and emotional insights. Many adults live a seemingly normal life—going to work, having friends, and visiting family—but live in complete romantic/emotional isolation. The residual fear of being left can cause lifelong emotional scars; create avoidance behaviors, personality disorders, and depression; and even engender suicidal loneliness. But never forget that these very problematic and personal issues of trust, romantic love, and hope can be resolved and healed. The key is to fully understand your ex-factor and all of its associated issues.

The key to coming out of your denial and healing your emotional whiplash is regaining your emotional perspective. This might require the help of a third party—a psychologist, a neutral friend, or someone who knows your relationship history with your ex. As part of the healing process, it is important that both of you explore the signs that indicated something was wrong in the relationship. *No breakup ever occurs in a vacuum*. There are always warning signs that the end is approaching, and every failed relationship has its own set of circumstances that led up to the breakup. The key is to recognize these signs in order to reduce your sense of confusion and rejection about the breakup. Many times there are relationship patterns, recurring themes about your prior love relationships, breakups that are important to recognize so you can make the necessary changes in your romantic life. The more you examine how and why the relationship ended, the more insight you will have for healing and for building a new and different future.

Relationship Ending Signs

The list below includes some common signs and relationship issues that, over time, become deal breakers for many people. Before reading this list, ask yourself: What do you think was the primary deal breaker in your relationship? What were the issues, ongoing problems, events, and other facets of your love relationship that ended it? Did you believe it would ever happen?

- Your sexual relationship became an issue. You stopped having sex with your partner. Your regular pattern of sexual intimacy decreased. You or your partner lost interest in sexual intimacy.
- You felt a sense that you were emotionally growing apart from your partner.
- You and your partner were too young when you met. Over the years you "fell out of love" with each other.
- Your partner announced on prior occasions that he or she wanted to divorce or break up.
- Having children was your sole purpose for marriage or an exclusive relationship.
- You were scared to address the relationship problems for fear that these very concerns would end the relationship.

- Your partner repeatedly told you that he or she needed to change things in the relationship. These changes never took place.
- You knew your partner was attracted to someone else. You never addressed the affair or infatuation. Your sexual relationship dramatically declined after this occurred.
- You didn't want to change the state of the relationship until your young children were older or your teenage children left for college.
- Your partner suffered the loss of a significant person (for example, a parent or sibling) in the past year.
- You and your partner began spending more and more time apart. You spent less and less time together.
- You and your partner stopped sharing personal issues and important information with each other.
- You and your partner continually struggled with power, control, and anger issues.
- Your normal style of intimate communication had been diminishing for a period of time. You and your partner hadn't talked in a long time. Silence replaced your intimate communication.
- Your partner had a relationship history of being "commitment phobic" and/or detached. He or she always told you that he or she didn't want to become exclusive or get married.
- You felt controlled by your partner—emotionally, mentally, socially, and/or economically.
- You and your partner had—and still have—different goals, values, and ethics.
- You didn't like your partner's parents, children, siblings, stepchildren.
- You didn't see how you could fit or blend into your partner's life.
- You always thought you could change your partner. You never did.
- You always knew that you and your partner weren't a good intimate or romantic match.

- You got married because it was the right time to do it, not because you found the right person.
- Your style of communication involved constant avoidance of discussing important relationship issues, vulnerable concerns, and intimate wishes.
- You knew the relationship should have ended long ago but didn't have the emotional courage to do it. You didn't think your partner was aware of the poor shape the relationship was in.
- You married or dated your partner because circumstances in your life (e.g., desire for children, age, loneliness) were pushing you to make a marital commitment. You didn't choose your partner because of great chemistry, mutual understanding, or a strong emotional bond between you.
- You sometimes secretly wished you were single again and regretted being in the relationship. You wanted out of the relationship but didn't know how to end it.

Questions of Denial

Many of us were standing in the kitchen, or sitting with our partner, having a drink, and talking when one or more of these signs finally became an undeniable reality and eventual deal breaker. He or she wants out of the relationship. The issues between you and your partner are no longer under the surface but are now the information for the divorce/breakup. The issues, tension, and differences can't be tolerated any longer. Many adults subsequently avoid relationships, with their attendant emotional intimacy and vulnerability, for fear of living through a relationship ending: *being left, rejected, and abandoned.* No one wants to face the hard, cold facts that one or several of the above relationship signs was flashing like a neon red warning light in the relationship. It is important to clarify that people generally don't avoid intimate relationships because of their issues but because they don't want to experience a breakup/divorce. The truth is that there are often several serious relationship issues brewing under the surface, and it was only a matter of time before stressful circumstances would expose these concerns. Given that you knew your intimate relationship had issues, what were the final signs, events, issues? If you had an idea of the problems, why do you think you ignored these signs if you knew about them? Knowing that there are numerous issues, complicated problems, challenges, and concerns in a relationship sometimes isn't even enough. Many times you and your partner will agree on the troubling issues but each of you feel differently about the severity of them. It is the degree of severity that many times leads one partner to terminate the relationship. Do you believe you could have changed the course of the relationship given the issues in it? The belief that you can change your partner can become an ongoing source of resentment on the other's part and lead to divorce/breakup. Divorces/breakups are very complex and have many layers of issues and concerns surrounding them. There is never one clear-cut reason or simple explanation for a divorce/breakup. It is a combination of many factors and elements between you and your partner. Pick four or five of the above signs or your own warning signs that helped contribute to the ending of your relationship, and ask yourself the following questions: What was the most powerful, obvious, and biggest problem/issue/concern in your relationship? What did you argue about the most with your partner? How did you handle this issue? Did you talk about it with any degree of resolution, insight, or compromise on your part? How often did blaming one another play a role in your relationship? Did you try to understand your partner's perspective about the severity of her/his concerns. Did you think that any of the "couples" issues were irreconcilable or unresolvable? Did you trust that your partner would never terminate your intimate partnership because of the tension?

All human interactions have a process and a pattern in adjusting to change, and our relationship endings aren't any different. The more we understand our individual processes for assimilating change, the better we can adjust to these life-changing relationship events. Going through the breakup of a romantic relationship almost always raises the question: *Why did this happen to me?* The basic answer is that all relationships go through changes. The problem is that we aren't always aware of the necessary changes our partner wants or needs. Our lack of awareness of our partners or ourselves can be a blind spot or something we avoid because of the consequences of dealing with it. We unfortunately may not be aware of what we want or need from our partner. Oftentimes the "couple" gets stuck in a frustrating phase for years at a time (i.e., arguing all the time, no sex, no intimate communication). The demands of "life" can overtake the priority of the couple and problems soon develop. The need for relationships to continue to grow and evolve can get lost, forgotten, or dismissed because the partners start growing apart emotionally. The emotional denial is not seeing or believing the relationship is declining rather than growing and expanding. Then we wonder why we can't move forward with our lives. Even worse, we may continue to blame our ex, or start to blame our colleagues, our friends, or our family for the relationship changes and heartbreaks. The more accepting we are of the process of separating, emotionally disconnecting from our former husband/wife/lover, the better we can genuinely heal, learn, and create a different future.

STAGE THREE: ANGER

Whenever we develop a deep emotional bond or connection with another person, we put ourselves at risk of later feeling as if our heart has been handed to us on a platter. The endings of these relationships are heart-wrenching encounters that happen to everyone and are impossible to avoid. It is crucial to never lose the perspective that your life is a collection of many powerful events—disasters, successes, brilliant moments, and painful learning experiences. It is the composite of these events that gives your life its substance, depth, and richness.

The fabric of your life is a composite of all your life events and lessons. Feelings of disappointment and betrayal are a natural part of relationships with loved ones—including our exes. I have worked with many brilliant adults who just can't believe or accept that their partner would want to leave them. They felt that they were immune to "rejection." It is this type of disbelief or narcissism that quickly turns into anger, rage, and revenge-motivated actions toward their ex. No one is ever beyond a relationship change (divorce, breakup, marriage). It is very common to experience disappointment and heartbreak in matters of the heart, but it is equally common to resolve these feelings and gain insight from the experience. Your goal is to gain valuable insight into the breakup of your relationship and not get stuck in the valley of anger and despair. This phase of relationship endings is the most problematic and ubiquitous.

It is ideal for all concerned when the relationship is ended with some degree of compassion. Unfortunately, the reality is usually quite the opposite. Relationships are often ended in either an angry or an emotionally detached manner. Time stops when you are on the receiving end of that powerful, life-changing pronouncement. Once the initial emotional whiplash and denial begin to wear off, feelings of anger often move front and center. Sadly, the anger phase can become a lifetime emotional state and psychological condition for one or both parties in the separation. Anger is a very strong emotional bond.

Anger as a Reaction to Personal Suffering

Throughout the ages, anger has been considered a very powerful and dangerous emotion. World history attests to the power of anger and its potentially destructive qualities. Even today, in the technology wave of the twenty-first century, nothing has stemmed its power. Anger is still a raw core emotion that can't be dismissed or underestimated because of its volatility and its power to destroy. The psychology of anger is very complex. Anger is essentially an emotional, mental, and behavioral covering for the uncomfortable, shameful, and painful core feelings a person experiences in his or her life.

During the breakup of a relationship, anger is usually aimed at the offending party: *your ex*. The anger phase is not only problematic and misunderstood; it is the most potentially dangerous of the five phases. Because of this, chapter 4 is completely dedicated to this particular emotional issue. It might seem obvious, but the majority of adults who have long-term problems with their ex-factor are generally never able to move beyond their anger, emotionally, mentally, physically, or relationally. It is important to remember that anger can be a very strong and deadly emotion when left unchecked and misunderstood.

Your feelings of rejection, abandonment, hopelessness, despair, and panic are real and legitimate, but they can't all be connected to your ex. Endings—particularly the end of a relationship—have the unique ability of bringing up every unresolved emotion, belief, and doubt a person has ever had. Your unresolved old issues, long buried, get confused with the present-day breakup. Anger blends past disappointments with the present moment of despair. *It is the blending of the past with the present that makes endings emotionally crazy, confusing, and painful.* The anger associated with the end of a relationship is like aiming a high-powered fan at your desk—with twenty-five years' worth of paperwork on it. It becomes very difficult to separate your past disappointments and unresolved anger from your present-day disappointments and reactions of anger.

One of the ways you can gain some clarity over your current despair is to recognize that a major problem with the anger phase is that you blame your partner for all of your pain and sorrow. No single person is to blame for the totality of your pain and suffering. *It is simply impossible for one person to be the sole cause of your anger, shame, disappointment, and personal insecurities.* If your partner were completely to blame, then you could be healed by that one person. You are solely responsible for your emotional reactions and responses to your ex. He or she doesn't control your feelings, even if it seems that way. Your personal issues, insecurities, and vulnerabilities were preexisting prior to your marriage or love relationship. It is critical that you become aware of your prior relationship concerns that influenced your current romantic relationship/marriage choices, behaviors, and emotional bonding. Your marriage or current romantic relationship played a role in how you handled or didn't handle your core emotional beliefs, reactions, and responses. You were a fully formed person prior to your romantic relationship and your ex-partner was part of your life. Many times adults believe that their exes ruined their lives but it is never that simple or easy. What is true is your ex-partner controls your life to the degree that you allow him/her to do so. The erroneous belief that your ex has control over your future is a common divorce/breakup myth. But relationships aren't that simple or linear. Your anger and despair are a combination of many variables, and your ex is clearly only one of these elements. It is rational to conclude that your ex can be a tremendous source of pain and suffering, but he or she isn't the whole reason for your anger. The details and depth of your residual anger predate your relationship. The personal history of your anger is something you must explore and resolve if your future emotional health and relationships are to be fulfilling. We will discuss your abandonment and anger history in great detail in chapter 4.

The reality is that the end of your intimate relationship was the result of experiences collected over a period of months, years, and maybe even decades. Your angry response at finally being told—verbally and nonverbally—that the relationship is over is reasonable. It is understandable and acceptable to be upset about the ending of your romantic bond with your ex. Anger often takes the place of emotional clarity during the ending of a relationship. But a problem occurs when your anger turns into a raging fire, consuming your entire life, emotions, and energy. When you are consumed with your sense of righteousness and your partner's wrongness, you are stuck in a never-ending cycle of misery and hopelessness. The cycle of anger prevents you from ever emotionally or mentally separating from your ex and rebuilding a new life.

Family law attorneys know that when a divorcing couple starts to litigate every aspect of their relationship, it is a way of staying emotionally connected. The litigating process has absolutely no time limit; it can go on forever. In my professional experience, when couples start to fight in court, it is usually a sign that neither person wants to truly separate. Fighting about money, arguing, and blaming each other feeds the anger phase of the breakup and keeps both parties intimately involved. The tabloids are full of stories of celebrities who get involved in these very unfortunate public displays in which they act out their anger. But let us consider the role anger is currently playing between you and your ex.

Anger Questions

Consider the following questions and how your anger has stopped, prevented, or helped you from moving forward in your post-divorce/breakup life. It is very important to allow yourself to experience your complete range of emotions (i.e., love, hope, fear, and disappiontment), not just anger.

1. What role does your anger and resentment play in keeping you from moving forward in your life?
2. How often have you used your sense of victimization as an excuse to be angry with your ex?
3. As compared to your initial whiplash breakup/divorce phase, how much has your anger kept you from moving forward into another relationship?
4. Do you tend to completely blame your ex, or do you accept your role in the ending of the relationship?
5. Does your anger scare you, your ex, or other people in your life?

These questions are only a sample of the issues you need to consider in order to resolve your anger and not allow it to become a major source of energy and fuel for seeking revenge on your ex. Even if you remarry and build a life with another partner, you can still be highly invested in emotional torture—such as withholding money, creating custody issues, invading your exes private intimate life, taking legal actions against your ex's, passive/aggressive behaviors, and outright raging at your ex. Just because you have a new love relationship doesn't necessarily mean you have genuinely moved on. All you may have done is brought your ex into your current relationship. Men are notorious for bringing past relationships into their next romantic union. Women, on the other hand, often don't believe they have any anger issues toward their exes. Rather, they suppress it. Women have been socially conditioned that any expression of anger is "bitchy" and unacceptable. Men have been conditioned that any expression of "soft" emotions (i.e., crying, grief, sadness) is non-masculine. Both stereotypes are very inaccurate and problematic for men and women. But neither gender is above feeling intense anger and its many forms of painful and explosive expression.

STAGE FOUR: RESOLUTION

The fighting has stopped and reason has replaced anger. This is the stage when couples who have been emotionally embroiled in arguing, finger-pointing, and committing character defamation suspend the fighting. Ex-partners rarely get to this point within the first five years after they separate, although some do. And it is my hope that you will be one of them. Resolution implies that you have been able to heal your emotional whiplash, address your denial and fear, let go of your anger and resentment, and start to create a new life. Your ex may never get beyond the sense of being "wronged" by you, but that isn't your issue or concern. Your primary goal is to keep yourself from engaging in or doing things that will hinder or stall your personal development and growth. This stage is the precursor to building a better life and a solid intimate relationship. The secret to gaining and developing a wider perspective is to incorporate your new insights about yourself and intimate relationship knowledge—experience you have gained from your romantic love history. When the emotional heat starts to diminish, you will begin to see patterns and old themes from your past emerge. It is at this point that you need to determine who and what you want to be in an intimate relationship, and at this time, making changes is easier. The easy part is that you have been released from a difficult intimate relationship that wasn't working for you. But you don't want to fall into the trap of repeating negative, self-defeating habits in your future intimate relationships.

Your romantic future hinges on your ability to put the past behind you. The key is to live in the present and not continually replay the trauma of your ex in your mind, life, relationships, and all the issues surrounding him or her. You have found, or are in the process of finding, the ability to detach yourself and your ex from the emotional bond of anger, resentment, and disappointment. Releasing your partner from the relationship may sound counterintuitive, but it isn't. It is easier to file for divorce and fight over property, money, and the children. The most difficult part is emotionally letting go of the unfulfilled dream of marriage/love. Though it may be hard to believe, many people hold onto their exes for years after those relationships have ended. It sounds ridiculous, but we all know people who are still emotionally carrying their exes around, many years after the breakup. This is true for some who were the one being left and who fought with everything to salvage the relationship. It is also true of the person who left the relationship but didn't leave it emotionally. Because a couple is divorced, live in different houses, have new friends, and have remarried doesn't always equate with emotional resolution. Emotional resolution with your ex is much more than signing divorce papers and shaking hands "good-bye."

It is possible to allow both yourself and your ex to move on even if you have children together and have constant contact and communication. Wanting and letting go of past resentments, misunderstandings, lost dreams, unfilled wishes, and cruel actions is a vital part of resolution. This is that moment when you know it is time to emotionally, mentally, spiritually, and physically move forward and let the past go. This can happen for any reason, but it needs to happen; it is critical to your romantic future and present-day happiness.

Fulfillment in future love relationships hinges on your ability to put the past away and to develop compassion and empathy for yourself and your ex. All your future partners and intimate connections depend on your choice to do this. Sometimes it is very difficult; adults from all backgrounds have expressed to me the pain and agony they have endured at the hands of their exes. But regardless of your intimate circumstances, it is necessary to get closure and resolution with your ex. Your ability to have an intimate relationship will be based on your ability to let go of past disappointments, resentments, and grudges. Your future intimate communications, emotional connections, and physical relationships will be directly impacted by this process.

True Intimacy Equals Self-Acceptance

True intimacy can be achieved only when two people allow each other to be imperfect. The need for perfection in a relationship is one person's psychological issue impacting the other. Demanding perfection is a form of self-loathing and, in severe cases, self-hatred. When we accept, understand, and work on our own imperfections, we can accept our partners' shortcomings and mistakes. The critical voice in your head—and we all have one—will be silenced only through personal acceptance and understanding of your own humanness.

These few sentences may sound very neat and easy, but they will provide the foundation to building the life, family, and intimate relationship you crave. Resolution will always start and finish with you. *All endeavors in personal growth, spiritual practices, religious exercises, and psychological insights will lead you back to one place: self-acceptance.* This concept is especially important when you are recovering from a major transition or change in an intimate relationship. It is normal for your self-esteem to be low after the ending of a romantic relationship, but it is important to resolve your dislikes of yourself, your personal insecurities, and your shame-based beliefs about yourself when you're on the receiving end of a breakup or divorce.

Many times we have an unconscious need for our partner to be perfect. This unconscious projection is about our own personal insecurities and feelings of inadequacy. These projections become very painful when a breakup occurs. The breakup is an acknowledgment that the relationship was not perfect, and that means that you aren't perfect. Your identity is directly tied to how your partner views you. The relationship and you are one emotional unit, which now feels like a huge failure. It is important that your core identity and self-worth are understood to be more than your relationship. Develop this perspective that your inner self-esteem is made up of many parts of your life internally and externally. If you can forgive yourself for the divorce/breakup, then all the negative emotional energy from it will not be part of your future romantic relationships. The inability to forgive—blaming your partner for your unhappiness—is all about *you* and your feelings of imperfection. Realize that the pursuit of perfection is untenable and hopeless. The more you understand and accept your emotional needs, wants, and desires, the less likely you will be to expect a future partner to be perfect. Your self-acceptance of your imperfections is the key to having a more satisfying and fulfilling relationship. If you don't have to spend your emotional energy and time with the need to be perfect, think what you could do with all that free time and energy.

Finding the ability to overlook the things that would only cause further fighting and arguing is reaching resolution with your ex. Choosing not to argue about the money, the custody arrangement, or what you feel your ex owes you emotionally is a clear sign of your relationship resolution. Looking at your ex and yourself and understanding what you both needed and didn't understand during the relationship is resolution.

Your emotional pain, regardless of its severity, is an informational sign that you need to make some important changes about your romantic relationship life. Fortunately, we are all wired to seek change when our level of personal pain and suffering exceeds our comfort zone. Resolving our own self-loathing and imperfections allows us to make room in our relationships for other people and their own imperfections. *Emotional pain is the catalyst for the changes we all want to make, though they may seem daunting.*

Resolution Barometer

Consider the following questions and how much or little you feel about each. Your goal is to become increasingly less reactive and more responsive to the issues surrounding your divorce/breakup.

1. Can you picture yourself in an intimate relationship in the future?
2. Can you name three positive things that you learned from your ex? If you can't find something positive to say, don't panic; just keep reading.
3. What is the major personality or emotional issue about yourself that you can now accept?
4. What could have you done differently with your ex that you will do differently in the future?
5. What is one change that you want to make in your next intimate relationship?
6. Can you accept your role/responsibility in the issues you had in your last relationship?
7. Do you still hold anger, resentment, or vengeful feelings toward your ex for leaving?
8. Do you verbally bash your ex to your children, friends, and/or family? If so, when and why do you do it?
9. Do you accept the "good" and the "bad" about your relationship?
10. Do you still secretly fantasize about being with your ex, even if it is circumstantially impossible?

How do you think you did on your resolution questions and current reactions to your ex, the divorce, and all the circumstances surrounding your romantic life today? Your goal is always to be moving toward resolution and personal self-acceptance. Remember that resolution is a process, not an ending point. If you find yourself arguing less frequently, not creating situations where you can be verbally aggressive, and doing positive (or at least neutral) things for your ex, then you are moving in the right direction. If children are involved in your prior relationship, you must take their well-being seriously. Your children can't bear the brunt of your disappointment and resentment toward your ex. I can't emphasize enough the long-term damage that is done to children when their divorcing parents have an ongoing battle and relentless tension. Even if you and your ex don't have kids, this stage is still critical to your future. Your answers about your process to the questions above all point to your resolution and your movement toward a greater degree of understanding of your life and responsibility for your actions. No matter how "awful" the circumstances of your divorce/breakup, you are always responsible for your actions and reactions to it.

STAGE FIVE: HOPE, INSIGHT, AND CREATIVITY

You will know when you have reached the phase of insight, hope, and creativity because the breakup of your relationship won't consume your life. You will get up in the morning and your first thought won't be about your ex or the breakup. You will start to see new things—literally and figuratively—in your life. As my client Tom told me: "Steve, I just noticed one morning that there was a beautiful red rosebush growing outside my bedroom window. I think it had been there for years. I just never noticed it—or a lot of things in my life—while I was going through my divorce." Another client, Christine, told me: "My divorce felt like it would never end, and one day it was over. All the fighting, court stuff, the kids—and then it was done. I felt like I jumped off a merry-go-round and landed on my feet. It was very surprising." It was at these precise moments that both Tom and Christine knew that the crisis had passed and the emotional pain and feelings of loss were declining. They now had the energy, time, and interest to pursue the next chapter of their lives.

When you enter this stage, you are realizing that your life is no longer centered around, consumed by, or obsessed with your ex and all the extenuating circumstances of the breakup. You are really living your life, not enduring the pain and shock of the end of your relationship. You are now finding a new path for yourself. You are building a new life, going in a new direction, and living a more fulfilling existence. You are finding that there are things in your life that you have never considered or pursued in the past. You might even find yourself wanting to change careers and do something that is more to your liking. Your changes aren't motivated out of revenge or envy of your ex, but out of the genuine desire for a different future.

There are many common assumptions about divorcing adults. One is that after a divorce a woman will lose twenty pounds, get breast implants, and start to do all the things her ex always wanted. These can range from taking up sports to working full-time to creating a new business. Likewise, a man will go buy the Porsche, Corvette, or Harley-Davidson motorcycle he has always wanted, date a woman twenty years his junior, and get hair implants. Instead of working long hours, he comes home earlier, spending more with the kids. But the changes for both men and women are in fact more internal than external. Their momentum in creating a new life often includes new cars, physical changes, and new hobbies. Some may make changes that seem radical (i.e., changing careers and taking a huge pay cut, having cosmetic elective surgery) but truly aren't. These changes are all about feeling personally empowered and confident enough to try new things that you were reluctant or afraid to do while in your relationship.

It is reasonable to assume that given the emotional, mental, physical, and psychological elements involved with separating from your partner, creating a new life for yourself will not happen overnight. You will find over time that you now have the energy and interest to consider a new path in your life, rather than just surviving the day. According to a number of sources, for every three years a person has been married or intimately involved, it takes one year to recover from the end of the relationship.[2] My professional experience has shown that the healing and resolution process doesn't really start until the divorce is finalized, the breakup is complete, and all the paperwork and money issues are settled. At that point it is usually a two-year process to move through the five stages of separating and gaining a new perspective on and direction in life.

It is almost impossible—I hate to say never, but there might be the one exception—to start a new and successful relationship while simultaneously ending another one. This commonsense approach to separating without complicating matters may sound wise, but it often isn't followed. People are people, everyone reacts to the separation process differently, and the need for companionship might be mistaken for love. *It simply doesn't work to bring another romantic partner into your life during this transition period.* I am not implying that having friends of the opposite sex is wrong or should be avoided. Adults underestimate the emotional toll that a divorce/breakup takes on them and developing a significant love relationship during your transition period is difficult. Rather, it is imprudent to become romantically involved and move toward another exclusive intimate relationship during this time. Developing another significant relationship makes the separating process that much more difficult and painful. Many times the new lover becomes the sounding board for how "awful" your ex is and your new relationship is focused on your old relationship. This new romantic partner becomes the "dumping" ground of your divorce/breakup. The new relationship never has a chance to develop naturally because it is in the shadow of your ex. We will discuss this all-too-common self-soothing behavior choice and avoidance style in section II.

REALITIES AND MISPERCEPTIONS ABOUT DIVORCE AND BREAKUPS

One of the realities about reaching a new place in your life is how you resolve, address, and understand—consciously and unconsciously— the common misperceptions about divorce and breakups. People ask me all the time: "How do I know I am able to move forward after my breakup? What are the tangible issues or beliefs I need to understand? How will I be able to know in the future that my intimate relationship is in trouble? I don't want to make the same mistakes again." The answers to these questions will be different for everyone, and you will answer them for yourself and understand those answers more fully in chapter 10. You are learning about the truth of your former relationship and your responsibility in love relationships.

Please mark each statement true or false, and make note of your personal explanation. Then compare your answers to what we have discussed so far. There are no wrong answers. The goal is to expand your level of insight and increase your movement forward. The explanations might or might not agree with your beliefs, but consider the new insights.

1. Breakups/relationship endings are unavoidable.
2. Rejection is toxic.
3. Feelings of betrayal and abandonment are abnormal.
4. I will never get over the emotional pain and loss of my partner.
5. I hate and love my ex.
6. My heart will forever be broken and my life is over.
7. Men always leave.
8. I will never again be vulnerable to a lover.
9. My ex is completely to blame for our breakup.
10. Intimate relationships should be avoided and relationships should be kept emotionally distant.

Answers

1. **True.** Relationship endings are normal and should be viewed not as failures but rather as a tool for personal growth and learning. All relationships have a beginning point and an ending point. It should be noted that ending a relationship through a divorce or a breakup is a different process than the ending of a relationship through the death of a partner. Losing a partner to death is a different emotional dynamic than the circumstances discussed here. (See the bibliography for suggested readings on death, dying, and being a widow/widower.)

2. **False.** Rejection is painful. What is toxic is not allowing yourself to see your own role and responsibility in the relationship. No one can reject you other than yourself. What may seem like rejection is simply the fact that you and your partner weren't, or were no longer, a good match.

3. **False.** It is normal to feel abandoned and betrayed when a relationship ends. These emotions, which are typical feelings when going through the process of separating, tend to have their roots in your childhood parent/child relationship. Childhood experiences of love, conflict resolution, significant attachments (your mom/dad, relatives, family friends, childhood pet, school friends), and socialization all help form your emotional template for relationships. It is this early template that you formed for relationships that will be re-examined in the following chapters.

4. **False.** We all have the gift called *amnesia*. The amnesia effect allows us to eventually forget the severity of our pain and the intensity of our heartbreak. What will not change over time are the core issues, beliefs, and hatred, unless we actively pursue resolution. Changing our core beliefs is possible by considering the responsibility we have in our marriage/romantic relationships. The diminishing of

pain allows us to deal with our deeper intimacy issues. The emotional bleeding will eventually stop and allow us to regain our perspective.

5. **True.** If you find yourself holding on to loving feelings toward an ex who was anything but loving, don't panic. Mental health and emotional intelligence allow us to feel conflicting emotions for the same person. Your ex will never be all bad or all good. You built a life with this person and there were great things in the relationship, regardless of its ending and the circumstances surrounding it. Unfortunately, the breakup is so painful that all the good memories are temporarily erased. Some positive memories will reappear months and years later, but you will likely be grateful that you are no longer with your ex.

6. **False.** Your life is different, changed, transformed—but not over. It is understandable that the absence of a strong intimate relationship may make you feel sad. However, your life is the sum of all its parts. Your life is more than your marriage, divorce, or ex-partner. It might feel as if you have a huge hole in your heart that nothing will fill, but ultimately you will fill in the gaps in your life with new challenges, activities, interests, and future relationships.

7. **False.** People leave! Men and women leave relationships every day. It is essential not to bash the opposite sex. It is very common in divorce to become cynical about the opposite sex. Engaging in this very negative and narrow-minded practice is destructive and toxic for you. You suffer when you adopt these types of negative, fear-based attitudes. There is no new information or widening of perspective gained in being angry and bitter toward the opposite sex. Adults who get in this rut are broadcasting to everyone that they are stuck in the anger phase. Gender isn't the cause of your divorce or breakup.

8. **False.** You don't want your emotional pain to make choices for your romantic life. Left unresolved or unprocessed, emotional pain will

turn into fear, which leads to emotional isolation. You can and will learn, grow, and move forward in being able to develop a stable, significant intimate relationship. You wouldn't be reading this book if you didn't have the drive, motivation, and ability to move beyond your ex.

9. **False.** Life would be so much easier if one person were the sum total of all our suffering and issues. But you know by now that your ex is only a piece of your puzzle, not the whole puzzle. It is critical to go beyond blaming and start seeing the relationship from a wider perspective and a position of expanded understanding. People who insist that their ex is the whole problem are walking into a cement wall. Blame, finger-pointing, and accusing your ex of ruining the marriage or your life is only half the story. It takes courage and insight to acknowledge and look at your role in the final outcome of your marriage/romantic relationship. Blaming your former partner will never heal or reduce your emotional pain. *No one is responsible for your life other than you.* You had a role in the relationship and you can't be completely uninvolved or considered an innocent bystander. Never underestimate your role or influence in the relationship; every relationship has two participants.

10. **False.** Intimate relationships are the only place in our adult lives where we can create a safe, supportive, and nurturing environment with another adult. Intimate relationships are where we can have genuine support and the sense of being understood and accepted. Maintaining emotional distance from our partners only cheats us of the opportunity to create the kind of intimacy that we crave.

All of these questions, themes, insights, and perspectives will be discussed and reinforced throughout this book. In the next chapter we will shift gears and discuss the breakup process from the other perspective: the partner leaving the relationship.

Chapter 3

THE PAIN OF LEAVING

The Guilt Syndrome

I felt like I escaped with my life. I moved from San Diego to Los Angeles and couldn't get away from him any faster. It took me at least one year to get on my feet and begin to start a new life. My ex-husband still hates me for leaving, but I had to do it. I was dying.
—Christine, age forty-three, mother of three, married for fourteen years, divorced for two years

The relationship had been dead for years. We went to counseling and it only pointed out our differences more. I filed for divorce because I didn't want to spend the rest of my life hoping my husband would change or notice me. The timing is awful, but I just needed to do something.
—Karen, age fifty-one, mother of two, married for twenty-two years, divorced for one year

I felt the pressure to marry Rose, but I knew it would never work. We lived together and did everything possible to make our relationship right. She was ready for kids, and I didn't know if we could make it past the honeymoon. I still feel horrible about the breakup, but I couldn't stay with her. We weren't a good match.
—Pete, age thirty-three, engaged for two years, broke off the engagement three months before the wedding

WHEN DO YOU LEAVE?

The question of leaving or staying with your partner is one of the toughest dilemmas facing many in adulthood. Unplugging the life-support system on your intimate relationship can feel like committing yourself to a slow and painful death. The layers of issues, emotions, circumstances, shared history, children, finances, fears, and doubt make the decision to leave an intimate relationship transformational. There can be no doubt that the person on the receiving end of a breakup has many difficult issues to contend with and to understand. But the partner who is contemplating leaving—initiating the separation action—has his or her own set of emotional circumstances, psychological concerns, and conflicted feelings. Both parties in the breakup will go through the five phases of separating, but they will experience these from very different vantage points. Neither person is spared the emotional pain and heartbreak associated with disconnecting lives and forgetting old memories. Sometimes the loneliest person in the separation cycle is the one doing it. The paradox is that both parties in a love relationship will experience the trauma of both sides of the breakup, and often the only person who gets emotional support, empathy, and understanding is the one who has been left.

I have professionally met all three of the people in the vignettes that open this chapter. Each of them struggled with, questioned, and anguished over the idea of ending their significant romantic relationship. *All three adults loved the partner from whom they were separating. The strong feelings of concern, love, and despair were independent of the surrounding issues and dysfunction.* Yet the circumstances of all three adults were as different as the desert summer is from the northern winter. An outsider might say that Pete had the easiest time, Karen had a tough choice, but Christine had the most difficulty. Christine would be the first to admit that her story was awful, but she still feels fortunate for having three great kids. Her marriage was great for the first eight years and became increasingly abusive the last six years. No one who is contemplating leaving an intimate relationship believes it is an easy task. The truth is that the decision to break up is one of the biggest ones any of us will ever make and is often one of the most difficult to execute. It takes a lot of courage, energy, emotional clarity, and psychological strength to initiate the ending of a relationship. A 2008 article in *Parade* magazine included the following statistics.[1] These numbers indicate that leaving or staying in a relationship is something that many partners consider at some point. It isn't abnormal or problematic to consider your options when your relationship is going through a difficult period. Considering "leaving" a marriage or romantic relationship doesn't necessarily imply that you should or shouldn't. The point is a large number of men and women do consider different ways (i.e., divorce, broken engagement, couples therapy) to resolve and work out their intimate relationship challenges and issues.

Numbers—Nobody Really Knows What Goes On behind Closed Doors

- Forty-four percent of married women have thought about leaving their husband.
- Thirty-one percent of married men have thought about leaving their wife.
- Thirty-one percent of all married couples have sex less than once a month.
- Forty-eight percent of married men say they don't have sex more often because their spouse isn't interested.
- Thirty-three percent of women say they don't have sex more often because they're tired.
- Twenty-five percent of married couples describe their marital sex life as either tolerable or terrible.
- Twenty-four percent of couples have kept an important secret from their spouse.
- Eighty-four percent of all married men say they would marry their wife again.

- Seventy-eight percent of all married women say they would marry their husband again.

These numbers show that almost half of all married women have considered leaving their marriage, and almost a third of all married men have considered that option. The figures relating to sex and intimacy show that many couples have become emotionally disconnected, either through a lack of sexual intimacy or emotional dissatisfaction. Based on the clients I've seen, I'd say that the emotional discontent continues to grow and breeds an increasing level of tension in the relationship. Missing from these statistics is the forgotten fact that deciding to end a significant relationship is not an easy choice. *Sometimes the circumstances and tension become so severe that the choice is made for you.* For instance, if your partner has crossed your tacit line of trust and the personal violation is beyond description. The relationship is over. Every relationship has a breaking point and when that point is reached the marriage/intimate partnership is over. It can be about infidelity, finances, physical/emotional abuse, drug use and/or anything that the partner views as a violation of the intimate relationship. Couples many times will never directly express to each other what that point of "no return" is, but they each know it.

It may take years for the separating action to materialize and come to completion, but there are certain actions that start the movement toward it. Every couple can look back and see certain points when it was clear that their relationship was moving toward its ending. These behaviors range from abuse, affairs, money laundering, drug abuse, fraudulent behavior, indifference, boredom, emotional negligence, child molestation, and endless other destructive relationship behaviors. There are much less dramatic events such as falling out of love with your partner, or feeling depressed and emotionally trapped in your marriage. All of these situations regardless of the severity can lead a partner to consider the termination of the relationship. Typically the most difficult decision for a partner is when the other partner is a "good" person and there is no tangible reason to "leave" the marriage/relationship. There is always personal information that each partner can either use to move toward an ending or continuing to build a future together. Romantic relationships, regardless of their formal title (i.e., married, living together, engaged, exclusive dating, etc.,) all have moments of decision to resolve issues or to ignore them. The relationship decision process is mostly subconscious.

RELATIONSHIPS ARE VALUABLE

It is worth mentioning, for the sake of avoiding misunderstanding, that it is important, whenever possible, to work through issues, resolve conflict, and build a deeper commitment in your relationship. Our discussion here isn't about relationships being disposalable or easily replaced but the complicated process of continuing to build a future with someone. The goal of this book is to help you develop the type of intimate relationship you want. Many times this process is impossible until the existing relationship has ended. The realization that leaving your current relationship in order to continue to grow and develop the depth of intimacy that you are craving can be very overwhelming. In order not to be repetitive about the importance of staying in a relationship, it is important to think through all your options with your current or ex-partner. Staying in your current relationship, however, isn't the focus of this book. It is assumed that by the time you are reading this, all the possible tools, solutions, and hopes for the relationship have been completely exhausted and attempted. My personal, professional, and social position isn't advocating a no-fault, "easy" divorce/breakup theory, but rather the opposite. It is presumed if you're reading this book that you had no other choice and hope of restoring your marriage/intimate partnership. There are volumes of outstanding books on how to save your marriage. I recommend those books and their approaches to saving romantic relationships. My approach and perspective is different. Our discussion is about where, how, and what you do when all else has failed and the relationship has ended.

There isn't much in mainstream psychology or relationship theory about the power and staying power of an ex. The increase in the last thirty years in the number of blended families is staggering. People are remarrying at a higher rate than ever before. The need for people to resolve, understand, heal, and create stable relationships is critical for society as a whole.[2] But there isn't much practical support or emotional insight on how to resolve the overwhelming negative emotions produced by a breakup. People going through a breakup—whether it is a divorce after twenty years or the end of a six-month love affair—know the power of all the changes taking place. Endings are always transformational. But endings don't have to be catastrophic or emotionally fatal to you. It is important to remember that *endings are inevitable in all relationships*. The endings we are discussing are what seem as premature and tragic (divorce) to the people involved. The death of a partner is a completely different subject and topic. In cases of death, you or your partner had no control over the ending of the relationship. Control and free will between the partners play a big part in the continuation and termination of a marriage/love relationship.

My goal in this chapter is to assist you in navigating the waters as you move forward in the wake of a tremendous personal loss; to help you overcome your disappointment, heartbreak, and feelings of anger and despair; and to help you create a new life. You still have needs and desires that do not cease to exist just because you are going through a major breakup or divorce. Our core emotional, mental, physical, sexual, and survival desires all center around our ability to have intimate relationships, connections, and bonds. *We will never stop wanting, needing, and creating intimate, loving, supportive relationships in our lives.*

But no one wants to keep repeating the same dysfunctional romantic patterns in their next intimate relationship, and no one wants his or her ex involved in the relationship future. There is a saying I heard recently from an older family friend that sums up the point perfectly: "You can have many marriages, but you only get married once!" In other words, we often keep repeating the same behavioral and emotional patterns of frustration, anger, emotional dysfunction, and wrong partner selection. If we never learn from our intimate connections or realize what we really want and need in our love relationships, the result can be that we have many disappointing love affairs in our lives. What truly matters is not the number of marriages or significant relationships we have had, but the depth of connection and the degree of intimacy and love that we develop with our partners. When we achieve the degree of closeness, intimacy, and emotional safety we crave, then we have finally married. This might happen after several significant dating relationships, or it might take two or three marriages before we recognize our needs, wants, and desires in a relationship. Marriage has always been symbolic of our deepest human need for loving attachment, approval, and understanding. People can call marriage-type relationships by many other names (i.e., living together, life partners, exclusive lovers, soul mates with no contract, etc.), but the dynamic and function of intimate relationships will never change. Our need to feel loved, supported, and accepted is the emotional equivalent of oxygen. Without this element, our lives may become filled with irrational paranoia, personality disorders, and loneliness.[3] Our bodies die without oxygen, and our hearts die without love and a sense of belonging.

Once you have reached the limit of your tolerance and your primary needs of love, acceptance, and safety aren't being met in the relationship, you unfortunately will likely announce to your world (including your partner) that you want the relationship to end. The choice to finally address the decision to leave the relationship doesn't make it any easier or less painful to follow through on it.

In many cases, the relationship's ending is calm and passive, and there is no drama or overt conflict between the partners. In fact, the rest of the world may think it makes no sense to end the relationship. Your relationship may look great to everyone else, while inside you may feel empty, psychologically suffocated, and emotionally dying. These types of silent endings are difficult to initiate because you have no particular defining moment to seize on or act on. The other extreme—chair throwing, name calling, and police intervention—may look like an easier way to end things, but it isn't. Regardless of how you got to this fork in the road in your relationship, you are there. As in real life there is no easy choice. All three people whose experiences were shared at the outset of this chapter had different circumstances, but they all had one thing in common: guilt. No matter how clear it was that their love relationships were over, they all struggled with their own feelings of guilt for "hurting" their partners. The impact and staying power of guilt can be very perplexing and not always a good indicator of how to proceed. Guilt feelings aren't always a good indicator or moral compass that you should stay in relationship that needs to end. (Obviously, to do something destructive or mean-spirited to your ex is not what I'm talking about.) The concept that you are changing the relationship with your decision to leave can be very guilt producing, even though it is truly in everyone's best interest to do it.

THREE STORIES OF CONFLICT

Christine

Christine didn't want to move out of her house and not live with her husband even though her marriage was one of physical, mental, and psychological abuse. She knew that her husband wasn't a good influence on her or her children. Christine still found the process of separating extremely painful and traumatic. She didn't want the marriage to end, but she couldn't tolerate the abuse or craziness any longer. When she discovered her husband having sex with another woman in their home, she finally ended the marriage. This wasn't the first time he had behaved in such a flagrantly disrespectful manner toward her, but it was the last time for Christine. Her husband clearly wasn't interested in the marriage, or her, any longer. After she found her husband in bed with another woman, Christine immediately moved out of town, taking her children with her. When he threatened her with physical harm, she took out a restraining order against him. Her ex-husband, who lived ninety minutes away, never came to see the children (Christine drove the kids to her ex's house for custody visits) after she moved with them to Los Angeles, and he blamed all the family struggles (i.e., custody arrangements, finances, divorce proceedings, extended family concerns) on her. Her children were seven, nine, and eleven years old.

The kids missed and wanted to spend more time with their father, but they supported their mother's decision to divorce him. The kids had witnessed the verbal and emotional abuse, and the extreme mood swings of their father. Christine felt like a failure as a mother, a wife, and a person for having stayed for so long in such a dysfunctional relationship. Now, two years later, she still struggles with feelings of guilt, anger, and resentment toward her former husband. This was her second marriage, and it wasn't supposed to end this way. For his part, her ex-husband still feels betrayed and abandoned by Christine for ending the marriage. He has since remarried a woman twenty-two years his junior and refuses to pay child support. Christine feels that she escaped the marriage with her life—and with some degree of sanity.

Christine feels very guilty for being "one of those women" who allow their husbands to walk all over them with chronic extramarital affairs and deceptive behavior. At the same time, Christine—who is a very smart woman—knows intuitively that she saved herself and her children from a rapidly disintegrating situation. Regardless of the dire circumstances and the flagrant abuse she suffered, she is still very sad about the outcome of her marriage. But her guilt is irrational since she made the best decision for herself, given the reality of her life, marriage, and young children.

Karen

Karen's situation is very different and much less dramatic, and she is conflicted by her feelings of both guilt and emotional relief over her divorce. As seen from the outside, she had the "perfect" marriage. No abuse, a nice husband, poor communication, easy daily life, and plenty of money. Karen had a house with a white picket fence, a country club membership, and all the associated luxuries that go with a comfortable lifestyle. She and her ex-husband were both Ivy League graduates and very well connected, socially and professionally. She had no wants financially or materially. *But she was comfortably miserable and felt like she was dying emotionally, psychologically, and mentally in the marriage.*

Karen had spoken to her husband, Charles, on countless occasions about the terrible state of their marriage and the need for more time together. The concept of spending time together would hopefully generate more emotional connection and intimate communication. Without spending time together there was no possibility of anything changing in the marriage. These talks took place on a regular basis over a ten-year period but never yielded any changes or different action. In fact, Karen and her husband took separate vacations and did "couple activities" only with other couples. They rarely spent any time together or shared intimate details of their lives with each other. Their sex life, as a barometer of their emotional distance, was nonexistent. Charles repeatedly accused Karen of quitting the relationship, even though he appeared completely disinterested in developing any type of closer emotional bond with Karen. But when she tried to arrange activities the two of them could do together, they never seemed to engage him. She felt that all the marriage counseling, relationship books, and countless talks had only postponed the inevitable.

After a holiday weekend, Karen announced to Charles that she wanted a divorce. He immediately left the house and golfed for the entire day. They didn't discuss the separation issue for another six weeks, until their sons left for summer camp. Charles had all of his friends' wives—the women in their social circle—call Karen and tell her how stupid she was for wanting to leave the marriage. Several of these women told her to grow up and face the reality that being single in your fifties isn't easy, and it certainly wouldn't be any better than her marriage. But many of the other women said they secretly admired her strength, encouraged her, and said they wished that they could do the same even though they publicly agreed with Charles. Karen didn't feel she was looking for "greener pastures," but rather wanted to start living again. She felt like a desperate housewife—without the drama and affairs. She felt as though she were sleepwalking through her life, and Charles didn't want to wake himself—or her—up.

Karen became very depressed and anxious about pursuing the divorce. Charles blamed her for the damage the divorce would do to their two teenage boys. But both of her sons thought it was a good idea for their parents to separate because of all the tension at home they had felt for the last five years. Neither son resented their mother; they wanted both of their parents to "get a life."

Pete

On the outside, Pete's situation looks very different from the previous two. Christine and Karen are both middle-aged women venturing out into the world with their children after ending long-term marriages. Pete is a single man (never married) who found himself with a woman who wanted a family and he was a convenient choice for her. Pete didn't completely feel like he was adored or loved by his girlfriend/fiancée but rather was a good mate for her dreams and wishes. But below the surface, the issues that motivated Christine and Karen were ultimately the same ones that made Pete reexamine his relationship with his fiancée. Pete knew that part of his problem was that he was marrying his girlfriend, Rose, only because she wanted to have a family. Pete wanted a family but never felt that Rose truly wanted him. She said the right things, but their relationship styles were very different. Pete liked to be emotionally close through conversation, while Rose liked to keep her feelings to herself. Consequently, Pete felt like a puzzle piece in her life plan. He loved Rose and wanted her to be happy, but he could never resolve his nagging feeling that he was marrying her for the wrong reasons. The *concept* of having children and building a life together was a priority for him. But Pete felt the relationship lacked energy, open communication, and emotional closeness. He found himself saying yes to everything to keep the peace, but never really knew what he wanted or needed. All of his friends were either married or were getting married, so he unconsciously felt pressure to move his relationship forward. Moreover, his relationship with Rose was scarily similar to his parent's marriage relationship. Pete didn't want to go through the "motions" of having a family and being an emotionally discontented husband like his father.

One morning, while lying in bed, Pete asked Rose if she were twenty-four years old instead of thirty-five, would she marry him? Without pausing or even seeming to think about her answer, she replied, *"No way."* Pete knew immediately that this was a moment of truth. Pete instantly flashed to what his father had told him before he died that he had gotten married too young, to the wrong person, and he regretted not waiting. Pete knew that Rose's answer was a reflection of his own gut feeling about their lack of intimacy, poor sex life, and distant emotional bond. Rose wanted to get married and Pete was the guy to do it. On paper, Rose was a great catch, but she didn't meet Pete's needs and desires. Two weeks after that conversation, Pete called off the wedding.

Within six months of their breakup, Rose was engaged and living with another man. Pete, on the other hand, didn't date for almost two years. He felt guilty, demoralized, and heartbroken about the breakup. Pete knew he had done the right thing for himself and for Rose, but he couldn't get rid of the feeling that he had done something wrong.

THE GUILT SYNDROME

Guilt Distorts

In all three of these stories, the end of the relationship wasn't easy to initiate, and in no case was it a sudden decision. These stories illustrate the anguish and confusion involved in trying to figure out the inner workings of an intimate relationship. Even though Christine, Karen, and Pete made good choices and allowed their intimate relationships to end, it still took an emotional toll on all parties. It is important to remember the struggles each individual goes through in the ending of a relationship; it is an arduous process. *Whether you are being left or doing the leaving, the ending process affects you.* The key to reducing your internal conflict is to understand the purpose and role of your guilt. Many times the guilt might be feelings of grief or loss about the relationship ending. Guilt feelings can be mistaken for other deeper unconscious emotions such as grief, sadness, despair, fear, and hopelessness. None of the three people in our discussion did anything to purposely hurt or abuse their partners. Yet all three adults felt like "bad" people for ending their intimate relationships. None of their partners were initially supportive of the divorce/breakup but eventually all three former partners accepted the new relationship status.

Guilt Creates Fear

The primary role of guilt is to enable someone to feel, think, and know when he or she has done something wrong. Guilt has no regard for emotional boundaries or misguided beliefs. For instance, you might have the belief that you should never divorce. Your marriage is very abusive and not capable of being "healed." You divorce your partner because it is an act of self-preservation and emotional safety. In spite of your choice you still feel guilty that you violated an old belief about marriage and divorce. Your feelings of guilt are highly personal and very subjective. It is your internal feeling that is individual and can be socially influenced. For example, your husband, family, and in-laws might all believe that you shouldn't divorce your husband because of his most recent affair. The atmosphere of your relationship is abusive, but your support system reinforces the feeling that it is wrong to change it. As a result, you feel guilty about your decision. Your guilt complex can be exaggerated by allowing others to dictate your behavior and feelings. Your opinion about your choices, relationships and family is the most important and valuable. It is crucial to recognize when you have given your personal power away to other people (such as your partner and your family), allowing them to control and to make decisions for you. Only you know what is truly right and wrong in your intimate relationship. No one outside of the relationship can really understand the circumstances surrounding it or judge your behavior. For these reasons, your feelings of guilt can't always be trusted or considered completely accurate. The more you objectively evaluate your relationship, the easier it is to see the issues, tensions, and challenges aside from your feelings of guilt. Moreover, it is very easy to disguise your fear of moving forward in your life and taking a new direction as a moral or guilt issue. Next to love, fear is one of the strongest forces in human relationships, and it can't be dismissed as a minor concern or issue. *Guilt is fear's first cousin!*

Guilt Can Be Misleading

Feelings of guilt are often among the most misleading emotions in a breakup. In spite of her horrendous circumstances, Christine still struggled with her decision to end the relationship. Karen felt that she would die a slow death if she didn't do something to wake herself and her ex-husband up. Pete also knew that his girlfriend of four years wasn't the right match emotionally, psychologically, or spiritually. These high-functioning adults were criticized by friends and family for leaving as a result of the actions they took. *Upon closer examination, it is clear that they were really the ones who stopped the denial, read the ending signs, and took appropriate action.* None of these three were looking for the "easy way out" or for "greener pastures." When you finally decide to end your relationship, it is an emotional challenge for both partners. Divorce, the end of a long-term relationship, and the breakup of a dating relationship will be emotionally painful and heartbreaking. It is unavoidable—relationship endings are traumatic to a greater or lesser degree. It doesn't matter who is at fault; the decision to end a relationship is always life changing. The person leaving is often portrayed as the villain, but the truth is often more complicated. In nearly every circumstance, no one is the total villain and no one is the total victim. Both parties are contributors and participants in the relationship, and both are partly responsible for the breakup. Don't lose sight of the perspective that *it takes two people to have a relationship and to create dysfunction.* When and if you have strong feelings of guilt, it is important to remain mindful in those moments that every relationship is never "ended" or terminated by one partner. You might be the person to end the marriage, but you aren't alone (your partner was there also) in the relationship for you to take this action.

How Guilt Works in the End

The person who initiates the divorce or breakup takes on a lot of extra responsibility. You automatically become the "bad guy/gal" because you are moving the relationship to its conclusion. The denial is over surrounding the problems in the relationship that led up to the divorce/breakup. Partners who are feeling abandoned or rejected, regardless of the role they played in the breakup, usually become defensive, laying blame and attempting to evoke guilt in the other. Also, partners who are being left usually get a great deal of support and sympathy from the outside world. This might even include *your* family, friends, business partners, neighbors, the children, and your own best friend. Never underestimate the power of desperation and the sudden need to "fix" the relationship on the other side of your decision to divorce/breakup. Because you have reached the metaphorical "end of your rope" doesn't mean you will not feel awful, guilty, and depressed because you are done with the intimate relationship. These actions are usually too little, too late and serve no other purpose than to cover up the bigger problems in the relationship. My clinical experience has repeatedly shown that women will attempt to work on the issues, problems, and tensions in relationships prior to a divorce/breakup. If the issues aren't resolved or adequately addressed (this is highly subjective and personal), they will eventually decide to end it. Men on the other hand generally don't view the problems in the relationship as serious until their wife, girlfriend, or fiancée has divorced/broken up with them. These are two different approaches to "endings" but very common among couples. For instance, the husband becomes incredibly motivated to "fix" the relationship after being told by his wife that she is filing for divorce. The wife no longer has any interest in working on the marriage/relationship. The other partner, usually the husband, will spend a lot of emotional energy trying to "win" back the other partner (wife), but unfortunately it is usually too late. The relationship is done and she has emotionally moved forward. Men tend to have a very difficult time emotionally accepting that their partners have made the decision to leave.

Don't be surprised at how the people in your life take sides in your breakup; often, the sides picked and the people involved aren't what and whom you expected. It is amazing how often the family takes the side of the physically or emotionally abusive husband when his wife leaves him. Christine's own family was upset when she left her husband because they felt she didn't "work hard enough" to save the relationship. *You can't "save" an intimate relationship or have one when there are more than two people in it.* Christine was clearly fighting for her position among a number of other women and that was another form of emotional abuse and demeaning to her. Her family's response is very typical because no one wants to acknowledge (denial) that "abuse" of any type is occurring with their nuclear or extended family.

Families often react to a divorce or breakup with anger and frustration. Your movement can cause a ripple effect in the greater family system. The decision to change your relationship status is always yours, regardless of the social and family pressure to maintain the status quo. Your decision to move the relationship to its conclusion is the beginning point for many changes in your life. Changing the status of a marriage or romantic relationship will always generate a wide spectrum of emotions, ranging from guilt to relief for all parties involved. Taking action always creates feelings, thoughts, and changes in all the people surrounding the couple, including the two partners. Unfortunately, guilt tends to dominate the feelings and thoughts of many well-meaning people attempting to create a better life for themselves and their partners.

Purposeful Guilt

We have seen and discussed the negative aspects of guilt, but it can also have a positive side. It can be a very useful barometer for self-feedback and monitoring your anger and your desire for revenge. When children are involved, the role of guilt is invaluable. Guilt is the emotional feedback that indicates that you might be committing character assassination (demeaning verbally) toward your ex. When children are involved, regardless of age, it is imperative to control what and how you talk about the other parent. Your children are 50 percent of your ex and 50 percent you. This is always a good thing to remember before verbally "blasting" your ex in front of your children. Use that reminder as a means to control and contain your negative feelings about the relationship. For instance, if you have crossed the line and told your kids that their other parent is a "loser" and you feel awful afterward, take notice. The feedback loop of guilt always includes your honest evaluation of your own actions, words, and intentions. When you are seeking revenge, emotional retribution, or punishment aimed at your ex, be aware of your sense of guilt about these actions. These negative behaviors are all emotional signs that you are in pain, fearful, and heartbroken. Use your guilt as a means to resolve your feelings about your past relationship. If you find yourself verbally assaulting your ex, it is important to pay attention to these feelings as information about your current mental, emotional, and psychological state. Guilt can be useful when viewed as a source of information about your behavior.

However dire the circumstances or necessary it is for the relationship to end, guilt will likely follow—regardless of how purposeful and productive the choice is for you. The ending of a relationship always involves some element of guilt. There is a cultural myth that "good" girls or boys never leave a relationship. Religious communities don't generally endorse or support the separating process, even when the relationship is far from normal or healthy. The guilt syndrome is based on the feeling that you are doing something wrong, regardless of the evidence to the contrary. The syndrome is the constant internal dialogue in your head about what you should or shouldn't do. It is a relentless internal mental battering of how you have "screwed up" your life, your family, and partner. These cyclical thoughts have nothing to do with the reality of your relationship but with your fear of doing something "wrong." On the other hand, you might be doing something that will cause your family, your ex, and your support network to change and heal. This is possible because if the marriage or romantic relationship is problematic, it usually impacts more than just the couple. The most common underlying guilt element is produced when one partner isn't in agreement with the relationship change—termination. His or her disapproval automatically becomes the strongest guilt-producing stimulus in the other partner. Strong feelings of guilt may tell you that you are doing something wrong, even though you logically know it is the right thing to do. Ending a marriage or any type of romantic relationship is very necessary for the partner initiating the change. In spite of your partner's refusal and acceptance of the problems, it is important to retain your sanity and common sense about the entire relationship history.

There are many circumstances that will push an intimate relationship to a breaking point: affairs; abuse—emotional, physical, or mental; financial issues; untreated personality disorders; lack of sexual/physical contact; poor communication; loss of respect; addictive behaviors; and so on. All of these very potentially self-defeating behaviors; by your partner over time become the reasons for separating. So why is the process of separating so complex and problematic? The fact is that walking away from a relationship creates so much emotional tension in the person seeking to end the relationship that his or her reasons for leaving can become at times very confusing and unclear to the other partner. The irrational element of guilt is the underlying reason why many adults stay in bad marriages, intimate relationships, and common-law marriages that they truly wish to end. The fear of changing your life and your partner's life becomes the emotional feeling of guilt. One clear purpose and intent of being emotionally bonded and intimately involved with someone is not to resent him/her or to wish you were elsewhere. When this basic premise of an intimate relationship is lost, that is a clear sign that the relationship has ended. The need to feel loved and being loved is many times lost when the paralyzing feelings and nagging thoughts of guilt overwhelm you. The power of guilt is that it can emotionally "mute" you from your need to be loved, supported, and cared for. Guilt if left uncensored will also "mute" you from pursuing a fulfilling and "safe" relationship.

REDUCING GUILT—READING THE SIGNS

One way to properly identify, understand, and see how your guilt operates is to examine your inner thoughts, verbal statements, and conscious and unconscious wishes you have about your intimate relationship. What is really going on between you and your partner? Why are you so irritable and depressed? Why are you so scared about leaving your loveless, sexless, and emotionally cold relationship?

What is your guilt complex about? What is the worst thing that could happen if you ended your intimate relationship? To help you better understand your own intentions—spoken and unspoken—as you resolve your process of closure with your ex, ask yourself about the validity of the following statements.

1. You have a well thought-out exit strategy. You want to leave the relationship.

2. You have exhausted every plausible option to improve the relationship.

3. You can't tolerate the abuse—emotional, mental, or physical—any longer.

4. Your partner threatens you with divorce or breakup whenever you argue or discuss problems in the relationship.

5. Your sexual contact and all signs of physical affection are non-existent.

6. You have no sexual, physical desire, or attraction for your partner.

7. Intimate communication and disclosures are no longer a part of your relationship, if they ever were.

8. You are living separate lives while still sharing a living space with your partner.

9. You have your own social network aside from your partner.

10. You are contemplating having an affair or have had one while involved with your current relationship.

11. You are having a romantic and/or physical affair. You think your partner knows but you aren't willing to end the affair or address the reason for it. This type of behavior creates a "wall of denial" between you and your partner.

12. You want to develop more intimacy, a deeper connection, and more understanding between the two of you, but your partner isn't interested in developing these critical elements in the relationship with you.

13. Marriage counseling isn't an option, or you have tried it and it didn't resolve the relationship issues.

14. You have lost respect for your partner.

15. Your partner has violated the relationship with his or her actions (drug abuse, unemployment—can't keep a job, affairs, abuse, or other irresponsible self-defeating behaviors).

16. You have lost all interest in and energy for the relationship. You feel like you are simply going through the motions of a marriage/romantic bond.

17. You are emotionally and psychologically done with the relationship.

18. If you didn't feel guilty, you would separate from your partner immediately.

19. The only reason you are staying in the relationship is for the sake of the children.

20. You can't support yourself financially and don't want to lose the lifestyle to which you are accustomed.

These twenty statements are a combination of many deep issues, beliefs and feelings, and conscious and unconscious behaviors that indicate that your relationship has run its course. If you agreed with more than five of these statements, then you are likely either in the process of ending the relationship or are very close to initiating an ending to it. What question or statement above best describes your current emotional state regarding your partner, your relationship, and/or your future? If you have already divorced or ended the relationship, what statements above played a major role in your decision to leave? How did you or will you manage your sense of loyalty and guilt with leaving the relationship? What was or is your "breaking point" with your partner about the relationship?

Guilt Resolution

Only you know the whole truth about your intimate relationship. If you have either left your partner or plan to do so, don't allow other people—such as family members or close friends—to influence or control your decision. This includes your ex, who might not have even valued you or the relationship until it was gone. Remember that your personal growth can be shaped by emotional heartbreaks and healings. *Remember that your choice to be honest with yourself and with your partner may be one of the greatest acts of love in the relationship.* Being completely honest as hard as it may feel with your partner about the true state of affairs between you both is something he or she knows but might never address. The truth is critical to all relationships: The relationship is done, but that isn't the end; it is the beginning of a new chapter in your life and your ex-partner's as well. Don't expect your ex to agree with your decision initially. Just because your heart feels like it is going to explode with pain and grief doesn't mean you did something wrong or made the wrong choice! Emotional pain is a sign of reacting to disconnecting from your ex, not a sign of a wrong decision or poor choice. Psychological pain is a result of changes in your life and the expansion of your emotional "comfort" zone.

Reducing Your Guilt

Stacy is a thirty-two-year-old woman who came to see me about recurring issues that had plagued her during her ten-year marriage. She had left her husband on three prior occasions and felt a tremendous amount of guilt and shame each time. When the guilt got to be too much to bear, usually after about three months, she would move back home. During marriage counseling, her husband, Mark, stated that he didn't want the marriage and regretted ever having married. But because of his family of origin and the children, he would never file for divorce or separation. He was essentially trying to force Stacy to take the action of ending the marriage.

Stacy wanted to figure out why she couldn't follow through on her deep desire to file for a divorce. She had two small children (a six-year-old son and a four-year-old daughter) and wanted them to have a stable home with both a mother and a father. Based on his current actions, the great deal of time he spent away from home, and his numerous affairs, Stacy knew that Mark wasn't interested in being married to her.

Stacy related the following after she moved back home for the third time in eighteen months: "I have had it. I feel guilty because I am more concerned about Mark's family than I am about myself and the kids. I love his parents and don't want to disappoint them."

I suggested that Stacy meet with her in-laws and explain the current state of her marriage. The goal was for her to stop making choices based on other people's ideas, perceptions of who and what she should be. Though paralyzed with fear, she knew she needed to do something different. Stacy met with her in-laws and later told me:

> Mark's mother held my hand and told me she would always love me regardless of what happened to our marriage. His father wondered why I worried about their opinion so much and hadn't divorced their son after the first year. Both of his parents knew about our problems and didn't understand why I hadn't acted sooner. They were very different than I had expected or imagined. I was worried they would hate me for splitting up the family and hurting their son. I was wrong. They gave me their full support and were very upset with Mark for his behavior and disrespect of me and the kids. I left their house with the weight of the world off my shoulders. I had projected all my disappointment on them when it had really been my feelings about the marriage ending. I hadn't been ready for it.

Three days later Stacy and Mark had a couple's therapy session in my office. Stacy said, "Mark, I am filing for divorce, and this is the last time that I will live with you. We have had problems for nine years. I love you, and will always, but I can't be married to you. We will be much better friends than lovers. We have two kids to raise and we need to be better parents." Mark surprisingly agreed with Stacy that it was for the best that they end the marriage. They continued therapy to resolve the issues of separation and to keep the tension, anger, and disappointment between them and avoid involving the children.

Stacy represents so many women and men stuck in relationships with the million-pound rock of guilt around their necks. She realized that her feelings and perceptions of guilt were her own distortions and irrational insecurities, not the reality or the truth of her situation. She had been raised to always be the perfect daughter, sister, woman, wife, and mother. Perfection for Stacy meant not having her own opinion or going against the perceived proper behavior. Her new personal action was a result of individuating and separating from her mother-daughter relationship and the expectation of perfection that came with it. Stacy resolved her guilt—and, interestingly, never left the relationship but rather brought the truth of it out. Expressing her true feelings allowed intimacy and a deeper connection to develop between her and Mark. The relationship also changed because Mark no longer was involved in extramarital affairs and made Stacy a priority. This story is an example of how a relationship needed the overarching guilt of a partner to be resolved. Stacy did it by being honest with herself and her husband. She might eventually leave the relationship but it is now working better than it ever has.

Chapter 4

THE POWER OF DISAPPOINTMENT, BETRAYAL, AND AFFAIRS

How They Break Your Heart

I just couldn't believe that Hank wanted to break up before the holidays. I hate being alone during New Year's Eve and going to all the parties without a date. I am going to skip the holidays this year and go to a cave and come out the second week of January. I can't take this breakup. Men just can't make commitments or follow through. I hate being single, and I want a baby!

　　　　—Amy, age forty-four, single, never married

I saw Debbie with another guy two days after we broke off the engagement. She is a bitch. I knew I was a fool for believing that she wanted to marry me and start a family. I am so lucky that she left me; now I can have a good woman in my life. I don't trust women or their true intentions. I knew she was no good.

　　　　—Mike, age thirty-seven, divorced for three years, engaged three times since the divorce

My husband left me for his coworker. She is younger, prettier, and a slut. I knew he was having an affair for years. I got rid of him, but I still feel

awful and angry about losing our marriage. We had
a good one. I can't believe he did this to me. I will
never forgive him.
—Claire, age fifty-three, mother of three adult daughters, divorced seven years, married for sixteen years

RESIDUAL EFFECTS

When they came to see me, Amy, Mike, and Claire had more in common than just their disappointment about their intimate relationships. They were both very angry, bitter, and deeply disillusioned with their love lives. None of these three adults had any insight into or perspective about how their prior disappointments and past relationship frustrations were currently affecting and directing their love lives. They didn't believe that the emotional residue of betrayal, heartbreak, and disappointment was negatively impacting their intimate relationships. Mike's, Amy's, and Claire's ex-factors were running their romantic lives and futures.

Let's review the working definition of your ex-factor: *The accumulation of lost dreams, broken promises, disillusionment, regret, emotional setbacks, disenchantment with past romantic partners, and unrealistic expectations all make up your ex-factor.* All these elements—acting singly or together—are impairments to your future satisfaction and fulfillment in relationships. It is very difficult to create any emotional distance from your pain and anger when the same issues and outcomes keep occurring over and over in subsequent relationships. All three adults were in a cycle of despair and desperation in their styles of dating, their partner selection, and their inability to develop and sustain intimate relationships. Their desire for safe, loving, nurturing, and secure emotional connections was becoming more of a dream than a reality in their current romantic relationships. The question was: *Why?*

The short answer to this question, as it relates to you, is: *Your unresolved emotional history will always repeat itself in your romantic relationships.* The only people who don't believe this powerful concept are the ones who are in a current cycle of repeating their relationship history with the same type of man or woman. The romantic partners picked will have different names and be in different settings, but there will always be the same outcome: *disappointment.* But regardless of your prior intimate relationship history, you can write and create a different future! In order to change your course, overcome your grief, and resolve your deep disappointment over never getting what you really want, you must first look at yourself. You are the only person who can direct a new relationship to a level of contentment that will be fulfilling to you.

Building and creating a different relationship template requires your internal skills (insight into your emotional needs and personal desires), attention, insight, and effort. *The hardest part of creating a new relationship is stopping the old, negative emotional patterns and old styles of intimacy and connection.* Don't be deceived or disillusioned by your previous marriages or old romantic relationships. It is possible to move beyond your heartbreak. Many women and men unconsciously decide that it is "better" or "easier" to stay angry and seek revenge toward the person who let them down. The alternative course of action is dealing with and resolving their anger, which has only been covering up their disappointment and sense of rejection. As previously discussed, anger is only a symptom of deeper emotional issues and unresolved concerns. Choosing anger is a very limiting course of action, and a guaranteed formula for future failure in intimate relationships. The road of anger, rage, and bitterness between ex-partners is a very crowded highway, with millions of participants and new members joining every day. Getting support from friends in focusing your anger on your ex is easy. But your goal—to change direction and to spend as little time as possible on the road of despair and anger—is more difficult. The deceptive nature of emotional wounds is that they can serve a short-term purpose as a source of personal information. But you shouldn't allow anger to define your psychological makeup or to become a personality style or "belief system" (the feelings and truths you believe about yourself and your relationships, it is how you make sense and meaning of your world). Everyone knows this. Instead, your anger can become a pathway toward unloading your old issues and leaving them in your past. Holding onto all the wrongs, screw-ups, disappointments, and failures of your ex assures that you will bring him or her into your next relationship. If you want a new loving relationship and a clean emotional slate, seriously consider the option of leaving your ex *in the past*.

AFFAIRS—THE NUCLEAR BLAST TO THE HEART

The single issue that tends to be the most difficult for women and men from all walks of life to leave behind is an affair. The deepest and most damaging aspect of the relationship for many couples is when one partner leaves the relationship to be with a third party. Under the best of circumstances, being abandoned is a very distressing and traumatic event. But the amount of anger, energy, and fear that is ignited when the secret is out that an affair has taken place can be overwhelming for everyone involved. It has been my professional experience that no one involved in an affair—either the betrayer or the betrayed—ever feels good or empowered by the experience. You don't need a research study to understand that affairs can blow up relationships and the lives of the people involved. In many cases the relationship needed to end, but the exit strategy of an affair is not a healthy or positive one.

The raging anger the betrayed partner feels about the actual affair usually passes with time, particularly after the divorce has taken place. It is the long-term negative effects of the betrayal (broken trust) that can cause endless pain unless they are properly understood and psychologically addressed. No discussion of relationship healing from an affair can exclude the element of betrayal within a romantic bond. The sense of betrayal is the outcome of breaking the bond of trust and fidelity between two people. It is the loss of trust that is so devastating because we are wired genetically to want to trust and bond with the people we love and care for. Betrayal is the "emotional fracture" to the bond of romantic trust. It isn't a natural human response to not trust your romantic partner. It is this counterintuitive action of not trusting that becomes the emotional wound for many sufferers of an affair. Inherently people want to regain their ability to trust their future intimate partner. Many times the affair is strictly an emotional encounter, with no sexual involvement or physical contact. Still, the bond that is created in these types of relationships can be very powerful. Many people dismiss the power and magnitude of an affair in which there is no physical involvement, but any type of affair—romantic, emotional, physical/sexual, or psychological—is a seedbed for disappointment, despair, and hopelessness.

It is common sense that affairs simply don't work in the context of any type of intimate relationship. Affairs are complicated, and they must be understood and deciphered by the people involved. The primary reason that a partner strays from a marriage/intimate relationship is based on his or her unmet emotional needs not being met in the intimate bond. The key is to know what these needs are/were and understand them better for yourself (where you had the affair or were betrayed by one). My purpose here is not to render a judgment about affairs; the goal is to emotionally resolve and learn from these devastating, life-changing events. Unfortunately, affairs have the ability to wipe out all the people involved. No one involved in an affair feels good about the secrecy of the relationship, nor do those involved completely get their emotional and relationship needs met. Affairs create a triangle and no one has a direct connection with the other person. There is no two-way direct communication, there is always a third party in the relationship. For this reason alone affairs are problematic and counterproductive to building a solid intimate bond with either partner.

> *I'll never get over my husband who made me feel so special. Why did he do this to us? Why the other*

woman? We had such a good relationship for years.
Why did he throw away our relationship?
—Martha, age forty-nine, mother of three grown chil-
    dren, divorced for five years, married for eighteen

Martha is representative of many of the people I see in my practice who
are recovering from the nuclear blast of an affair in their relationship.
The secondary damage of the affair is the emotional devastation and
heartbreak it engenders. As a clinical psychologist who has been
treating distressed couples in different types of relationship configurations for more than twenty years, I am frequently asked one question,
which is always posed in an agitated emotional state of despair, anger,
and fear: *Can I survive infidelity?* The answer is always yes. Whether the
couple can make it through this shattering experience and recover their
relationship isn't the topic of our book. In fact, the subject of recovering
from an affair and staying with your partner is a complete book in itself;
please check the bibliography for excellent resources on that subject.

It is assumed in this discussion that you, the reader, are on the
receiving end of this relationship breach. Couples can recover from
an affair, and it requires a lot of work and understanding on both
parts. It is critical for you to know, however, that most relationships
don't survive the violation and residual impact of an affair. This is
true of any type of intimate/romantic/marriage-type relationship
that is based on fidelity and monogamy. Though the statistics vary
widely on the subject,[1] one of the most recent and reputable studies
shows that as many as 37 percent of married men and 20 percent of
married women have been unfaithful in their intimate relationship.[2]
No one knows the exact percentages, but I suspect that someone
who lies to a spouse or significant other might also lie to a
researcher. But even by the most conservative estimates, we can say
with some degree of confidence that in the United States, 1 in every
2.7 couples—some 20 million—is touched by infidelity.[3]

These numbers are astounding and a very serious issue for all
intimate relationships. An affair can be a major roadblock to

rebuilding any type of romantic life. The fear that this type of betrayal could occur again is enough for many people to avoid any type of intimate relationship—however secure and loving—again. It is assumed that your anger, betrayal, and disappointment are greatly fueled by your partner's betrayal. The violation of trust is devastating to the betrayed partner.

After the affair is revealed and the emotional whirlwind has died down, it is important to give voice to your feelings and thoughts. It is crucial to keep in mind that affairs can make you feel crazy, like you're losing your mind—but you're not. You're one of many who have experienced the same pain, confusion, and betrayal—so you're not alone.

The strong emotional and psychological reaction to the emotional pain of betrayal is common in the context of any type of intimate relationship. Separating the ending of your relationship from the affair itself is necessary, however. The relationship ending includes the affair (or affairs) but didn't happen solely because of it. The residual feelings of disappointment is the realization that the illusion of love and security are gone forever. *But your relationship embodied many aspects, and infidelity was only one aspect of it.* The common mistake many women and men make is to lump all the relationship problems onto the issue of the affair. The violation of trust—this lapse—is a symptom of deeper unresolved issues within the context of the relationship and the individuals involved. *Your marriage or love relationship didn't end because of an affair.* Intimate relationships are much more complicated and much stronger than a one-night stand or a crush on a coworker. The affair is only another symptom of the underlying problems in the relationship.

DISAPPOINTMENT'S BIG SECRET

Mike, Amy, and Claire represent a large majority of newly single adults: those who were never formally married, those who have been divorced, and all the other combinations of relationship status (including sexual orientation). *The first step in changing your relationship landscape is learning not to underestimate or ignore the power of your emotional disappointment from the past.* When the whiplash-shock, denial, and anger have diminished, the underlying issues of disappointment (i.e., loss of your intimate partner and all the consequences from that change) will always come to the surface. This might happen as soon as your ex moves out, or it might not happen until the divorce is finalized, but profound feelings of disappointment will arise and continue to surface at various points.

Your disappointment contains the truth—the real meaning of what, how, and why you feel the way you do about your ex. Regardless of how "awful" your divorce/breakup was, it is understandable that you might still have loving feelings, thoughts, and unfulfilled wishes with your ex. Those repressed feelings are the substance and fabric of your emotional disappointment. The things that you are disappointed about are also the very things that you want, desire, and need in your intimate relationship. Don't forget that your feelings of disappointment are also your key elements to knowing how to rebuild your romantic future (we will explore this further in chapter 10). Many times people avoid acknowledging their feelings of disappointment and use other emotions to cover them up and keep a distance from them. Anger is the primary cover-up for the deeper pain and frustration within the ending of any relationship. Anger, as we have discussed, acts as a fuel to get you past the initial shock over the change in your relationship status. The problem with anger is that it can become a style of relating to the world, a personality pattern, and a toxic friend. Over time, if you hold on to your anger, it will become very destructive to your mental, emotional, and physical health.[4]

If you don't provide your anger a proper outlet/expression, it will create its own problems, including psychosomatic health issues. Some of the common physical health problems that can arise include increase in blood pressure; anxiety issues, including panic attacks and insomnia; immune system deficiencies; Epstein-Barr illness; chronic headaches; weight gain or loss; problems with sexual function; infections; eating disorders; destructive drug use; broken bones, strokes, and even death.[5] Many times anger, which is closely linked to physical health, is misunderstood by its victim: *you.*

EXPLORING YOUR DISAPPOINTMENT

Consider the following questions about your heartbreak as well as your current emotional state. These questions are designed to assist you in uncovering and exposing your hidden emotional links to your ex. Try to answer all of the questions with your first thoughts and immediate feelings.

- Do you feel depressed—sluggish, hopeless, emotionally flat, feeling bleak about your future?
- When you think about your ex, what is your primary thought?
- What are your regrets about your relationship?
- How much do you hide behind your anger, emotionally and psychologically?
- If you weren't angry with your ex, what would you be feeling instead?
- Do you ever allow yourself to feel the full emotional, mental, physical, and financial loss of your marriage and your ex?
- Do you believe that any positive emotional feelings you had in the past have been "crushed" and "devastated," and are nonexistent now?
- Do you find it difficult to trust members of the opposite sex in a romantic setting?
- Do you blame the ending of your relationship entirely on your ex?
- Does it seem impossible to ever consider an intimate relationship again?

- Do you privately (and only you know the truth about this) feel absolutely devastated, rejected, and/or abandoned because of your divorce or breakup?
- Does it seem impossible that anyone will ever be as close to you as your ex was?
- Do you date or get romantically involved with people who are completely "wrong" for you? When did this pattern start?
- Do you blame yourself for your partner's affair?
- Do you feel emotionally stuck with angry emotions about your past?
- Do your friends tell you that you are "angry," "hostile," and "bitter" toward the opposite sex since your divorce or breakup?
- Do you believe that you had any responsibility or role in the ending of your relationship?
- What are your coping skills (emotional insight, patience, perspective keeping), behaviors (new activities, individual therapy), and actions (exercise, new job, making new friends) to move past your ex?

Which question or statement above best describes your current state of disappointment? What would it take for you to finally let go of your disappointment and replace it with hope? What happens when you are no longer feeling, thinking, and acting disappointed? What psychological, relational, and emotional changes would occur in your life if your disappointment dissipated? The idea of disappointment turning into something useful might seem illogical. But when we actively move past our deepest disappointments, there is emotional, mental, and psychological room for our dreams, hopes, and desires to reappear. So it is important to understand—and resolve— your emotional roadblocks to overcoming your disappointment.

The discussion of anger is an excellent starting point for any and all concepts of change in your relationship life. In order for you to continue to move—emotionally and psychologically—through the five emotional phases of separating, you must let go of your anger! Anger and emotional healing are incompatible. In chapter 2 we discussed each of the five phases—whiplash, denial, anger, resolution, and hope/creativity—and their paramount importance to your life and future. *The most problematic sticking point is phase three: anger.* I am frequently asked, why is anger such a tough emotion to resolve and heal? The answer is simple: *Anger is a mind-numbing emotional state.* There is no drug or alcoholic combination on the planet that is stronger than anger.

When you are angry, you can barely feel any other emotion. You also likely have a great reduction in mental clarity and emotional perspective. But anger, as we've seen, provides you with a way to avoid feeling or dealing with your underlying feelings of despair and disappointment from your divorce or breakup. Anger also keeps your feelings of despair, panic, and bewilderment far away from your conscious mind. Anger has no regard for your role in the breakup. Anger is a response many times to your unfulfilled wishes, hopes, and dreams of a dynamic marriage/relationship that turned out differently than you expected. Unrealized expectations are usually expressed emotionally as anger and bitterness. You can be the one leaving or the one being left in the relationship—it doesn't matter, you will feel some degree of disappointment and anger.

Depression, anger, anxiety, panic attacks, and other strong negative emotional responses to the breakup are cover-ups, defense mechanisms to help you avoid dealing with your underlying feelings. Defense mechanisms enable us to unconsciously block out the painful feelings of despair, isolation, rejection, and abandonment, to—however temporarily—protect us from these powerful feelings. Though anger can be purposeful to get us through the initial stage of a breakup, we can't let it become our daily emotional fuel for addressing, building, and creating our future. Prolonged anger keeps us from building productive intimate relationships. It is counterintuitive to developing a loving, emotionally safe relationship when you have a lot of angry emotional energy toward your ex. The negative "anger" energy will adversely impact your next intimate relationship(s) until it is resolved.

In order to start moving past your ex and all things associated with your former relationship, you must *put aside your anger and allow your "softer" emotional side to have a voice.* We all have a soft side. It might be buried under twenty-five tons of anger, resentment, and self-righteousness—but it's there. Your soft side might feel so foreign to you that it has become a stranger in your life. Accessing it may seem easier for women than for men. The truth is our emotional health is deeper than gender stereotypes or self-imposed limitations on self-expression. If a woman is sad about her divorce, it doesn't mean she is overly emotional; nor does the tight upper lip of an unexpressive man mean he isn't suffering a tremendous amount of pain and grief. *Stereotypical gender styles aren't an accurate indicator of emotional pain and the impact that pain has had on a particular person.* After a breakup, your heightened sensitivity, feelings of emotional loss, change in family circumstances, economic changes, stress-related health issues, and sense of despair are very important to understand and address. Everyone in a breakup faces these very common issues to some degree. Whether you or your partner initiated the breakup, facing your disappointment is a very big part of the rebuilding process in your life. No one is exempt from the disappointment felt as a result of this process of transformation and its far-reaching impact on your life.

A LETTER OF DISAPPOINTMENT TO YOURSELF

Writing is one of the most powerful tools known to humankind. Scholars over the centuries have advocated that writing allows a person's creative nature and repressed thoughts to have expression, voice, and freedom. Writing is one of the most productive ways to hear, see, and resolve your unconscious conflicts and buried disappointments. Even if you don't consider yourself an expressive person, you should still sit down and write a letter to yourself from the perspective of your disappointment. Doing this gives your disappointment a voice. This may sound a bit far-fetched, but it works.

Try to imagine your disappointment talking to you like a trusted old friend. Now, allow your disappointment to write a letter to you about your relationship ending. Bear in mind that the particular divorce or breakup might not be the most recent one, but the one that your mind keeps drifting back to. Allow your disappointment to discuss your marriage, expectations, personal changes, hopes, and fears. The examples below are interesting because disappointment can ultimately become a source of hope and insight about your life and future. There is no right or wrong way to write this letter. If you are at a loss as to how to start writing your letter, consider how different your life feels compared to how you thought it would be at this point. And remember, your writing doesn't need to be rational, logical, or organized in complete thoughts; it just needs to be straightforward, honest, and unedited.

Examples of Letters of Disappointment

Mark, age fifty-two: I can't believe that you ever had the courage to finally ask for what you wanted in your marriage. I know you never wanted to be divorced. You had a successful marriage. You have now become aware of your own needs and wants. I know you are terribly disappointed with your life. Karen screwed up and divorced you. Even though she thought it was the right thing to do. The delivery was rough. I know you are devastated.

Lisa, age forty-seven: Your marriage was a wreck. You were unhappy and Frank wasn't good to you or the kids. You should be relieved about the growth and changes in the whole family. You have done so much with your life since the divorce. You will have a wonderful relationship again. You are moving forward, stop worrying about being "good." Your pain and sadness will eventually end.

Terri, age thirty-three: Stop blaming Mike for the breakup. You needed to grow up and move toward a more serious relationship and marriage. You have the right to feel the loss but your future is just starting. Don't cry over the past. Mike isn't going to ever get married, stop trying to convince him to marry you. You look desperate.

Patty, age thirty-nine: I know you are really depressed about not being married to Don. You will get married someday and have children. Don't allow your panic about kids and marriage to become your full-time occupation. You will have children. Sperm donors, adoption, or stepchildren are all possibilities. It might not be the way you would have imagined. You might never have children and that is very disappointing.

John, age forty-four: If you hadn't allowed the relationship with Jean to end you would have never met Maggie and married her. I know you really wanted to marry Jean. She didn't want to marry you. Now you have a wonderful woman. Let Jean go and stop thinking of her. You wanted to be perfect so Jean wouldn't have broken up with you. You aren't perfect, get over it.

Margo, age twenty-seven: I know you couldn't move into the new house with Jeff. He wanted marriage and you knew it wasn't the right time for you. Now you can do whatever you want and become who you want. Your dream for children and a husband will happen. Jeff didn't appreciate you and all you did for him.

Liz, age thirty-one: Jason moved across the country and I couldn't believe it. I know you were forcing the marriage issue. Accept the breakup but you keep fighting it. Stop it! Having a relationship with Jason isn't going to work. He has a new girlfriend. You knew there were issues in the relationship but ignored all the signs. Now you can date men who want to be with you. It is all right for relationships to end. Your life isn't over. Jason is gone.

Stan, age sixty-three: I know you worked hard for thirty-five years to build a great life, family, marriage, and retirement. Don't think it was all in vain because it wasn't. Your kids are happy, healthy, and each one successful. People love you and you are never alone even though Sherri left you. Sherri never appreciated you.

Peggy, age fifty-eight: The kids are gone, the house is empty, and your ex is also gone. You have no regrets or embarrassments. You know it was time for a change and now is your time to find your life. Being single sucks but it is better than a dead marriage.

Shannon, age thirty-six: I hate my life. I know you never expected to be single with three small boys. You can handle the challenge and raise them to be wonderful adult men. Don't be mad about the divorce; it was an event and now it is over. You are desirable to men regardless of your circumstances.

Start to write your letter on this page with pen and ink. It is important to allow your inner voice, your intuitive nature, and the buried emotion about the romantic status—past or present—of your life to come out. There is no right or wrong way to express your loss, pain, or despair. It is worse to avoid your despair rather than directly address it. Your sense of incomplete dreams, unfulfilled wishes, unmet emotional needs, and loss of positive expectations and hope for your future are all important elements of your disappointment. When you understand your disappointment, it can push you forward to create, build, and develop your future intimate relationships.

Dear _____,

What does it feel like to go inside of your deepest fear? Finding emotional resolution and relief from a broken heart starts with letting go of your unspoken disappointment and sadness over the divorce or breakup. Coming to terms with and being honest about your romantic loss is a large part of the process of resolving your disappointment and despair about your past relationship(s).

Once you lift the lid off your deep unspoken emotions, what is inside of you that isn't being given a voice? How much is your anger covering up your heartbreak? You may think that despair and disappointment aren't issues in your breakup, but rather that your residual anger itself is the issue. *Remember: anger is always a reaction to our feelings of abandonment, betrayal, broken trust, rejection, and perceived emotional injury.* You would have never invested so much emotion, love, time, and energy into your relationship with your ex if it wasn't important and meaningful to you. It is a distorted, "bitter" perception to believe that all of your efforts were a waste of time. This perspective is misrepresentative because you aren't allowing yourself to remember any of the positive moments, events, and feelings associated with your relationshp. Allowing yourself to recall the positive things about your relationship isn't wrong or delusional; nor is it "living in the past" or trying to reconcile with your ex. Remembering your relationship in its entirety—good and bad—is a way of getting beyond your emotional wounds and resolving your anger.

Love and Anger—same coin, different sides.
Which side are you living on?

Don't make the common mistake of forgetting that disappointment/anger is the flip side of love. You wouldn't be so disappointed about the end of your relationship if it hadn't had some great things, moments, and memories about it. You might have amazing children, a new career, better health, or any number of other remarkable things as a result of your prior intimate relationship. Your unconscious defense mechanisms—anger and denial—will not allow you to start longing for the relationship and really miss your ex. It is when these positive feelings come to the surface that your subconscious pushes them away, and you avoid them by focusing on your anger. Your pain and feelings of loss are so strong that they just don't leave any "air time" or emotional space in your conscious mind for happy positive memories. The waves of disappointment feel emotionally paralyzing. The solution to overcoming this cycle of denial, disappointment, and anger is to address your emotional pain. The next step is to consider writing the letter of anger and what information it might contain. First we are going to consider some other elements of anger before you write your letter.

REDIRECTING YOUR ANGER AWAY FROM YOUR EX

In order to find and maintain a proper emotional balance with your ex, you have to let go of your resentment, anger, and rage. The circumstances and conditions surrounding the end of your relationship might have been horrible. You were left with a heart full of anger and resentment toward yourself and partner for tolerating such a dysfunctional partnership. In chapter 3, Christine struggled with her rage after finding her husband having sex with another woman in their family home. This wasn't the first time her husband had cheated on her, but it triggered Christine's final emotional break with her husband. The emotional fallout from this final disappointment was horrendous, tragic, and overwhelming. She couldn't reconcile her husband's lack of respect for her with the fact that they had three brilliant children and many years of marital stability. There was no tangible reason or rational psychological explanation for the way Christine's husband continually acted out to end the marriage. His self-defeating (serial cheater/sexual addict) behavior signaled to Christine that the marriage was over for her. *When people don't have the emotional insight to cope with their fears of leaving or losing the relationship, destructive types of "insane" behaviors become the pathway to end the partnership.* There are sometimes no words or psychological explanations for the cruelty done by partners to each other in the process of breaking up and separating.

It is the lack of emotional clarity, insight, and maturity fused with ambivalence about leaving that creates tragic endings to relationships. The needless emotional pain so many adults endure is beyond sad. But in these cases, there is always an underlying reason, cause, or deep-seated emotional fear that is being replayed in the relationship. People who act out their aggression or anger often aren't aware or conscious of the long-term impact their behavior will have on their exes, themselves, and other innocent bystanders to the relationship—including children, relatives, and friends.

It is important to avoid the common pitfall of labeling your ex as "evil" in an attempt to make yourself feel better. Pretending that your ex is a horrible person will not make you any stronger or less disappointed. Chronically criticizing your ex only delays your ability to evolve, change, and move forward. One of the easiest ways to avoid your emotional pain, loss, and despair is to hyperfocus on your ex's irrational behavior, the ex's new relationship, and ways to get revenge. The more time and energy you spend hating, blaming, and raging against your ex, the more time you are spending in the past with him or her. Your primary goal is to move forward and re-create your life. Don't be deceived or blinded by your anger that you are resolved and clear minded about your ex. Your continued emotional investment (anger) and mental preoccupation about your ex-partner is a clear sign that you haven't moved forward from the marriage/romantic relationship. If you find yourself thinking and speaking only negative thoughts about your ex, then you are still strongly attached to your prior relationship. Until you resolve it, your disappointment will keep you closely attached and bonded to your ex. Your life will be on a treadmill until you extinguish your anger, disappointment, and resentment toward your ex.

Your goal is to redirect your emotional and mental focus to whatever chronic childhood issue, fear, and/or long-term personal concern the end of your relationship has activated in your life. If you can't think of anything, consider your feelings of disappointment as a clue to your deeper feelings about your sense of personal loss. Developing emotional distance and a clearer perspective on your ex allows you to regain your own psychological balance. Those who commit aggressive acts (i.e., verbal, emotional, physical, and financial) toward an ex are motivated by the inability to resolve their own sense of rejection, helplessness, and despair. It is the unguided vengeful behavior, vindictive attitudes, and irrational thinking that are emotionally and physically dangerous to all parties involved in the separation process.

A SERIES OF ANGRY EVENTS

Passive-aggressive actions and vindictive behaviors are the only way many partners feel they can force the termination of a relationship they want to end. These behaviors tend to be far more damaging to you than the actual preexisting relationship was. The bitterness and resentment that can be created by a once-trusted partner is sometimes beyond belief and often becomes the final lasting memory of the relationship. It is very common for partners to make egregiously self-destructive choices as a way to "blow up" the relationship, leaving no opportunity for reconciliation. If you left an abusive relationship, for example, you might be very disappointed, angry, or resentful that you were forced to finally stop the abusive behavior and take action to end the relationship (by moving out, filing for divorce, or getting a restraining order). Your partner may have taken no responsibility for his or her reckless actions, words, cruelty, and outright abuse toward you.

The endless stories of ex-partners committing character assassination are sad and unfortunate. These extremely upsetting, appalling, atrocious acts point to the harsh reality involved with attempting to separate lives. Because of these very emotionally complicated and trying circumstances, relationship endings are on par with death and terminal illness with regard to their psychological impact on individuals.[6] No one is equipped to have his or her world turned upside down by a lover who was, up to that moment, his or her best friend. Your disbelief that the person you had built a life with is suddenly trying to destroy you emotionally, relationally, and mentally (it feels that way) is beyond the boundaries of most people's capacity to understand. The sense of feeling "destroyed" is how sudden and drastic (i.e., married for twenty-four years and now divorced) your life has been permanently changed. Because of the deep emotional injuries that are—deliberately or inadvertently— inflicted by an ex-partner, many adults resolve never again to get involved in another intimate love relationship. Resolving never to be vulnerable again, they believe, is the heart and soul of overcoming their exes and their failed relationships. Don't be discouraged, but it takes a lot of insight and understanding to not allow your past to control and direct your present and future. The primary goal of this book is to systematically "walk" you through your ex-factor process. The rage that is unnecessarily created by either intimate partner during a divorce, post-divorce, or protracted breakup can be well documented beyond belief. The legal system has seen this dynamic and the irrational actions that can be triggered in these very tense moments (separating process—physically and emotionally). Law enforcement describes these emotional blowups as "crimes of passion." Neither of you should want any part of that. The key is not to take up residence any longer in the hopeless, painful place where this becomes possible.

AN ANGRY LETTER TO YOUR EX

Writing a letter addressed to your ex from the perspective of your anger is one of the quickest and safest ways to move out of the valley of despair. You have to allow your anger a voice and full expression. If you ignore your anger, it will find its expression in a variety of other ways. As noted, some of these include psychosomatic symptoms, sudden health issues, and chronic illness, because your physical body is being worn down by your anger.[7] Women have been traditionally advised not to express their anger because they will be viewed as a "bitch" or "crazy." Men are told that anger is only the masculine emotion they can express. Both stereotypes are very limiting and highly problematic for both men and women.[8]

Examples of Letters of Anger

The purpose of these examples is to give you some moral support in facing the fire of your passion. Anger can release untapped feelings and incredible emotional clarity that you might not ever have seen or experienced in your life. Allowing your anger to express itself is very sensible and pragmatic, but it is not something you should keep doing indefinitely. Very few people ever take the time or have the courage to deliberately express their anger. It is frightening to feel your own rage, relentless passion, and desire to hurt your ex-partner. Writing should allow you to short-circuit any desire you might feel to take self-destructive actions and move you to a higher level of understanding and resolution with emotional detachment. *If it does not, you should seek therapy.* When your anger is no longer consuming you and controlling your judgment and actions, then you will be able to start living your life again.

These brief examples of anger are from my clients who have had to let go of their anger and move forward in their lives, despite their ex-partners' poor behavior and insensitive actions. These letters give only a glimpse of the passion, disappointment, heartbreak, rejection, and sadness that their anger was concealing. All of these writers had to move toward resolution because their lives were drowning in their anger, despair, resentment, and disappointment.

Robert, age forty-three: I can't believe I ever allowed you to control me the way you did. I resent your attitude and arrogance for trying to always put me down. I am no longer in your orbit and will live a much better life without you. No matter what you say about me or tell our friends about our relationship, you didn't win. I didn't want the money, the house, or your grief anymore. You now live in an empty house and I never felt you could love anyone other than yourself. You are highly narcissistic and self-absorbed. You used my family against me and ultimately it didn't matter, we all know you are a rotten individual.

Carol, age forty-six: You are still trying to control me with the kids, custody, and the money. Cutting my alimony and child support will not get me to come back to you. I left you because you are piece of shit. I would rather be poor than live another day under your control. I left you and I know it was and still is the right thing to do. You can't hurt me anymore, my heart is hidden away and I will never allow you to be near it. You never loved me. You just love the idea of love. No one will ever love you or take care of you the way I did, you are a fool for ignoring me. You will die alone and you are a sad example of a man. We had an incredible life together and you had to go fuck it up and go fuck the twenty-two-year[-old] trainer at the gym. You are disgusting and I wish you were dead. You should have died in the car accident. My life would have been better. You are worth more to me dead than alive.

Bonnie, age thirty-six: You couldn't find the courage to tell me the truth and so you had an affair with my business partner. I hate you both for being cowards and hope you both die in hell. You are both useless and a waste of a human life. I will never forgive you, and the kids think you a jerk also. You were never a man anyway because you allowed your wife to be the breadwinner while you stayed at home. Real men work and you aren't a man, you are a scared little boy.

Tammy, age thirty-nine: You lied to me the entire time we were married. I feel so betrayed and hurt by you. How many affairs did you have? You did drugs, gambled, and violated our relationship all the time. You married my best friend and I can't believe you did that to me. Why? What did I do to you for such awful stuff? I will never give you my heart again. You are a huge disappointment and a royal fuckup. Your new wife is just a "gold digger" anyway. I hope you both rot in hell.

Carlos, age forty-nine: I fully intended to fight you over the kids and get custody away from you. I wanted to hurt you and I am glad I did, you are a horrible person, awful mother, and a train wreck of a person. You will never see the kids ever again. You don't deserve the money I give or the things you got out of our marriage. I wish you were dead and the kids would only have a memory of you. You are fat, a lousy lover, and really a desperate woman. You give ex-wives a bad name. I never wanted to have sex with you because it was awful. Your sister is really the better-looking one in the family, I should have married her.

In the space below, start to write your letter of anger to your ex-partner. This letter may take many hours, days, or weeks to complete. Again, there is no right or wrong way to do it. The goal is to give your anger full vent on paper. Writing about your deepest wounds and your feelings of rejection, betrayal, and despair doesn't require any action other than your honest expression at this point.

Dear_____,
You are a . . .

It is very wise and equally prudent not to mail or show this letter to your ex-partner. He or she doesn't need any more information, emotional ammunition, or personal empowerment over your process of detachment and healing. If you feel an overwhelming need to mail your angry letter to your ex, consider this first: Trying to get even and "air" out your feelings about your ex's behavior isn't going to do you any good. Your feelings are about *you* and your need to heal, not his or hers. You can't change, correct, or fix your ex-partner's behavior and lack of emotional sensitivity toward you. You aren't part of your ex-partner's healing or emotional recovery. *You aren't part of his or her solution.* It is good to vent your feelings, but you don't want to be emotionally stuck in a cycle of repetitive angry behaviors, hostile feelings, and negative thoughts with your ex. It is time to let him or her go psychologically and change the emotional bonds in your life. The only way you can heal is by detaching yourself.

BREAKING THE BOND OF DISAPPOINTMENT— THE FINAL FRONTIER

Few would argue that one of the best ways to break the emotional bond with your ex is through the doorway of forgiveness. *The problem with forgiveness is that some actions, behaviors, and choices in life seem unforgivable.* A former lover's mean-spirited and cruel actions might defy credibility or any commonsense understanding. There is no shortage of examples of negative, loveless behaviors. Given that we are all human, made with feet of clay, the imperative to detach might be the best we can do in the separating process. Then maybe—when the years have passed, kids are grown, money is no longer an issue, remarriage has taken place, and the heartbreak doesn't feel like a giant hole in our psyche—*then* we can reach total forgiveness. Total forgiveness means that our ex-partner no longer elicits any emotional or psychological internal response from within us. The ex-partner has become a *zero*, a nonentity, a cipher, a person in our past (and this *can* happen even with children involved).

The scale for your emotional reaction to your ex can be gauged. It can range from zero to ten. Ten represents raging out of control, constantly reacting, being consumed with anger, and desiring revenge and retribution. Ten is the worst emotional state we could be in and usually requires a third party—perhaps even the police or the courts—to contain us or to intervene for everyone's safety and sanity. You don't want to go there. Zero is the opposite end on the scale and that would be, for example, seeing your ex and not having your stomach drop or feel your face become flush with anger. Zero response would mean that you don't have a physical reaction or negative feeling about him or her. They can be acknowledged without you feeling overwhelmed, angry, or upset.

In our attempt to become increasingly neutral toward the person or events that have caused us such tremendous emotional and mental suffering, we need to strive for detachment. This is the first step in the process of forgiveness. If all you can manage is detaching, you still have accomplished an incredible feat, showing personal growth and self-empowerment. Becoming able to emotionally, mentally, psychologically, and spiritually detach is a means of healing and retaking control of your life.

Detachment enables you to make the deliberate choice to "unhook" yourself from all the pain and negative feelings about your ex and the awful process of separating. Detachment is your pathway to feeling hopeful and positive about your life, today and tomorrow. Once you have gained some mental and physical distance from your ex, then you can focus on moving your life forward. *Don't mistake detachment as a watered-down version of forgiveness.* It isn't that. It is merely your ability to stop plugging into your ex-partner's actions, past or present. Importantly, detachment keeps you from obsessing on the past, on the vicious, insensitive, or unloving acts of betrayal, and the residual pain these events created. If this idea makes you want to throw this book across the room and start screaming, keep reading.

DETACHMENT SECRETS

The list below is a practical way and approach to shift (gain new insight), expand your belief system, and stop giving your emotional power away to your ex. Remember that your daily choice to detach is for you and no one else. It is your form of practicing self-love and nur-turing yourself. In choosing to detach, you are no longer allowing your-self to be abused and emotionally tortured by your past, your ex-partner, and your own sense of inadequacy. The following ideas are intended as a foundation for you to expand upon and tailor to your per-sonal needs and beliefs. It doesn't matter how you detach—you just need to do it. You will likely find that your disappointment will dra-matically diminish and your sense of hope for your future will expand as your ability to detach grows. Remember, you aren't fully available emotionally, psychologically, or physically to develop intimate relation-ships in the future if you remain mentally attached to your ex. There is no room in your heart or your head for someone else if you are still attached to your ex-partner. This idea alone should be motivation enough to get you to immediately begin practicing detachment.

- *Your ex's behavior isn't about you.* It might be directed at you as if it were a nuclear missile, but it isn't about you. Your ex's negative reaction toward you is about his or her own past and unresolved issues. His or her problems and issues predate you and the relationship. You aren't responsible for his or her childhood rage and accusations.
- *You control how you feel and act.* No one can make you think or feel anything you don't want to. You control your own feel-ings and thoughts. If you believe someone can make you feel "bad," you are not appreciating your own personal power.
- *Stop giving your ex permission to hurt you.* You have the ability to hear your ex's statements as his or her own opinion and not yours. The most important opinion of you is your own. Your opinions, thoughts, and feelings about yourself are the only ones that matter. Your ex-partner's opinion of you isn't your business or interest any longer.
- *No one can define you or decide who and what you are except you.* It is your sole responsibility and duty to define your own life. Your ex has no role in you developing your personal identity.

- *Create your own mantras as reminders of who and what you are.* View yourself as separate from your ex-partner. An example is: "I control my life. That is his/her opinion, not mine. I choose not to argue anymore. This is a bad moment, not a bad life. My ex is angry and I am not the solution. My ex's anger predates our relationship."

- *Accept the relationship change.* Stop wishing or hoping things were different between you and your ex-partner. Stop fighting the reality of your situation and look to your future. Don't hang on to the fantasy that your ex-partner is your significant other when the relationship has ended. Denying the change is an attempt to stay emotionally attached.

- *Your life is in the present, not the past.* You are no longer married, dating, or involved with your ex-partner on an intimate level. You may share custody of your children, but that isn't a romantic bond.

- *Know your emotional triggers with your ex.* Remove your emotional triggers and don't allow them to be exposed to your ex-partner. For instance, don't allow his or her attitude to push the emotional button surrounding your need for respect. Don't expect your ex-partner to be respectful or positive toward you. Assume and know that you are responsible for your own sense of worth and damage control (i.e., not allowing yourself to lose your temper).

- *Develop strict emotional boundaries with your ex.* Don't discuss personal matters with your ex-partner. Keep your discussions to business—kids, finances, and the like—and away from heated emotional topics. Never discuss your new intimate partners or dating relationships. Talking about your new and exciting lovers only keeps you bonded to your ex-partner. Revenge doesn't achieve the healing and resolution that you truly want and need. The motive to hurt your ex with your new romantic life is misguided and will likely bring you more problems.

- *No sexual or intimate physical contact*. It is impossible to separate from your ex-partner if you are still physically/sexually involved. If you are sexually involved with your ex, then you aren't broken up. Regardless of your divorce status, sex equals an intimate bond. Ex-partners are never neutral sexual mates. Using sex to stay connected can be emotionally dangerous and a reckless short-term solution to a long-term separation problem. Resolving your ex-factor issues includes no sexual contact of any kind.

Please make your additions to this list to assist you in creating emotional, psychological, and mental distance from your ex. Living near your ex or having children together has nothing to do with your ability to detach from him or her. Using your children as a reason to stay emotionally bonded is another form of denial and resistance to your relationship change. We will continue to discuss these detachment points throughout the book. It is critical to continually focus on the emotional process of detaching from your ex-partner. Only after you have detached from your partner can you begin to experience your life again.

> *When you hold resentment toward another, you are bound to that person or condition by an emotional link that is stronger than steel. Forgiveness and detachment is the only way to dissolve that link and get free.*
> —Catherine Ponder, psychologist

SECTION II

THE VALLEY OF DESPAIR

"The game of guilt and blame is a tempting one to play in every relationship, whether it is personal, professional, or political. If there are any rewards to be found in this game, they are self-punishment and feelings of separation."

—Gerald G. Jampolsky, MD

Chapter 5

PICKING UP THE PIECES

Processing the Damage

You can be in a marriage relationship and never be married.
—Charlotte, age eighty-seven, married for fifty-five years, widowed for eight months

The quote above can be used to illustrate many long-term relationships and marriages. The realization that you might have been in a marriage but not "married" can be devastating and humiliating. When I met Charlotte at a friend's wedding, she made this statement about the agony she felt going through the motions of marriage for almost forty years. She said, "It wasn't until we both turned sixty-two that we finally became a married couple." It took her and her husband forty years to become fully committed (emotionally and mentally) to their marriage and enjoy the benefits of being loving, supportive partners. As odd as it sounds, a secure loving bonding took place in the fortieth year of their marriage. For many couples, this bond is developed during courtship and/or the early part of marriage or sometime during the course of the relationship; for others it never happens. Actually *being* in marriage—in a metaphorical, spiritual, psychological, and emotional sense—is about developing and having a loving bond between both partners.

It is clear from listening to her story that Charlotte always loved her husband, but it actually took him forty years to realize what a great woman she was. It was only then that he became fully involved in and committed to their marriage. Charlotte felt that, within their fifty-five-year marriage, they were married and divorced several times within the context of the relationship. Neither she nor her husband, Lenny, ever moved out of their house, but they did sleep in separate bedrooms for years at a time. Finally, in the fortieth year of their marriage, they finally developed an intimate, safe, and secure emotional bond. After their fortieth anniversary, they never again slept in different bedrooms. Charlotte told me about her marriage only two months before her death; she died ten months after Lenny's passing. She couldn't live without her lifelong partner and best friend. In the last chapter of their life, Charlotte and Lenny had a marriage that many envied, but it took them four decades to accomplish that intimate connection. Clearly, intimate relationships always require effort and commitment on the part of both individuals.

We all crave emotional safety and security.

An intimate relationship, by definition, is a safe emotional place where romantic partners can fully share their true selves with each other. A safe intimate relationship is one in which you can experience the transformational power of being loved and emotionally supported. Any type of intimate relationship that contains these elements—which are basic human needs and desires—is a marriage relationship, regardless of whether an actual legal ceremony took place. The inner sanctuary of safety and support is priceless and something that every adult needs and wants.[1] It is normal, natural, and very appropriate to want to be understood in an atmosphere of love and acceptance. *It is the pursuit of and the experience of falling short of these aspirations that can lead to the emotional hardship of relationship endings and divorce.*

It is a commonsense statement and belief that no one gets involved in a relationship leading to marriage or "falls" in love so that he or she can at some future point terminate it. Yet relationship "endings" occur and it isn't reason or cause to avoid or dismiss the value and benefit of an intimate partnership. The motivation for an intimate connection, both consciously and unconsciously, is to have a sense of completion in your love life. Our intimate connections, attachments, and bonds allow us to feel alive, valuable, and emotionally complete. Many times the most startling and devastating aspect of a marriage ending is the realization that a long-term love relationship fell desperately short of creating a positive, supportive, and loving atmosphere for both partners. One of the most painful parts of overcoming the trauma, disappointment, and pain of your relationship with your ex-partner is admitting to yourself that you might have *never* felt closely connected, fully loved, or properly understood. To some people, the idea that one can feel emotionally complete within an intimate relationship is almost laughable, which is a very sad reality. The pain of a breakup is in accepting that the relationship wasn't what you wanted or had hoped for. The fact that you had a role, a responsibility, and a choice in how you interacted and emotionally bonded with your ex-partner is a very powerful reality. Many times this insight comes with tremendous emotional pain, regret, and personal cost.

ASSESSING THE DAMAGE

> *My world no longer makes any sense to me. I feel lost and very empty. I never wanted to be divorced. I resent my wife and being divorced.*
> —Beau, age forty-three, married for fifteen years, newly divorced

It may be difficult to accept the fact that you have never felt like you were fully attached, loved/loving, and/or fully functional in your relationship. These honest introspective feelings have nothing to do with the length of your relationship or its context. You might have been together for five years, twenty-five years, or fifty years and never felt the relationship was "it" for you. This realization is very powerful and can become the impetus for making major changes in your relationship model and intimacy style. The quote above is blunt but a very accurate assessment of how many men and women feel about their prior romantic relationship(s), including Beau.

It is at this point of honesty and personal introspection in moving beyond your ex-factor that you begin to pick up the pieces of your life, heal your heart, and take control of your own destiny. Beau's quote illustrates the full realization that his marriage/love relationship had ended and that the truth about it was very troubling to him. Beau didn't recognize his world anymore, and he didn't know how he was going to put the pieces of his life back together. Everything felt different and very scary. Going forward after such a loss takes a lot of courage and clarity, and Beau could no longer live in the past (blaming his ex-partner) even if he wanted to. His marriage was over and Beau had to redesign his life and future.

Would you describe your love life and your relationships as exercises in frustration, pain, and/or misery? If this is the perfect description of your married life, your relationships, and/or the sum total of your adult love life, don't panic. Many people spend time in a marriage or an exclusive long-term intimate relationship in which they never feel they were emotionally connected or fully involved. Many people—women and men alike—comment that they were "going through the motions" while they were married or dating. *No one wants to be serving time and going through the motions of love— and there is no reason you have to, ever again.* In the aftermath of your divorce or relationship breakup, you now know much better, or are learning, what you want and don't want in a partner. You now know, or are learning, what works and what doesn't work for you in your relationship with an intimate partner.

It is safe to assume that you would like to be intimately connected to a new partner. You now have the motivation, insight, courage, and prior experience to be "different" in how you act and feel in your next relationship, and how you approach and relate to your next intimate partner. The more you can see, examine, and understand your intimate relationship style, the more control you have in rewriting, redirecting, and re-creating your future. Your expanded insight will enable you to stop repeating your old patterns of frustration, emotional emptiness, and despair. *You never again have to be in a relationship where you are playing a part rather than being a fully loving and fully loved participant.*

EXPANDING YOUR ABILITY TO ACCEPT LOVE

Your development of and participation in intimacy is exclusively contingent/dependent on you, along with your willingness to step outside of your comfort zone with regard to relationships. Your emotional and psychological comfort zone is the combination of your old relationship pattern, your style of intimacy, and your personal belief system. All these elements will be discussed in this section of the book. Your new insight into your romantic attachments will help you expand your level of comfort with regard to feeling loved and being loved—in other words, it will increase your emotional and psychological ability to accept that your partner sincerely loves and cares for you. This concept may seem foreign, an impossible reality, but it is up to you to accept these new loving gestures from a new intimate partner. When you allow someone to love and embrace you, you must also love and embrace yourself. Developing a higher level, a new standard, and a larger capacity for loving and being loved starts with overcoming and resolving the trauma of the ending of your significant relationship (present or past). It is important to note that your most recent relationship/marriage might not be the intimate relationship that has the "emotional" weight or negative residual impact on you. What intimate relationship holds the most energy for you? This could be a lover from high school, college, prior coworker, or your ex-husband. Who is it for you? Let's first outline the four basic elements to expanding your capacity for a loving relationship:

- First, believe that you deserve more and can have more fulfillment in your romantic life. Your past love relationships don't have to predict your romantic future. You are more than your past. Leaving the past in the past allows you to do things differently in the present and in the future. You can't be in the past and in the present at the same time. Your life is better served living in the present.
- Second, believe that you can have the kind of love relationship you want. You are the only person who can rebuild, rewrite, and re-create your romantic life. No one else controls your romantic destiny, regardless of your prior disappointments and heartbreaks. Start considering what you desire as well as what you won't tolerate or accept in your romantic relationship.
- Third, believe that there is potential for a significant love life after your ex. Regardless of the emotional insanity, mental intensity, and psychological trauma you withstood, you can rebuild your life. It is vital to never forget that *out of your pained heart, your new life will emerge.* The means to transform your core belief system about your sense of value (what is important to you—personal priorities, family, children, money, career, etc.) and self-worth starts with putting your heart back together. People who feel shattered forget that it is possible to be a whole person again. The agony of feeling emotionally, mentally, psychologically, and financially ruined is terrifying. But remember: There are good things to come.
- Fourth, believe and know that your feelings of pain, terror, hopelessness, and devastation will diminish. There is always and will be an ending point to your pain and suffering, and this is something you can control. Like all things in life, suffering has a beginning point and an ending point. You can seize on your willingness and openness to actively resolve your prior relationship trauma to move your healing process forward. Your deliberate choice not to completely blame your ex for your romantic legacy is critical to healing your broken heart

and shattered dreams. It is never too early or too late to pick up the pieces of your life and put them back together, but this time in a new way. It takes incredible courage and persistence to create the life and relationships you have always wanted, but you can do it.

NO LONGER SHATTERED

Oftentimes, the ending of an intimate relationship is so heartbreaking that those involved feel as if they've been shattered into a million pieces of pain and sorrow. Every part of life feels broken, fractured beyond repair. Feeling shattered is far beyond being shocked, numb, or stunned by your partner's sudden actions of divorce or a breakup. A shattered life is the feeling that your life is completely devastated, unrecognizable, and permanently flawed. You feel as if nothing is working, nothing feels safe, and you don't recognize yourself anymore (i.e., eating poorly, lose or gain weight, lost your relationship routine and stability). Your life feels and looks unfamiliar to you, including your inability to handle or cope with all the changes happening in your life. Usually these changes happen suddenly and with tremendous personal impact. There are books, tapes, and multiple workshops on how to put your life back together after a series of these personally devastating events. These may be helpful to you.

Our focus here, however, is also to help assist you in putting the pieces of your heart back together after your divorce or breakup. Regardless of how your relationship ended, you may feel like a glass vase that is broken beyond recognition or repair. Nevertheless, the experience of feeling "broken" is considered by many scholars throughout the ages as the pathway to lasting change.[2]

SHATTERING STORIES

The following stories are about three adults who believed that their entire lives were over, beyond emotional repair. These are true, painful, but very purposeful examples of people who have overcome their sense of being emotionally, mentally, and physically shattered. It is important to remember that none of the healing steps of personal repair and emotional renewal could be accomplished until these three decided to become emotionally detached from their crises. They understood the invaluable wisdom of no longer being attached to a former partner or the drama that was created by the relationship. They withdrew, becoming no longer emotionally plugged in to their ex-partners' opinions, actions, or moods. They stopped allowing their feelings to be pulled into the past. Their ability to stop the endless psychological pain and suffering started with staying in the present and dealing with the events of the moment. Their path of healing and re-creating their lives was as seemingly miraculous as the events that led up to it. Let's read their stories and then explore ways for you to continue moving beyond your disappointment and relationship pain.

Robert's Breaking Experience

Background

It was the last Friday in February, two days before the Los Angeles Marathon. Robert had recently been divorced after twelve years of a "marginal marriage" and had trained extensively throughout the divorce process to literally and metaphorically "run the race." Robert needed both physical endurance to actually run the marathon and emotional endurance to bear his divorce process. Robert, an orthopedic surgeon and a single father of two children (an eight-year-old boy and a ten-year-old daughter), struggled with guilt, shame, and anger about his divorce from his wife, Margo. The marriage was a codependent arrangement. Robert's codependent behavior was his constant seeking to please Margo, until he finally reached the end of his rope. Margo was narcissistic and very demanding, and couldn't understand why Robert would not always acquiesce to her desires. Robert's needs, wants, and desires were never acknowledged, valued, or addressed. The relationship was set up to meet Margo's needs; Robert had no needs.

Robert's Story

He related this story to me:

> I met Robert when he was in the middle of a family crisis. Robert had been reported by the family therapist for inappropriate touching of his son during a "wrestling" match. Robert had never been accused of or had any personal issues with physical or sexual touching with his children. His ex-wife felt that he was too physical and "playing" with their son and called the therapist. Robert was very scared when he recounted his situation to me: I got a phone call from our family therapist that she was reporting me to the Department of Children's Services for child abuse. My son allegedly told the therapist that I was touching his bottom while we were wrestling. This was ridiculous and very scary. I am not a pedophile or a child abuser. The therapist didn't believe me and called Children's Services. Three days later the social worker came to my house to visit me. I didn't have an attorney and I wanted her to see my new home for me and the kids. The woman was an African American Jamaican-born woman. She walked into the house and looked me straight in the eye and asked me three questions: Do you have a new girlfriend? Did you just buy this house? Did you tell your ex-wife that you weren't going to reconcile with her?
>
> My heart was pounding and I was so scared that I seemed very calm. I told the lady that I had just met a wonderful woman a few months ago, I had just bought this house three months earlier, and I wasn't ever planning on going back to my ex-wife. I mentioned that my ex-wife wanted the divorce but then changed her mind; I

had reached my emotional limit always trying to please her and chasing after her wishes and desires. The social worker told me to not leave the house and she was going to see my ex-wife right now (we live five minutes apart).

The social worker came back to my house an hour later and told me that the next time my ex-wife made a false child abuse report that she [the social worker] was going to award me with full legal and physical custody of the kids. I asked the social worker how she knew I wasn't a pedophile or a sexual creep. She said that no pedophile asks you to their home, sits down with you, and pleads for help in dealing with an angry ex-wife. "You are the one being abused," she said, "and I recommend you put a stop to that woman."

I have never felt so much relief and anger at the same time. The insanity of reporting me for child abuse was so painful and devastating that I had mild panic attacks for the next year. It took me a full three years to fully recover from that vicious attack on me. I have had a lot of trouble trusting women since then and haven't really developed a serious relationship since. My girlfriend at the time broke up with me and my kids were very distant from me for the next six months.

Robert's Recovery

Robert started attending therapy with a female therapist on a three-times-a-week basis to address his codependence and his profound fear of having to deal with his ex-wife. He was justified in not trusting his ex-wife, given her attempt to destroy his life and profession and to deprive him of raising his children. In therapy, Robert had to talk through and overcome his childhood fear of disappointing his mother and of her vengeful nature toward him. He also felt bad about being divorced and ashamed of how he allowed his ex-wife to terrorize him. It took him several years to find the hope, courage, and personal strength to consider the possibility of opening his heart to another woman again. He learned to manage the emotional and mental terror he felt when having to coparent with his ex-wife. He redefined his ability to love and be loved in an intimate relationship. He began to realize—and believe—that he could be an "equal" in an intimate relationship.

Robert fell into a pattern of dating women who were nice but were never a great match because of his unconscious fear of trusting or allowing another woman to be inside his inner courtyard of intimacy and love. He developed a higher tolerance for accepting and experiencing a woman's disappointment as her issue, not his fault or responsibility. Before, Robert would do almost anything not to have his ex-wife or past girlfriends get mad or disappointed with him. He now wasn't emotionally paralyzed and no longer avoided stating his own wants and needs in a relationship. He eventually remarried—after he stopped picking women who all were very similar to his ex-wife in their demands and reactions to him.

Robert didn't feel fully "safe" or "trusting" again until he became romantically involved with the woman who would ultimately become his new wife. It took him seven years to feel healed, excited, and hopeful about his future. He also had a decreasing amount of residual feelings concerning his ex-wife's malicious actions. Robert continued to trust his emotional ability that he would never be subject to her emotional and mental abuse.

Marie's Broken Heart

Background

Marie met her ex-boyfriend, Chuck, while on a business trip in New York City. They lived only two blocks away from each other in Santa Monica, California. The synchronicity of their single relationship status, age, living proximity, desire for marriage and children, career success, and family backgrounds (both raised Catholic) was unusual, and they quickly formed a very strong bond. The emotional chemistry, physical attraction, and overall attachment for both Chuck and

Marie was intense, a new experience for each of them. They both were newly single after dating others, never marrying, and were craving an exclusive romantic relationship. Within two months after they met, Chuck moved into Marie's new house. Chuck had a bicoastal sales job (travel two weeks out of each month) and decided to travel less and to spend more time at home in Los Angeles. Still, Marie never felt completely comfortable with Chuck's moving in so quickly, but she decided to be open-minded about the process. Marie was also concerned about Chuck's "short fuse" explosions over meaningless details and potential anger issues. But after they lived together for a while—and Chuck didn't pay for any of the household expenses—it became a relationship burden for Marie and made her reexamine her feelings about Chuck.

Marie's Story

I met Marie when she was attempting to end the relationship with Chuck, six months after they began living together. She related the following story:

> I can't take the verbal abuse—the insane immature behavior—anymore. Since the day Chuck moved in, he started becoming verbally aggressive towards me when he was upset or angry at me. I knew the relationship was wrong. I just couldn't stop the momentum of our relationship. Chuck wanted to marry me six weeks after meeting me. I knew it was wrong for a lot of reasons. The main reason was we didn't know each other enough to remotely make that type of life choice. Now I can't get him to move out or leave. I am paying for everything. I feel like I am with a little boy and I am the mother. I promised him I would buy him a new sports car if he moved out within the next four weeks. It is worth the money to get him out of my life. I had skin cancer two years ago and I don't want to become so upset that my body suffers another setback. I knew my cancer was related to all the years of drama and verbal abuse from my family. I knew Chuck was intense,

but his immaturity and narcissism is beyond anything I have ever seen or experienced. He makes my father look like a saint. I have always considered my father to be the most self-absorbed person I have ever met. Chuck is worse than my father. This is really a bad thought that Chuck and my father are very similar. I feel like I am losing my mind.

Marie was paralyzed by the fear that Chuck would become physically violent with her if she allowed an argument to escalate. Marie wasn't convinced that Chuck wouldn't impulsively kill her in a fit of rage. He became completely irrational, according to Marie, when she attempted to discuss their relationship issues. Chuck had no prior history of physical abuse or any violent behavior, yet Marie was concerned that Chuck would harm her if she didn't do what he wanted or demanded. She said, "I am acting and behaving like I swore I never would and resent being a scared woman and being in this type of relationship. I have always been critical of women who support their boyfriends. I am now one of those women. Chuck wants to have a baby with me and I think he has lost his mind. Last week, he informed me that he has lost his job and needs to borrow money from me. I feel like I am being held hostage in my own house. Chuck has his own house two blocks away and will not move out. I feel like I am going to lose my mind if he doesn't move out and leave me alone. I think I am going to tell my father and let Chuck and him figure it out."

Over the next six months, Marie attempted to improve the relationship and went to couples' counseling. She was in denial about the degree of dysfunction in her relationship with Chuck. She even caught Chuck cheating on her with numerous other women. Still, he refused to move out of her house unless she paid him for his emotional distress and heartbreak. Marie had no legal rights in California as a homeowner and couldn't evict Chuck from her house. Instead she moved to Santa Barbara for six months, leaving Chuck in her house in Santa Monica. Chuck finally moved out after Marie's father confronted him in front of her house. The emotional trauma of constantly fighting with Chuck about his leaving her home was extreme; Marie felt she had lost her life to an emotional terrorist.

Marie's Recovery

During her six-month sabbatical from Santa Monica, while living in Santa Barbara, she went to intensive therapy three times a week. Marie learned that she first had to emotionally detach from Chuck and not fear his reaction to her new emotional and physical boundaries and appropriate relationship requests. Then she acknowledged that her unfinished father-daughter issues were being replayed in her relationship with Chuck. She began to separate herself emotionally from her fears of failure, her prior traumatic father-daughter history, and the reality of her situation with Chuck. In Chuck, Marie had unconsciously picked a younger male version of her father. Chuck's abuse was similar to the verbal abuse she had endured from her father while she was growing up. Much like Chuck, her father had demanded that she be perfect and always support him emotionally. Marie's moods vacillated between anger, hysteria, and anxiety when she talked to either Chuck or her father. Marie began to separate Chuck and her father in her mind, where they were the same person, until she began to understand the connection between her present relationship and her past.

Over time, Marie was able to stop panicking about her emotional safety and was able to detach herself from Chuck and address her chronic codependence with Chuck. She was able to get Chuck to move out of her house and stopped financially supporting him. She terminated the relationship with him and refused to see him, and she now hasn't seen him for two full years. Marie then began to address her father's demands for her attention and began to set limits on what she could and couldn't do for him. Marie limited herself to speaking on the phone with her father to only twice a week (previously it was twice a day) and only seeing him for a meal biweekly (previously she saw her father five times a week). While she worked on healing and piecing her life back together, Marie didn't go on a date for three years after her relationship with Chuck ended. She knew she had to emotionally heal and develop a different standard for her love relationships before she could develop a successful connection with another partner.

Charlene's Series of Unfortunate Events

Background

Charlene's life started to unravel when her husband, Mark, staged an alcoholic intervention for her with her family (her parents and siblings; there were no children in the marriage). Charlene agreed to go to drug/alcohol rehabilitation for thirty days in Arizona. While she was in the treatment center, her husband filed for divorce, changed the locks on their house, emptied all their bank accounts, and moved his girlfriend into the house. He put all of Charlene's clothes into her parked car in their home's driveway. He also told her employer that she had a drinking problem and could never work again. Charlene, a corporate attorney, had been supporting the household. Mark, an unemployed actor, had a marijuana addiction and hadn't been regularly employed in about ten years. Charlene would binge drink (nonstop drinking for approximately seventy-two hours) about three times a year. Each drinking episode was connected to their impending divorce, Mark's lack of ambition, and his chronic "womanizing," which left Charlene feeling very insecure in their relationship. Charlene never viewed or understood that she had a responsibility in the marriage for her problems and personal issues. It just wasn't Mark's fault for her drinking and sense of feeling emotionally "trapped." Charlene and Mark had had a very high degree of anger and resentment toward each other for years. They were never able to resolve or let go of their resentments toward each regarding money (Charlene controlled it), Mark's actress girlfriends (infidelity), and the stress of building a new house.

Charlene's Story

Charlene was referred to me by one of her former law partners. During our first appointment, she told me:

> I was fired while in the rehab center. They [the law firm] can't do that. It is illegal, but my ex-husband scared them with my rehab stay. It makes no sense that my ex-husband would "blow-up" my career because he depends on me for financial support. Regardless, it is better for me to move on and take my clients with me to another firm. My ex-husband filed for divorce while I was in rehab three months ago. I am now living in an apartment in the valley and he is living in our newly built four-million-dollar home in the Hollywood Hills with his whore actress girlfriend. They are spending their afternoons around our new pool and I am looking for a job. You wonder why women hate their ex-husbands.

Charlene's anger suddenly turned to profound sadness. She started to sob, and between sobs continued to relate her heartbreaking story:

> The judge in our divorce trial has ordered me to continue making the house payments until the financial end of the divorce is figured out. Do you know how screwed I feel? I am paying for my ex-husband to live with his unemployed whore actress in our new house. I am so angry, but I am not drinking and I can't. If I drink right now, it will kill me. I want to go to sleep and wake up and have this awful nightmare end. I am so scared and feel absolutely lost. I am trapped, I have to make my life work or I will lose everything. I will end up being a street woman—a bag lady with a law degree—and no one really cares. Mark has set me up to pay for everything and I can't do anything right now. I am financially tapped out. I am using my savings, retirement funds, and family loans to keep the house and all its costs going. I am looking for a job in the midst of my meltdown. I cry at least two hours every day. I at least have a great divorce attorney, but he costs ten thousand dollars a month. My stepchildren will not call me back and my par-

ents are angry that I didn't leave Mark first and could have prevented this from happening. Dr. Poulter, call me crazy, but I really loved Mark and I can't believe I allowed this mess to ever happen or get this bad. I knew for years that my being the "breadwinner" was going to catch up with me and for constantly complaining about Mark's lack of work. He is really lazy and really smart; that is a bad combination. He has blown up my career, my family, my stepchildren, and me. I would run away if I had somewhere to go.

Charlene's Recovery

Charlene continued therapy to begin to address her personal issues. It was very hard for Charlene to see that her drinking problem was a secondary problem in her marriage. Mark's motivation for Charlene's alcohol rehabilitation stay was a ploy to get her out of the house and file for divorce. Charlene's serious emotional addiction to "fixing" her ex-husband—as well as the other significant men in her past—was the unresolved crisis in her life. Mark wasn't fixable (nor is anyone, it is an individual's choice, not the partner's) and Charlene had never accepted that concept. Mark wasn't the first lover Charlene had completely supported. Charlene had a history of rescuing men—all ex-lovers—and trying to fix their lives. Her secret hope and unspoken intent was to be loved in return for her exceptional giving and unconditional loving. But she never received the payback and was instead always devastated by their rejection and their insensitivity to her loving gestures. Charlene had two long-term relationships before her marriage to Mark, and all three ended the same way: *disastrously*.

The emotional heartbreak of her first two romantic breakups was tremendously devastating and shattered her self-confidence. Yet, by her own admission, she had previously refused to address her codependence as well as the self-esteem issues that were connected to men prior to her relationship with Mark. She began to binge drink in an attempt to muffle her feelings of hopelessness and despair when her partner/lover wouldn't be the man she wanted. Until now,

Charlene never addressed her underlying problem, issues, or addictive behavior with men and her constant need for their approval. She repeated her same romantic patterns with Mark, and the consequences this time were too painful to ignore. The circumstances of her divorce—her finances, his affair, and his lack of emotional support—were so extreme that she couldn't overlook her issues any longer. In the past, the binge drinking had been Charlene's way of avoiding and numbing her anger and her fear of being unlovable. In the past, she had felt emotionally safer to numb herself with alcohol than deal with her long-standing problem with the men she had chosen as romantic partners. She knew now that she couldn't drink, smoke marijuana, or do any other drugs and be emotionally clear, psychologically insightful, and mentally alert at the same time. So the sense of urgency to heal her life and rebuild it had never seemed so serious. Ultimately Charlene addressed her underlying father-daughter issues and was able to successfully resolve her divorce with Mark. Her first step was to become detached from Mark and extinguish her rage about feeling abandoned by him. She also needed to face her fear of being unlovable.

Over the next two years in therapy working with me, Charlene uncovered the emotional anger and resentment that she had toward her father for divorcing her mother when she was twelve years old. Charlene psychologically addressed her need for male attention as really the emotional "wound" from her lost relationship with her father after the divorce. Charlene worked on her unresolved grief (never allowed herself to talk about this tremendous loss in her life) about her father. She made the connection between her need to fix men, which was her unconscious attempt at "fixing" her father so he would not leave her or her family. Charlene also allowed herself to grieve the lost relationship with her father. She only saw her father four times before his death, when she was twenty-eight years old. Charlene began to feel a deep sense of relief knowing she didn't have to fix her ex-husband or any future intimate partners in her life.

YOUR NEW LOVE STANDARD

Expanding your tolerance for feeling loved, allowing yourself to experience love, and acting in a loving way are critical elements to developing and understanding your future intimate relationships. Another way of thinking about this is to uncover your desire and your personal need for acceptable and loving behaviors from your partner. What actions by your partner make you feel loved and adored?

The theory, practice, and application of love in romantic relationships have long fueled religious and psychological debate. The theme of love has inspired an endless supply of hit songs, Academy Award–winning movies, and epic poems through the ages. The element of love and its role in your life and relationships are topics that need to be further explored. A major part of your emotional, psychological, and spiritual recovery is to expand the role that love plays in your life. No one is ever beyond the scope of understanding the strength and transformational power of feeling loved and loving a significant other. We all have the human need to love and to feel loved. These basic needs never go away or diminish, although they may go underground after a painful divorce/breakup.

One key element that will help you put your life back together is your ability to understand your love factor. The love factor is composed of these elements, actions, behaviors, and gestures that make you feel loved, accepted, and understood. There are a lot of factors in life, and the love factor is the biggest one of all. Very few people can live a fulfilling and a complete life without feeling loved and loving others. The extreme consequence of being unable to develop the ability to love or feel empathy for others is the primary element of a fragmented personality—someone without a conscience or feeling for others.[3]

Being psychologically connected to your loving feelings, your capacity to experience love, and your ability to express love make up the emotional oxygen that fuels your entire life.[4] There is no way you can rebuild your life without the active ingredient of love as part of it. Your understanding of love, your experience of love, and your ability to increase your capacity to be loved are of critical importance. *Your entire intimate relationship future is guided by your ability to love and accept love—your love factor.* The concept of love may seem foreign to you given all you have been through in your divorce or breakup. But regardless of your circumstances and history, love *must* be part of your future. Accepting that romantic love can be part of your life again is a major step forward in healing your ex-factor—in creating hope and a different future.

Avoiding your need and desire for love will only isolate you and push you further into despair. Your fear of being rejected, betrayed, abandoned, and violated can only be overcome through your personal journey of expanding understanding of love in your life. Trying to control, manage, and explain away the need for intimacy is a dead-end discussion—it leads you to nowhere and creates more despair and fear. People regularly come into my office with horrendous stories of heartbreaking events. They adamantly explain why they can never trust or love anyone again. These same people pour their heart and soul into wonderful causes in the hope of never feeling emotionally vulnerable with another man or woman again. These endeavors are positive and many times are unconscious attempts to avoid romance and to fill in the void, emotional hole in their relational life. Yet these people all intuitively know—and begin over time to understand more fully—that their healing is directly connected to their opening their lives again to the experience of love. Healing your heart and rebuilding your life through emotional strength, courage, and hope requires you to incorporate love as the main ingredient.

WHY LOVE ALWAYS MATTERS

Robert, Marie, and Charlene all knew that their behaviors, relationship choices, fearful reactions, and panicked responses to their particular crises didn't bring out their best feelings; in fact, they brought out their worst. Their need to be loved and appreciated without asking for any give and take was the very fuel for their relationship failure. Another way to view your romantic pattern is to acknowledge that being a "doormat" and avoiding your emotional needs such as *"not asking anything in return regardless of what you have to put up with and endure,"* in hopes that your partner will throw you some small portion of love, doesn't work anymore in your life. It is this narrow belief of relationships, self-defeating behavior, and lack of value for your emotional needs that helps create a very lop-sided marriage in terms of love and support for you. *The need to be loved is natural. Your need for love and your capacity for love are two entirely different issues.* The need to be loved issue is a natural desire that is a result of your gender, family history, upbringing, and prior intimate relationship experience. What is problematic is when you are willing to take any emotional crumbs of kindness and compassion. The second love dynamic is a full understanding of your need and ability to be loved as an adult, giving and taking in measure. The more insight into your unspoken desire for love, the less your wounded inner child or rejected adult will make decisions for you. Your expanded insight into your desire for love and acceptance of love becomes the driving force in the romantic choices you make. *You also need to be aware of what you want, need, and can accept from your partner.*

All three adults had to stop their old automatic behavior patterns of feeling unloved because their lives had been broken, fractured, and shattered into a million pieces. They were faced with very serious circumstances that would overtake their lives if they didn't choose a different path to their future. Their old ways of approaching and seeking love were no longer viable or functional. Robert could have lost his medical career and his ability to support his children if he had continued to avoid conflict. Marie almost lost her career; fortunately, her investment firm gave her a six-month leave of absence to address her personal issues. Chuck used Marie's money and name to buy her company's competitors' investments. Charlene lost her law firm partnership, which had taken her fifteen years to achieve, and almost lost her ability to practice law because of Mark's vindictiveness about her binge drinking.

Each of these high-functioning adults learned—as a result of being heartbroken and emotionally smashed into the ground—that they need to understand the role of love in their relationships if they are going to have a different future. Their prior choices and decisions in romantic relationships had become dysfunctional to the point of catastrophic.

Over the next few years, they each very deliberately detached themselves from the insanity of their old relationships. Their emotional hearts and souls began to heal as they slowly moved forward in rebuilding their lives. The first issue they each had to individually resolve was their love issue. Robert, Marie, and Charlene spent the next two years expanding their understanding of what I call *the six faces of love.* In order to rebuild your life and put back together your sense of self, you need to begin the process of understanding these six love faces and how they can fully operate in your life. Each idea, insight, and concept is critical for you to appreciate in order to improve your relationship present and future.

THE SIX FACES OF LOVE

- *Believe you deserve more.* Your intimate relationships start and stop with your beliefs and choices. You are the only one who will decided when and whom the next romantic relationship will be with. You have more control and choices than you might feel or believe.
- *Transcend your emotional comfort zone.* Go beyond your old familiar style of love—expand it. Change always implies that you are willing to try new things and respsond differently to your future partner.

- *Rebuild trust.* Being vulnerable is your pathway to healing and expanding your love life. Avoiding relationships will never be the answer to a broken heart or emotional disappointment.
- *Stop blaming.* You are solely responsible for your past, your present, and your future. Blaming and finger-pointing only increase your inability to psychologically move past your ex and the old relationship.
- *No more self-defeating choices.* Understand how you haven't accepted love in your life. Learn to like yourself. Don't accept disrespectful and unfair treatment as if it is something worthwhile. Consider your old romantic patterns, choices, and what has worked and what hasn't worked in your love life.
- *Let go of your ex.* Embrace your life after the pain stops. Your intimacy history and legacy can change. Remarriage and love can be in your future, regardless of your current emotional and mental state. "Moving on" in your life requires you to look forward, not backward at the marriage/romantic relationship.

These six faces of love are the practical application for increasing your tolerance, your acceptance, for new experiences of love and being loved. One of the hardest things for people to accept in a relationship is that someone else considers them a soul mate—lovable, exceptional, and easy to be with. These types of loving, affectionate, and adoring feelings force the receiver to accept or reject the sender. Rejecting the sender is a very common pattern in women and men who are recovering from a profoundly disturbing emotional divorce or relationship breakup. *It is much easier—or so it seems—to dismiss your new lover as a wrong choice when he or she pushes you into new areas of love and intimacy.*

Going beyond your familiar patterns of intimacy is the foundation for rebuilding your romantic life. Learning to tolerate and accept romantic love in your life is critical. *Your expanding ability to love again starts with you.* The belief you aren't lovable, or you are defective, damaged goods, or not good enough is the old pattern creating another romantic tragedy in your life. It's time to do away with self-loathing, emotional insecurity, shame-based feelings, and rejection of the old perspective of yourself. To counter and change these self-defeating beliefs and behaviors, you need to incorporate the six transformational faces of love into action. Take your time, reread the list, and add your own ideas and thoughts to it. The goal is to start viewing your romantic life from a fresh new perspective. In the next six chapters, we will explore how to expand your repertoire for intimate love and fulfilling romantic relationships. We will elaborate on those six concepts in greater detail, using examples and incentives that you can apply to your life right now. Your romantic present and future, career, family, children, stepchildren, new partner, and overall health will all be directly impacted by how you incorporate these six new faces of love into your daily life. Your future will look like a series of new self-acceptance steps to enlarge your capacity for being loved and loving.

Chapter 6

WHICH PARENT DID I MARRY?

Lifelong Patterns

I knew I should have never married Brad. Everyone told me that he was just like my father but rather a younger version of him. We fought constantly and he turned out to be more of a narcissistic jerk than my father. I can't believe I married him!

—Karen, age forty-five, mother of three, married for fourteen years, divorced for three years

I always prided myself on being different than my parents. I swore I would never marry a woman like my mother. She married and divorced four different men while I was growing up. She was a disaster. My second wife became just like my mother after our marriage and she divorced me after ten years. My two marriages seem like my mother's life, not mine. I know better, but I still date women like my mother.

—Dan, age fifty-two, divorced twice

We tend to marry the parent that we have the most unresolved conflicts with and this has nothing to do with their gender.

—Salvador Munichin, MD, family systems research psychiatrist[1]

I remember exactly where I was sitting—in a lecture on a Wednesday evening many years ago—when I first heard the concept of the unconscious partner selection process. My heart immediately fell into my stomach. At the time, I was dating a great woman (not my wife-to-be) who was emotionally distant, depressed, and very moody at times. Other times she was loving and engaging, potentially a serious marriage partner. Her behavior was troubling and frustrating, but it felt very familiar and like something I could handle. I had no conscious idea why I found myself drawn to an intimate partner who wasn't a good match for me on many levels. The ending of that relationship two years later was a replay of my mother-son dynamic—cold, distant, codependent, depressed. My first thought was, I suddenly realized that I was doing exactly what the lecture was describing; dating a personality type similar to my father: critical, emotionally aloof, and unsupportive. Then immediately my second thought was: *No way I will ever date or marry either one of my parents*. I was wrong. I have dated and married both—and not very well, either.

WHY DID I GET INVOLVED WITH MY EX?

The basic premise of partner selection is that we pick our romantic partners based on the unresolved issues that we have with a particular parent. It doesn't matter if we are male or female or if our fundamental parent-child relationship strain is with our mother or our father. These parent-child tensions, conflicts, misunderstandings, and traumas will likely direct our romantic choices. But bear in mind that you can change this process. For instance, if a daughter has unresolved emotionally painful issues with her mother, then she will often instinctively pick men similar to her mother as romantic partners in an unconscious attempt to resolve those issues. All of our unconscious partner selections are blindly motivated by a core need for resolution and healing with that particular parent.

If we aren't consciously aware, healed, and beyond blaming our conflicted parent for all our ills, then we will likely choose partners like him or her in our romantic encounters/unions. It is natural to want resolution, love, and self-acceptance from an estranged, conflicted, or problematic parent. In an attempt to gain this, we may automatically pick romantic partners who have attributes that closely resemble the core problems, issues, and tensions that we have had with either our mother or father.

Now, this premise doesn't apply if we have resolved our conscious and unconscious conflicts with our parents. Unfortunately, for most of us—including me—it is only after a heart-wrenching relationship ends that we begin to gain insight into our process of partner selection. This insight comes as a result of our healing and expansion of personal boundaries and allowing someone to be emotionally close to us, thus accepting their love and support. It isn't for lack of strength or good judgment that our significant romantic partner selection may be directly influenced by our parent-child relationship. The need to feel loved and approved by—and at peace with—our parents is a powerful driving force in any person's life and choices. You must accept that this concept is most often valid so you can use it to acquire valuable insight into your love life and your choice of former partners. The primary question you should ask yourself is: How did your relationship with your mother or father impact, shape, and direct your adult romantic and married life?

MY MOTHER ISSUES

If you are a woman, your relationship with your mother may have been very conflicted, a source of constant pain in your life since you were a young girl. On the surface, your husband, boyfriend, or significant male lover might appear to be nothing like your mother. Yet under the surface, he may have the same or very similar personality issues, behaviors, attitudes, and/or values as your mother. The same patterns may hold true for men with their mothers or fathers. Many men who have problematic relationships with their fathers date, live with, and marry women who are the female version of their fathers. It is a mind-boggling concept to think we married a female version of our fathers or a male version of our mothers, yet the divorce and remarriage rates may indicate that many intelligent adults are repeatedly remarrying the same parent with whom they have a conflicted relationship. This unconscious act of selecting a partner has no regard for sexual orientation or the idea that "opposites attract" in a relationship. *What attracted us to our significant romantic partners in our lives often is our prior unfinished relationship issues with our mothers or fathers.*

Another piece of the unconscious partner selection puzzle is that you might have overreacted to your conflicted parent-child relationship and married someone who is seemingly very different emotionally and psychologically. On the surface, the behavior may look new, but the relationship may ultimately be the same as your parent-child dynamic. For example, Margaret was raised by an anxious, loving, overbearing, and very fearful mother. All her life Margaret, an actress/model, was constantly instructed and guided in her decisions by Lucy, her mother. Lucy's constant mantra—verbally and nonverbally—was the world isn't a safe place. Lucy continuously told young Margaret, starting at age five, that in fact the world was especially dangerous for attractive women. Immediately after college, Margaret met and married Ari. He was an extremely controlling and powerful personality. Margaret felt safe with Ari, but it cost her her psychological independence and her continued emotional development. Ari became increasingly abusive on all levels—verbally, emotionally, and physically—as he tried to control Margaret more and more.

The level of tension and control Ari exerted only increased throughout their four-year marriage. Ultimately, Margaret left the relationship. She didn't initially see the connection between her mother and Ari. Later, Margaret began to realize that she had married Ari for protection, as an unconscious reaction to her mother's constant fears and worries about living in the world. The irony is that Margaret never felt emotionally safe with Ari, though he shielded her from the world and from her mother's panic. Margaret recognized that she had actually married the male form of her mother. She unconsciously allowed Ari to control her because she didn't believe she could take care of herself in the world, based on Lucy's fears. Margaret learned by going through her divorce that she not only could take care of herself but that her ex-husband never knew what she needed or wanted in their marriage. Margaret's ex-factor process revealed that her hidden strength of being "safe" in the world was never her issue but her mother's and ex-husband's.

THE UNCONSCIOUS PUZZLE PIECES OF YOUR LIFE

Even if you don't see or believe that you married someone who is the opposite personality of either your mother or father, your response to your parent—even selecting someone with the different traits—shows that your parent had a tremendous impact on your intimate partner selection. This selection process is not a conscious act, but rather a very powerful unconscious dynamic that drives our core need for res-olution, love, self-acceptance, and emotional safety. The parent with whom we feel the most anxiety, abandonment, and conflict and from whom we feel the most emotional indifference, lack of love/empathy, and rejection will likely be the prototype and template for our choice of a romantic partner. Don't drop the book or start panicking. This unconscious process of partner selection can be resolved in your romantic relationships. By understanding the dynamics of the process, we can often see why and how we have married, loved, and built a life with a certain type of man or woman. Usually our closest friends and the people in our lives will wonder why we lived with and had children with this person. Adults resolving their ex-factor issues often find that their partner selection was very complex and more than simply "falling in love," and now appreciate their newfound ability to make more healthy and better-informed choices about their romantic future. Many others doubt this analysis about intimate relationship selection and believe it to be a new "psychobabble" myth. However, this is a viable family systems theory that is, unfortunately, commonly misunderstood and sometimes even dismissed.[2]

I knew immediately sitting in the lecture hall many years ago which issues I had with each parent and why I had picked certain women who were wonderful but not the right fit for me. Regardless of those powerful insights about my parent-child relationships, I still played out my issues with my romantic partners. It wasn't until these relationships ended that I made an emotional and mental connection to my core issues. There was no doubt in my mind that Dr. Munichin's research into parent/child relationships had tremendous insight into family dynamics and their impact on next-generation marriages. Most people, including myself, are generally perplexed by this very accurate concept of love, marriage, and the role our parents have in our romantic encounters. The psychological family systems theory contends that we will pick our partner based on the unconscious unresolved issues with our parents. *The idea that our parent-child history strongly influences the people we pick as partners may be a very troubling concept.* For the sake of our discussion, let's say that this concept is true and has to be addressed, explored, and understood by you. No one can continue to date, marry, or live with the same type of woman/man with any degree of success without a more complete picture of his or her parent-child relationship issues and concerns. Until you fully understand why you are choosing your romantic partner(s), these partners will not be a good fit. It is a repetitive cycle of disappointment and you can't sustain a fulfilling relationship without comprehending the reasons and motivations behind your choices. Applying the idea and theory of not "marrying our conflicted parent" and exploring it in relation to ourselves may help us.

Your ability to resolve your ex-factor, re-create your life, and have the type of intimate relationship you desire is greatly shaped by your parent-child history. The more you become psychologically aware of your core emotional conflicts, incomplete attachments, and relationship barriers, the better able you are to re-create your future. It is important for you to start thinking about what parental relationship issues and events have had the most powerful and lasting impact on your life. Don't dismiss something as irrelevant just because it happened thirty years ago; your unconscious stores these events in a "time freeze" matter (your memory isn't diminished over time). Your parent-child issues and concerns aren't tied to a linear timetable. Feelings of loss, rejection, and abandonment, for instance, are stored in your memory outside the reach of a calendar. These feelings can be reactivated by your intimate partner without your making any conscious connection to their source—all you know is that you feel very disappointed and deeply wounded by your partner.

It is important to note that this concept of unconscious process of partner selection also holds true when you have had a very positive relationship with a parent. Common sense would dictate that if you had a good relationship as a child with a parent, then you will select a partner who is similar to that parent. The parent-child relationship has farther-reaching influences than most people would imagine; the key is to become more aware of all the influences of your family of origin.

For instance, your partner might have chosen you because of your stability and lack of parental conflict. If you grew up with a mother-daughter relationship that was supportive and loving, and your father fully embraced you as well, then you will likely unconsciously pick partners who can create the same type of safe emotional atmosphere. Positive parenting creates a foundation for children to develop the same type of functional and loving relationships when they grow up. Another example is positive communication within your family of origin. If your parents fostered a safe environment for expression of feelings and thoughts, then you will likely unconsciously pick partners who have the same aptitude and desire for direct open communication. The focus here is what to do to change your unconscious attraction toward certain types of person-alities, counterproductive behavioral patterns, and incomplete emo-tional bonding that isn't positive or productive in your intimate rela-tionships. We all make relationship choices and our discussion is centered on the choices that are based on old dysfunctional experi-ences that lead to unhealthy adult relationships.

PARENTAL CAUSES AND EFFECTS IN YOUR ROMANTIC LIFE

The following list of residual effects from your childhood in your present-day relationships is a very critical jumping-off point for romantic healing. The questions are specifically designed to be a cat-alyst to help you develop a deeper understanding of the numerous connections between you and your parents. The old conflicts between you and your mother or father may have even diminished, but the painful feelings can linger for years. It is likely these uncon-scious residual beliefs and feelings are negatively impacting and directing your life without your awareness. The immediate goal for your present-day relationships is to reduce your internal conflict with the parent with whom you have had the most conflict. This doesn't mean that you should pick up the phone and verbally blast your mother or father. In fact, it is preferable that you don't involve your parents at all—that you do the internal core work yourself. Your parent-child issues are now *your* issues and your responsibility to resolve.[3]

Ask yourself the following questions:

- Which parent or stepparent do you feel has been, in some way, the most problematic for your romantic life?
- Which parent gets the strongest negative reaction(s) from you?

- Do you have present-day disagreements, conflicts, and/or tension with a particular parent?
- If so, what is the recurring issue for you?
- What keeps you emotionally attached to the conflict between you and your mother or father?
- What is your goal in fighting with your mother or father?

Mother-Daughter Conflicts

Consider how the lingering effects of a verbally critical mother can still affect you and how you speak to yourself, as well as to your new romantic partner and your own daughter. You may find yourself very critical of your daughter's weight and/or appearance. You may not consciously believe that your critical opinion and fear of being overweight have anything to do with your mother's obsession with your appearance while you were growing up. You feel that your mother wanted a perfect daughter, and you may have felt—and still feel— that you have never measured up to your mother's invisible standard of perfection. You know your mother was harsh at times about your appearance, but you don't believe that is the main issue between you, your ex-husband, and perhaps even your daughter.

In a continuation of this dynamic, if you have a teenage daughter who is very defiant with you, she is dating a very "troubled" young man as a way to create emotional distance between you and her. Your daughter knows that you are disapproving of her boyfriend because he isn't "perfect." The two of you argue just like you and your mother still do currently. Your ex-husband may have left you for a younger woman. His explanation for the sudden divorce was that you were no longer slim, attractive, or interesting—never mind that he also has aged but that wasn't an issue for you. In addition, your last two boyfriends have suggested that you should consider breast augmentation and some other minor cosmetic surgery.

These unfortunate circumstances may seem unrelated, but they all likely stem from your mother's constant need for perfection. You may still feel insecure about your attractiveness to men as your mother reminds you all the time of your advancing age. At the same time, you have great difficulty believing and trusting that a man would find you interesting and intelligent. You are very attractive, smart, and accomplished, and men find you desirable and want a relationship with you. But because of your insecurity, you choose only men who find you imperfect and lacking. Your mother, in the meantime, has already had numerous facelifts and elective cosmetic operations; your teenage daughter tells you that you are just like Grandma. Your strained relationship with your mother is still impacting you and directing every area of your life. You feel like a failure with your daughter because of all the tension and conflict, and your mother reminds you of your "shortcomings" as a mother.

Father-Son Conflicts

Consider how a smart, accomplished, loving family man might unconsciously marry a female version of his father. Your father might have passed away years ago, or he might live far away, or you might call or visit him once a week in his nursing home; whatever the situation, he still matters in your life. Your father may have withheld his acceptance and approval of you throughout your life. You feel like whatever you do is never "good enough" and you find yourself constantly seeking others' approval as an adult like you did as a boy growing up. Your father has never been verbally or emotionally supportive of you and your life choices. Now your father's health and mental capacity might be declining, but regardless of his current life circumstances, wealth, age, or health concerns, his emotional impact on your life continues to the present day.

The Father Issues

Mike has had a long history of finding himself very attracted to sarcastic, smart, and narcissistic women. Mike's dating history prior to his marriage repeatedly proved that these women weren't a good match for his life or his mental health. In spite of the rejection, abandonment, and wasted energy involved in these relationships, he always found himself trying to please them and seek their approval. Mike was always motivated to convince them that he was a good guy, as he tried to do in his father-son relationship. When Mike first met his ex-wife, her immediate criticism and distain for his father felt refreshing and emotionally protective.

Fourteen years later, Mike divorced his wife because he could no longer tolerate her verbal abuse and constant criticism of his life, his friends, his family, and his parenting skills. Unconsciously, Mike had chosen a wife who was a female version of his emotionally distant, withholding, and narcissistic father. Mike constantly found himself the target of his wife's rage and disappointment about her life, their marriage, and their lack of material wealth. Mike's father, Pete, always criticized him as a child for being the reason he was married to Mike's mother. Mike blew up one morning after being told by his wife that she was moving from the East Coast to the West Coast to seek a better life. Mike exploded and told his wife that he had been done with the marriage for years and wanted a divorce. In a period of twelve weeks Mike moved out, filed for divorce, and, in an emotional reaction to his feelings of insecurity, met and began dating another woman.

Mike felt his wife and father were very similar—emotionally, mentally, and psychologically—during his fourteen-year marriage. After college, Mike got fed up with his father and didn't talk to him for five years—yet unconsciously, he still wanted his father's approval. Interestingly, Mike reported that his sex life with his wife was always strained because he didn't want to be vulnerable or emotionally close to her. The self-protective automatic defense mechanism Mike had developed with his father—distancing himself while desiring approval—was the same one he developed with his wife. Moreover, Mike often found himself feeling like a young boy with his wife, much the way he did when speaking with his father. Prior to his death, Mike's father reprimanded him for not being a good guy and suffering through his marriage—like he had.

Mike always felt that nothing he did for his ex-wife—including sharing joint legal and physical custody of their three children—was ever good enough. Neither Mike's father nor his ex-wife ever expressed any loving, accepting, positive feelings toward him. He felt that he had grown up in a loveless, emotionally negligent, and insensitive atmosphere. His marriage reflected his unresolved feelings about the lack of acceptance and open communication in his relationship with his father. Mike found himself in a loveless, sexless, and emotionally abusive marriage, with the same feelings of anxiety in dealing with his ex-wife about a conflict as he had in dealing with his father when he was growing up.

Mike never felt emotionally, mentally, or psychologically safe with either his father or his ex-wife. He kept himself from telling either of them his true feelings or expressing contrary opinions about any matter. Mike's self-protective behavior was based on years of feeling abandoned for having a contrary opinion or different belief than his father, and he continued the same pattern of behavior when he married his ex-wife. When Mike divorced his ex-wife, his father agreed with her that Mike wasn't a good father—even going so far as to provide written testimony against Mike during the custody trial.

Mike began to realize the underlying connection, similarity, and emotional commonality between his father and his ex-wife. As part of healing from his past and creating a different romantic life for his future, he fully acknowledged that he had married a female version of his father. In the six years after his divorce, Mike had increasingly less difficulty in communicating with both his ex-wife and his father.

MOTHER/FATHER CONFLICT RECOGNITION

Many women can identity with the father-son conflict, just as there are men who can identify with the mother-daughter conflict. Both scenarios are important to understand in order to gain insight into your relationship history. The parent we carry in our hearts is usually a very different one than is in our lives in reality. It is the parent in our minds who causes the most conflict and impairment in our present-day relationships. Drawing a connection between our current relationship choices and our relationship with either parent while growing up is the key to changing our future for the better. Our prior partner selections, past marriages, and ended relationships have their roots in our family history. The effects and consequences of our childhood, teenage, and early adult parent-child relationships can have long-term unconscious consequences.

For instance, you might have never questioned or considered that you can state your own opinion or voice with a partner without being fearful of a blowup from it. Your automatic behaviors, beliefs, and reactions have caused you to make choices and decisions that aren't always in your best interest. Your goal is to uncover your unconscious issues and make them conscious so they can be changed for the better. This process may sound daunting, but it isn't. As an adult, you are now able to amend, change, and redirect how you choose to respond to and emotionally bond with your partner. These core changes are the foundation for any significant long-term intimate relationship.

Your expanded understanding of your prior automatic/unconscious choices, beliefs, and feelings make them subject to questioning and reexamination. You are old enough and wise enough, and have been heartbroken enough, to make the changes you need and desire. If you can't seem to grasp what your core issues might be, don't be alarmed. Whatever you do, don't ask your ex-partner about your mother-father issues, because he or she will usually take the opportunity to lecture you. Remember that everyone has at least a few residual core issues that will keep reappearing in various contexts until they are addressed and resolved. The most powerful context for our parent-child issues to come out is within our deepest and most significant relationship in our adult lives: marriage or marriage-type commitment.

It is worth repeating that it is only in the supportive atmosphere of your love relationship that your deepest wants, desires, and hopes will be met and fulfilled. It is also true that your deepest core issues and faulty beliefs about yourself will surface in your exclusive love relationship. It is very exciting to start allowing someone to love and cherish you when your prior experience of intimacy was compromised. A careful reading of the following list may help you flesh out which parent you have struggled with, unconsciously and consciously. Ask yourself which statement best applies to you and connects with a particular parent. Please note that the words in parentheses provide an analysis of why you might feel that way. These statements have a present-day application with a link to your family history.

The Intimate Partner Application List

- Mistrusting of the opposite sex (parental alienation by one parent to the other; you were taught to hate the "other" parent).
- I am not "good enough" (parental narcissism and perfectionism).
- Your greatest asset is your appearance (parental neglect of developing your inner qualities and inner strengths).
- Fear of rejection (parental indifference toward you and your interests; you didn't feel important to your parents).
- Marriage is a trap (parental relationship dissatisfaction and unresolved parental intimacy issues).
- Strong independence and inability to trust (parental dependence on you and emotional engulfment of you).
- Living through your father's or mother's affair (fear of abandonment created by the parent leaving the marriage).
- I don't feel lovable, my partner doesn't love me (lack of parental expression of love).
- Emotional deprivation and neediness (parental narcissism; your emotional needs were never addressed, understood, or met).
- Needing a perfect partner—physically, mentally, and emotion-

ally (parental narcissism; appearance is more important than substance).

- Codependence; needing to fix our parents (parental dependence on us).
- Uncomfortable with emotional, physical, and verbal affection (parental perfectionism; nothing is ever good enough).
- Feeling inadequate, shameful, and/or phony (parental indifference, lack of emotional support of you and your interests).
- Picking violent and volatile relationships (terrorized and/or abused by a parent).
- Anxious and fearful about your future (parental instability and anxiety).
- Inability to make or maintain a secure relationship commitment (insecure, unstable, and unpredictable emotional parental bond).
- Tolerating abusive behavior—physical, verbal, and psychological (parental fear and a childhood history of abuse).
- Avoidant of conflicts and arguments (parental narcissism; need to always be a people pleaser).
- Feeling unlovable and not worthy of a great relationship (parental neglect; lack of affection in childhood).
- Anger issues (parental indifference, neglect, and physical abuse).
- Commitment phobia (incomplete/unfinished parental separation).
- Desirous and fearful of having children (parental caretaking; always took emotional care of your parents).
- Feeling abandoned in your marriage/romantic relationship (unstable parental emotional bonding and a lack of emotional separation from your parents).
- Picking the "wrong" man or woman (unresolved issues surrounding your personal value with your parents).
- Fearful of men or women (parental emotional engulfment of you and having no emotional space for yourself).
- Angry at your father (women; emotional and physically distant father).

- Angry and aggressive toward others (men; rejection and indifference by your father).
- Marrying or dating emotionally absent or unavailable partners (parental negligence, parental depression).
- Traumatized by the parental tension in your home growing up (inappropriate tension and verbal abuse toward your partner).
- Men want only sex; women want only money and status (parental depression and lack of self-worth).
- Being resistant to change and emotionally inflexible (parental criticalness of you).
- Alcoholic, drug abuse, and addictive behaviors (parental instability and inconsistent love/security).
- Lack of sexuality in your intimate relationship (parental repression of their sexuality).
- Greed, selfishness, and exploitative behaviors (parental withholding of love and support).
- You have to be perfect in order to be lovable (parental criticalness).

This list isn't about blaming or putting your relationship issues at your parent's feet. Your parents aren't part of your healing or the solution for creating healthier functional relationships. *You* are the solution, with your conscious choice in picking the right kind of partners and developing the type of romantic relationships that you desire and deserve. Your expanded awareness and understanding of your parent-child blind spots and their residual connections will help you bring about permanent change.

Many of the statements in this list are derived from childhood. They represent unfilled wishes that have guided your behavior and feelings in the past with your ex-partner. These old unconscious emotional reactions and skewed personal beliefs that derive from your tension with your mother or father can be redesigned and rewritten. We will address the problems above in depth in the chapters that follow, but first we have to recognize what particular issues are short-circuiting your present-day significant love relationship.

After reading the list and thinking about your childhood, adolescence, and adulthood, ask yourself: Which parental relationship holds the most tension, conflict, and disappointment for you? How have you handled your frustration with that parent? Do you see some of the emotional threads between your parental conflict and your current romantic feelings, insecurities, and conflicts, as well as your partner selections? Can you begin to acknowledge that your feelings about this conflict with your parent are shaping the way you approach and interact with your partners in present-day relationships? It is important to note that many adult children have ongoing resentment toward a parent who left during childhood. A parent's absence from a child's life is often highly traumatic, and the long-term impact can't always be assessed until later in life. These adults may have little to no contact with their estranged parent, but the impact of the abandonment is not limited to childhood.

But this book isn't about your parents' marital status. It is about your emotional bond/connection to your parent(s). This can include any combination of blended families or adopted parents (i.e., adults you had in your life growing up who acted in a supportive and loving manner toward you). So again, ask yourself: Which issue(s) in the above list felt like the most accurate description of your former/current intimate relationship? Can you see any correlations between your behaviors, insecurities, disappointments, and anxiety, and your parent-child relationship? Your present-day emotional challenges usually have their roots and beginnings in trauma or unfinished business from your childhood. The issues and concepts above are now going to be addressed in your present-day life and romantic connections. The ideas, questions, and thoughts below are worth considering as they relate to healing and finding a parent-child resolution that will assist you in changing your intimate relationship behavior. When you consider reentering the "relationship" world, what is your core fear or insecurity about being romantically connected again? Which parent do you feel has shaped your relationship life the most? Why hasn't your other parent been more of an influence in your romantic relationships? Try to allow the first answer that comes to mind to be unedited after reading the following statement or incomplete sentence. This exercise is considered "projective" in nature because it provides you the chance to see how you might really feel and think about certain issues that normally you would never consider or examine.

Fill in the Blanks

Fill in the blanks with whatever thought or feeling you have (try not to edit your answers) in the following statements about your rebuilding of your romantic life. Don't edit or second-guess your answers; the key is to access your true feelings, values, beliefs, wishes, and hopes. One of the goals of this list is to continue expanding your emotional, mental, and psychological insight that will allow yourself to be loved differently. Allowing someone to love you starts with your knowing how love operates in your life. It might seem very odd, uncomfortable, and unfamiliar to consider these statements. But it is necessary to move out of your emotional comfort zone and break down old psychological barriers in order to gain new and deeper insight.

What would your marriage or love relationship be like if you were

_____ ?

What or how would it feel to be _____ ?

The one thing I have never told my partner or ex-partner about is

_____ .

What would you do or act like if you felt completely confident with your partner_____ ?

What is the most_____to me in a relationship?

If you could remarry/be romantically involved with anyone, it would be _____.

Who was your most important lover _____ and does he/she know it?

What is your greatest _____ in a relationship?

I act like my _____ when I get mad.

I have been told all my life that _____.

My _____ told me to never _____ in a marriage!

I hate when _____.

My idea of love is _____.

I wish my _____ knew _____.

I regret _____ with my ex-partner.

My mother was _____.

My father was _____.

My parents' marriage was _____.

Everyone told me before I got married _____.

I secretly felt _____during my divorce process.

I believe men and women _____.

Arguing and chronic conflict causes me _____.

I hope my children know this about me: _____.

I hope my children know this about my ex-partner _____.

When I get sad about my _____ I do
_____.

In a love relationship, I _____.

I picked my ex-husband/wife because _____.

I wish I had _____with my ex-partner.

The next time I become romantically involved I will do _____.

I am scared to be in a love relationship again because _____.

I can't let go of my ex because _____.

I have let go of my ex and I wish _____.

I would love to have sex with _____.

When I had sex with my ex _____.

My sexual desire is _____.

I believe intimacy and sex _____.

My parents' sexual relationship was _____.

When someone tells me he/she loves me, I _____.

I believe my future will be _____.

My greatest fear is _____.

No need to dismiss any of your answers about your unconscious wishes and desires for romantic love. Your understanding of the parent substitute you married and your unresolved feelings, beliefs, and personal commitments about relationships can provide a wealth of information. All these questions and statements are designed to access the unconscious, unexplored, and hidden desires that direct your significant and daily choices. The more you understand your true feelings and have the courage to embrace them, the more choices you will have in the future. We could spend hundreds of pages exploring how to undo these behaviors, but it is more crucial that you spend your energy on realizing them. Change is the easiest part of this insight-oriented process. Your recognition of these inner connections is the greater challenge. From there, it will be easier.

YOUR PARENTS' MARRIAGE

Much like touring a new country or visiting a remote vacation spot, you have to investigate certain points of interest; one of them is your parents' marriage on your trip to understanding. You are currently on a very exciting, at times painful, and other times courageous trip into your core development of love and being loved. *The personal benefit of getting to this place in your life can't be measured, and you are already on your way.* It is crucial that you let go of your self-recriminations and self-loathing for your past decisions. There is no psychological room in your life or chance of healing if you are still blaming yourself for past choices. Your life is in the present, and it requires your complete undivided attention and patience. The relationship change that you crave—along with complete resolution of your past—is in the process of happening. One of the stops along your exploration of your ex-factor includes a brief stop to examine your parents' marriage.

As you were growing up, what were the stories, myths, and family folklore about your parents' wedding, honeymoon, and first year of marriage? Whether your parents were married for sixty years, divorced seven times, or had a common-law marriage, there are stories that describe these and other events. Believe it or not, these stories and beliefs influenced and shaped your current relationship status. You learned more about intimate relationships while watching your parents than you are consciously aware of. Regardless of how your parents' marriage worked—positively, tragically, painfully, abusively, or lovingly—you were an eyewitness to much of it. In observing your parents' interactions with each other, you learned how love relationships function between two adults.

Your conscious mind may have blocked, ignored (denial), rejected, and dismissed certain traumatic or stressful events regarding your parents' marriage, but your unconscious mind has been working entirely differently. The unconscious mind is a non-stop twenty-four-hour-a-day video camera that never shuts off or ever runs out of film. Your unconscious mind made decisions to protect you and guard you from feeling scared, rejected, unloved, and abandoned. Because of this built-in psychological protection, you will need to dig deep to bring to the surface your core emotional wounds so that you can heal them. The healing process can't be one-dimensional (only subconsciously driven); it requires your full awareness and deliberate, willful participation. The problem is that your conscious mind and your ability to think, reason, understand, and have insight have to be actively involved in the healing process with your subconscious mind (unresolved issues from the past). No one can heal the heart and expand the six faces of love without an all-out conscious and subconscious effort. You can get to your subconscious by asking yourself the kinds of questions we just asked.

What were the problems, issues, and conflicts in your parents' marriage? The relationship between your mother and father may have seemed normal to you, since children often don't know that chronic yelling or abusive behavior is unusual or dysfunctional. Children often protect parents from each other or become representatives for one parent or the other in a strained union, much like Margaret—whom we met at the beginning of the chapter—was her mother's confidante and emotional support system while growing up. Margaret's parents' marriage didn't improve until she moved out of the house and went to college. Many children unknowingly had a major role in their parents' marriage—as well as its ending.

In stressed marriages, children often unwittingly and automatically become active participants in the power struggle and conflict between their parents. This fact is based on approximately all adult children reporting that about 85 to 90 percent of their parents' marriage to be problematic, conflicted, and dysfunctional.[4] Since so many adults today come into intimate relationships after having been exposed to their parents' strained marriage, it is not difficult to see why they replay the same dynamics. But you want to have a different marital experience and intimate connection than your parents had. For that to happen requires you to develop the emotional insight discussed earlier. You also need to examine the role you played in your parents' marriage.

When your conscious mind becomes aware of your old roles in your parents' relationship, that insight brings about healing. Did you play the "caretaker," the "peacekeeper," "Mom's representative," "Dad's protector," the "perfect daughter/son," the "rebellious child," the "silent child," the "emotional supporter," the "parent," and/or the "dependent child"? The possible roles are endless, but the ones you played often come back to you when focusing on behaviors that are problematic in your intimate life today. Until you become consciously aware of your need to change certain things in your relationships, as a result of your parents' marriage, you will continue to drive forward blindly in your romantic relationship. It is extremely problematic for your entire being to be constantly repeating the same mistakes in your love life without gaining new insight and developing greater wisdom. Your heartbreaks are a valuable source of personal information about all of your past relationships. Your parents' marriage and your roles in it provide another significant source of information about you and your ex-partner.

Developing more insight includes exploring your childhood, your siblings, your mother-father bond, your development of self-esteem, and your core feelings about love. Having a better and fuller understanding of your parents' marriage is a great starting point for understanding how you view women and men in an exclusive relationship. Many times we were witnesses to things that children shouldn't see, hear, or experience. The important point is to see the multiple connections between the current emotional challenges in your intimate relationship and their far-reaching roots in your parent-child relationship and your parents' marriage. These are all related and connected.

It stands to reason that any in-depth discussion about your ex-factor includes investigating your parents' marriage. Your first exposure to love and marriage was likely watching your parents interact. For many people, recalling their parents' marriage is a very psychologically loaded, heavy, and painful recollection. Many of your own values, life messages, and conflict resolution abilities, as well as your sexuality, communication style, and attitudes toward money and fidelity were played out in front of you in the context of your parents' marriage. It is difficult to measure the full impact your parents' marriage had on your core sense of relationships and the influences it had on the roles that you play in your own relationships. It is important to understand that your parents' marriage had a significant impact on you and is well worth exploring further.

WHAT WAS YOUR DREAM OF MARRIAGE?

If you had to describe your parents' marriage to a stranger, what would you say about it? Was the marriage tension free, strained, or even something you don't want to repeat in your life? What was one of the most positive aspects of your parents' marriage? What was the lesson you learned about relationships from your parents' marriage? When you were growing up, did you ever wonder why your parents were always arguing or avoiding conflict? What would you say about your mother's love and devotion to your father? What would you say about your father's emotional bond and expression to your mother and you? Do you know why your parents got married? What was their relationship with their parents—your grandparents—like?

Since so many children grew up watching their parents' marriage end with an incredible amount of tension and conflict, it is understandable that you might fear the same outcome in your own relationships. It is a natural response to want to correct not only your parent-child relationship, but your parents' marriage as well. In terms of avoiding conflict and minimizing relationship tension, what did you learn from your parents? If you could have magically done anything for your parents' marriage growing up, what would you have done and why? Your wish as a child for your parents' marriage can become a very strong value that you developed for your present-day marriage/relationship.

CHANGING THE RULES FOR YOUR LOVE LIFE

The discussions, questions, problems, and issues surrounding your parents' marriage and all the different facets of it could very easily fill four volumes and still not exhaust the topic. Your parents' marriage is part of the explanation of why you have selected the partners you have. The purpose of understanding your partner selection is to bring your focus back to *you* and your own development and change. Letting go of your ex can be done in a moment, but it can take a lifetime to fully process the impact of that decision. Many people are stuck with residual resentment over having built a life with someone and seeing it not turn out the way they had hoped. Understanding the subconscious issues between your parents and between them and you is critical to your movement forward. Gaining emotional perspective and insight into your interactions in intimate relationships is the overall purpose of this chapter. The more you can see and begin to comprehend the numerous connections between you, your parents, and your former partner, the less frustrated and angry you will be with yourself and your ex.

Your reasons for having chosen to be with your ex-partner are very complex and are more than simply a bad decision made when you were young and naive. Your choice had many subconscious reasons, motivations, and purposes stemming from your parent-child relationship. The other major contributing factor in your choice is what you learned from your parents about the roles men and women play in intimate relationships. *These two perspectives about your upbringing and childhood can explain volumes about your intimate relationship and its beginning and ending.* All your issues and personal concerns come together when you begin to look at the relationship legacy left to you by your mother and father.[5]

The six faces of love are always involved in moving past your parent-child history, your parents' marriage, and the issues that have held you back from enjoying a fuller intimate romantic life. We will explore fully the new rules for your love life in the next chapter. It is discovering the new ways that you need to feel loved and accepted. It isn't about how you should love someone, but rather understanding what makes you feel loved, adored, and emotionally safe. These issues make up the foundation for rebuilding your romantic life and relationships in the present and future.

Chapter 7

REBUILDING YOUR LOVE LIFE

Expanding Your Ability to Be Loved

I have never understood why I got mad when my ex-husband would touch me or hug me. It seemed very sweet but I just didn't feel like it was loving. He never got that I liked to talk rather than be touched. I know this was one of the main reasons we got divorced. Neither of us felt loved. Yet I know we meant well. My ex is a good guy.
—Jane, age fifty-two, mother of two, married for twenty-one years, divorced for five years

My wife would never come near me, hug me, or touch me. I thought she loved me. I felt like an idiot that I had to tell her how to love me. We never got around our issue of communication and how I felt unloved. When we divorced my ex told me that she was never comfortable with sex or physical affection. She wanted to communicate. I thought our sex life was communication.
—Brandon, age thirty-nine, married for seven years, divorced for two years, currently engaged

LOVE IN *ACTION*—LET IT IN

Walking out of the painful valley of despair and overcoming from your breakup or divorce requires a deeper understanding of how romantic love works in your intimate attachments. The more you know about your needs for feeling loved, adored, and accepted, the more you can experience these qualities in your romantic life now and in the future. It is a valuable, worthwhile, and necessary exercise to expand your understanding of what makes you feel loved. If you don't take the time to notice, observe, expand, and process your ability to accept love, your future relationships will be a continuation of disappointment and disillusionment.

You will inevitably repeat the cycle of despair and frustration in future relationships if you don't take the time to recall your part and remember your concerns and problems. The idea of love in action may sound a bit simplistic, sophomoric, and elementary. Don't be deceived by the idea or this very powerful concept of what makes you feel loved. It is necessary for you to be able to accept love if you want to build positive, healthy relationships in the future. A big piece of your healing is based on expanding your ability to be loved. It is also crucial that you learn to allow someone to be intimately close with you again. Rebuilding your life isn't about living in quiet desperation and in isolation from others. The concept of being loved, respected, and loving will always be part of any romantic, family, social, business, or parent-child relationship. Maximizing your own relationship potential and personal fulfillment will always include intimate relationships and loving gestures.

Why is it so important to know and explore what makes you feel loved and cared for? The short answer is that the role of love in your relationships starts with you. *If you don't understand the role of love in your own life, it is very difficult, if not impossible, to understand it in another person's.* Recall for a minute what it is like not to feel loved, supported, or understood by the important people in your life.

How does it feel when your partner doesn't show you empathy in the way you need it? When your partner doesn't know or forgets that you need to talk after an emotionally upsetting day rather than giving into his or her demand for emotionally detached sex, how do you feel? You know the frustration! The culmination of many moments of not feeling loved, understood, or supported can soon develop into a Grand Canyon–sized emotional gap between you and your partner. The ongoing frustration and reactivation of your subconscious childhood issues of abandonment, neglect, and rejection will soon evolve into an angry relationship between you and your partner.

A powerful association of anger can soon replace the peaceful bond of love and emotional safety. Once the emotional glue between a couple turns from empathy, understanding, and love to rage and resentment, it is very difficult to restore the previous positive emotional connection—the bond. Unless the couple is able to step back from their increasing resentment, the intimate relationship will suffer and in most cases will ultimately end. The residual emotional wound that occurs as a result of not feeling loved, misunderstood, or unsupported is devastating for both partners. One partner begins to feel unloved while the other partner doesn't know what to do to solve the problem and reduce the emotional distance from widening. Feeling wounded by your intimate partner is a very difficult psychological barrier to resolve and overcome.

Knowing what types of actions, behaviors, gestures, companionship, gifts, affection, and discussion you need from your partner in order to feel loved should be as natural as breathing. You can't survive without breathing *or* without having a sense of feeling loved. But you become aware of your breathing problems only when you are suffocating or having an asthma attack and not getting enough oxygen. Unfortunately, many marriages and long-term relationships can be described as emotionally suffocating, lacking love and understanding. Many relationships end because no emotional room or allowance has been made for a person's specific needs regarding love. *The type of loving actions that you need and want in your romantic relationship is as important as the person you marry, date, or live with.* If you don't know what love means, looks like, and feels like for you, it is nearly impossible to find a partner who can meet those needs. Your chances of having and developing a fulfilling relationship are left to chance and random luck. *No one needs or wants to depend on luck in his/her love life. You want informed, smart choices instead.* It is never too late to begin to understand what your choices are and to start making better decisions about your romantic life today and for the future.

We have discussed in great detail the powerful dynamic of our subconscious partner selection process based on unfinished business related to our parent-child relationship. Don't be critical of yourself because, although you haven't lived with your parents for thirty years, you still have strong conflicted feelings about them. Your healing process isn't connected to a linear calendar or a timetable. (My professional clinical experience is that the half-life of most emotional issues is thirty years.) We have also examined our response to our parents' marriage(s) and the feelings generated by that union. Our past relationships with former partners are also a valuable source of information of what works and what doesn't work. The key is for you to understand how love works in your life. Once you know that, it should become your spoken and unspoken connection to your next significant other. In other words, your goal is to make your emotional and psychological needs more conscious, less hidden from your mental processes—and known to your partner. The combination of these seemingly separate events from your childhood and adulthood can join together to become the fabric of your sense of feeling loved, cared for, and adored. *This collection of your life experiences shapes your feelings, behaviors, needs, beliefs, and emotions—which, in turn, translate into how you feel loved.* Feeling loved is the primary step to loving others. You can't do the second step—loving your partner—without first allowing love into your life. The goal is to further expand your ability to allow someone to love you and become intimately connected to you. This process will allow you to reach out and extend love and support to your partner.

WHAT ACTS OF LOVE DO YOU NEED?

The practical aspect of feeling loved can be broken down into five basic categories and/or actions: *verbal, physical/sexual, gestures and actions, companionship, and acceptance.* We will discuss in detail how each of these styles works, and in chapter 9 we will also discuss how to use and apply your new personal knowledge in order to allow someone to become intimately close to you. Understanding your primary style, needs, and level of comfort in allowing your partner to express love to you is very powerful and transforming. It is critical to your future relationships to accurately know what actions, gestures, means of communication, touches, and signs of affection make you feel loved. It is very important to never lose sight that all acts of love are their own language. It is clear from the two quotes at the beginning of this chapter that Jane and Brandon knew what made them feel loved, but this wasn't clear to their partners. They were unable to communicate their needs to their partners. This breakdown in the understanding of what they needed in order to feel loved in their marriages resulted in divorce. Brandon and Jane both feel that if they had known better about their own individual needs (acts of love), there is a very good chance that their relationships might not have ended.

An excellent way to better understand how love works in a relationship is to consider the analogy of speaking a different language than your partner—perhaps you speak English and your partner speaks French, or some other language that you don't understand. If neither of you understands the other's language, symbolism, syntax, cultural expressions, and nonverbal meanings, there is no possible way the two of you can develop a relationship much past the level of acquaintance. The frustration, disappointment, and anger generated as a result of this basic language barrier are serious, and together they act as a primary cause of many intimate relationship breakdowns. Adults often assume—wrongly—that their partner should know exactly what they like, need, and want in order to feel loved. *Men and women of all ages assume that their partners speak and fully understand their "language" and actions of love that they need.* This erroneous assumption that love works the same way for you as it does for your partner is very risky. Your partner is at a great risk for unknowingly creating a romantic disaster in your life that neither of you wants or deserves.

It is an extremely difficult task to build a love relationship with your partner if you do not know exactly which actions make him or her feel loved, adored, and cherished. You might make a very generous gesture, give a gift, or plan a surprise trip for your partner, and you may feel rejected if he or she doesn't seem to appreciate or feel your love behind the act. If you both speak a different language of love, the amount of intimacy and closeness between the two of you will be dramatically reduced and become a potential source of conflict. This is a very simple concept: If you don't feel loved and understood by your partner, your romantic relationship will soon be in a state of decline. *Intimate relationships can grow, develop, and stand the test of time only when both partners feel loved.* This issue of understanding your partners needs for feeling loved and adored is one of the biggest areas of conflict in marriages and intimate relationships.[1]

Consider the following five basic acts, gestures, and feelings of love that you need in your life to thrive and grow. Everyone needs a certain degree of each, but you need to know what each one's level of importance is to you. You have a good sense of what acts and gestures make you feel loved in your romantic relationship. It is important that you don't dismiss or minimize what you need, want, and desire from your partner. The success of your relationship starts with your ability to address and communicate with your intimate partner the priorities that you have regarding these acts of love. If you don't believe that someone would do these things for you, stop immediately and recall your parent-child relationship and what you wanted from your mother and father growing up. Many times our needs and desires for love and acceptance are based on the things we didn't receive enough of in our earlier development (birth to age ten).

Today, you can have your needs and wants addressed by your intimate partner. It is appropriate and necessary to describe to your partner what makes you feel loved and ask him or her to provide it. The explanations and practical examples of how each act of love works will be discussed in the context of an existing or prior intimate relationship.

WHAT IS YOUR PRIMARY ACT OF LOVE?

Verbal—Communication

This is one of the areas that creates the biggest emotional misunderstandings in couples. Verbal affirmations, supportive words, expressions of empathy, and talking are all avenues for building intimacy and emotional safety. All relationships (i.e., intimate, social, professional, family) have to have some degree of open and direct communication to build a sense of trust and security between the parties. All forms of verbal communication help to create an emotional bond between people. Men and women who regard communication as their primary act of love must have a partner who understands this dynamic and can fulfill this need. For these people, verbal expression is the "warm-up" for the development of intimacy and emotional closeness. All types of verbal communication help in processing and understanding one's feelings, thoughts, and ideas. Verbal communication is how many people figure out what they and their partners are feeling and thinking about on a particular subject. The verbal component of a relationship is the most important aspect for many people because it becomes the emotional glue for the relationship. Communication allows you both to know what, why, and how you are feeling and thinking.

The better you understand each other's thoughts and feelings, the greater a sense of attachment will develop between you. All couples need to communicate, and understanding the importance of communication in your life is invaluable. What is "enough" time for talking? When do you like to talk? When you are upset, how do you talk out your anxiety, panic, or fear? It is important to know that talking enables you to process your complete range of thoughts, feelings, and emotions.

Women and men who hold communication as their primary act of feeling loved need a partner who has the ability and is willing to communicate. This doesn't require that your partner be as articulate as you, but rather that he or she has the ability and desire to communicate and interact with you verbally. It is possible you are in a mismatched romantic partnership if you need verbal contact/intimacy, for example, and your partner values only physical contact as a means of intimacy and love.

Dialogue between partners is very important for the emotional atmosphere of any relationship. If anger is the only verbal expression you or your partner can engage in, it is a major problem and roadblock to intimacy. In an existing relationship, a therapist might be required to help partners develop good communication. A neutral third party, a therapist, can help you and your partner to understand each other's need for communication. For instance, stopping the cycle of feeling rejected, emotionally abandoned, and/or the butt of passive-aggressive behaviors requires a fuller understanding of what forms of communication make you feel loved. These forms are casual conversation; verbal affirmations of concern, love, and affection; dialogue to process feelings; intimate discussions during physical contact; phone calls, e-mails, and text messages; and regular "nuts-and-bolts" conversations. These forms of verbalization are critical. Intimacy is built through talking, which creates a deeper emotional connection and understanding.

Mike and Kim—"We Just Don't Talk Anymore"

Do you enjoy talking throughout the day with your partner? Do you like to talk immediately after an emotional event, or do you wait until you have thought about it for a while? Mike and Kim are an excellent example of how the questions above became a primary source of conflict in their marriage. Communication for any intimate couple can become a classic misunderstanding of the verbal act of love. Mike is a postgraduate student at a university in Los Angeles and his girlfriend, Kim, is a representative for a large pharmaceutical company. Kim talks about medications all day to doctors. Mike sits in lectures and craves an emotional connection with her. Mike came to see me because he was having communication issues with Kim, and because of these issues he didn't feel loved. Mike and Kim had been dating for more than eighteen months. Mike was a very verbal person and needed and wanted the same in his partner. Mike told me the following story:

> I will tell Kim how much I love her, share my feelings, and always ask her about her feelings. Kim usually will tell me that she feels the same way as I do. She never offers anything new about our relationship or how she feels. I feel like I am the talker in our relationship and she is the listener. Kim is really good at always calling me back and returning my gestures. But I am becoming very resentful of her lack of sharing and expressing her own feelings and thoughts. I know she loves me but doesn't talk very much.

I asked Mike if he knew what Kim's primary act of love was. Since he felt loved by making a verbal connection, he believed it was the same for Kim. The next week we met, Mike explained the following:

> Kim considers listening and being with me as her way of showing her love to me. She knows I need to talk. Kim feels loved when I spend time with her and hang with her for the day. She feels that spending time with me is her way of showing her affection and commitment to me. It never occurred to me that she had a different idea of how to show love. I was a little naive in thinking that communication was the same for her as it is for me. Kim is really trying to be more verbal but she is more comfortable just sitting with me and talking very little. She feels loved by the amount of time I spend with her.

Mike and Kim are now enjoying the deeper connection they developed by understanding each other's romantic needs and wants. Each now understands the other's style better, and this has created less tension.

Physical/Sexual—Intimacy

How do you feel when you are touched and embraced? Do you like to hold hands, kiss, and cuddle? How important is sexual intimacy for you? What is "enough" sexual contact for you? How do you feel emotionally after being sexually intimate with your partner? When you want to be emotionally connected to your partner, how do you express it? How do you like to express your sensuality?

Physical touch is important for all couples. The concept of "skin hunger" indicates that we all need to be touched on a regular basis.[2] We all need a certain amount of physical touch that is our daily amount of feeling loved and loving. Much like the standards for nutrition, we have the needs for physical touch and human contact. What is your daily requirement? Numerous studies have indicated that everyone needs some degree of physical contact to feel connected and bonded to his or her intimate partner.[3]

People thrive when they are held and affectionately touched. Numerous psychological studies have shown the correlation between physical touch and uninterrupted mental and emotional development of infants.[4] These studies have repeatedly shown that physical touch is imperative for our overall health and well-being. Babies who aren't held, touched, or physically soothed will stop developing normally and in some cases even die. At the end of life, hospice care operates under the belief that we all need a loving network of physical, emotional, and supportive people around us, even when we are dying.[5] These studies are very telling because as adults we need to be touched, lovingly embraced, and kissed, just like infants do. Our partners are critical to the satisfaction of these physical cravings.

Regardless of our body image, weight issues, physical challenges, abuse history, and prior sexual history, we all need to be touched to some degree. We need to be soothed physically when we are upset, whether with a hug, a pat on the back, or cuddling next to someone in bed. Knowing what you need, want, and desire for physical contact is crucial. It is also imperative to understand that your partner might not share your priority on physical contact, though he or she still needs it to some degree. It is important to know the importance each of you places on physical contact and how you have your physical cravings met.

Dave and Lucy—"Sex Means You Love Me!"

Lucy came to see me about her husband's relentless need for sex and the frustration she felt about it. Forty-four-year-old Lucy and her fifty-one-year-old husband, Dave, had met while attending a divorce recovery group eight years earlier. They had been married for five years and enjoyed a very healthy, active, and fulfilling sex life. When they were first married, they both felt that sexual and physical contact was their primary act of love. They both had previous marriages where the physical component wasn't a priority and their sexual desires were never fully addressed or met. Two years before, Lucy was diagnosed with breast cancer; after a double mastectomy, she was now cancer free.

After her cancer treatment and breast reconstruction, Lucy lost a large portion of her sex drive and need for physical contact. Lucy felt that verbal expression was now her primary act of love. Dave felt rejected and wanted a divorce because of their substandard sex life. Lucy related the following:

> I love Dave, but he only feels loved if I have sex with him. Unfortunately, I am sexual about once a week, and it isn't enough for Dave. I'd much rather talk and be emotionally close that way. My body and breasts don't feel the same to me anymore. I have no feeling in my chest, and sex just isn't that exciting. I no longer feel that sex is that important and I could very easily go without it. I know my marriage hinges on our sex life. If I have sex with Dave,

then everything is fine and we can talk and resolve our issues. I feel
awful because I want Dave to go beyond sex and develop a deeper
bond with me.

I suggested that Lucy bring Dave with her to discuss the impact of
her cancer process on their marriage.

Lucy and Dave started couples therapy to discuss their sex life.
They addressed for the first time the nonverbal change that had
occurred in their marriage regarding how they each expressed and
experienced love. During therapy, Lucy revealed her secret fear that
her cancer would return; as a result, she just couldn't enjoy or trust
her body anymore. Dave learned for the first time about Lucy's fears
and her lost sensuality following her breast operation. She began to
see that she hadn't lost her sexual appetite or her need to be physical;
she had simply never resolved her trauma about her cancer and how
her body had changed. Dave realized that he didn't understand Lucy's
changed feelings because she looked perfect and was cancer free. As
a result of therapy, Lucy rediscovered her need for physical affection
and Dave learned to spend more time and energy talking and processing Lucy's feelings. They both felt emotionally closer as a result
of discussing what initially appeared to be an impending divorce.
Dave and Lucy incorporated a new degree of verbal connection,
problem solving, and companionship into their feelings and expressions of love. Their sexuality and physical connection became more
fulfilling as a result of their expanding ways of showing love.

The Act of Affection

The act of experiencing love can be summed up with the old adage:
Actions speak louder than words. Actions are the main commodity of
this timeless expression of giving and feeling love. The types of loving
actions are as varied as the people doing them. The act of expressing
love through affection is important because your actions have to be
consistent with your words and feelings. Men are typically comfort-

able showing love through their actions and deeds, including giving gifts.[6] I've seen this in both my professional and personal experience. Men are typically socialized to express only anger and frustration, not sensitive emotions (love, disappointment).[7] It is much safer emotionally for most men to show love with their actions than with their words. Young boys are told not to cry when they are upset. The problem is that these young boys grow up and become men who can't cry or show any type of "soft" emotion to their wives or lovers. Many men feel emotionally illiterate regarding verbal expression and find it difficult to voice deep feelings of love and concern. These same men may be very smart academically and professionally and may be excellent fathers, but they just can't talk. Many times their marriages end because they can't articulate their love, despite the fact that this articulation is of supreme importance to their wives.

Many women feel unloved in their relationships because of their partners' inability to express love in ways other than through action. These men know that the real issue isn't about love; it is about learning new ways of expressing love, empathy, and concern. My waiting room is full of these men who have never learned about other ways of showing and experiencing love. It is important to note that anyone can learn another person's language and the desired acts of love. Many times affection isn't physical, but demands verbal support and empathy. Other times, touching and doing little meaningful things are what matters to your partner. *Your history isn't your future, and showing affection and love needs to become a new and enduring behavior.*

No relationship can properly function without some degree of loving actions, gestures, and positive affection between partners. Your romantic relationship future must include all five acts of love, not just a focus on one particular action. Giving cards, sending flowers, cooking your partner's favorite meal, making coffee in the morning, fixing things around the house, going to work, and providing a stable home are all loving actions that are necessary for any intimate relationship. These collective actions build a deep trust and emotional security in the person receiving them because the giver's actions are consistent with their words and feelings. Men who feel comfortable with their expression of love know how to show love for any and all occasions to their partner. Knowing what makes you feel loved, makes it much easier to know what your partner needs and wants.

Frank and Susan

Frank is a great example of a wonderful man who feels loved and shows love through his gestures. He is fifty-one years old, a divorced father of two teenage boys, ages sixteen and eighteen. His girlfriend of three years, Susan, who is thirty-nine years old and never married, recently broke off their engagement because of their lack of emotional contact/attachment. Susan liked Frank's boys and found them to be great guys who were very respectful. She had been involved in the boys' lives, and they wanted her to marry their father. Since Susan was unable to have children, she felt that Frank's boys were her own. Both Frank and his sons were devastated by the breakup.

What was incomprehensible to Frank was how Susan could feel unloved or emotionally disconnected. Frank believed that he showed his love, support, and affection for Susan by the things he did—for example, planning trips, taking Susan to parties and movies, and taking care of her car when it needed servicing, gladly paying for all of it. Frank paid to have Susan's house repainted and her new air-conditioning unit installed. He felt that she knew how much he enjoyed her company, intelligence, and ability to be spontaneous with him and the boys. He felt that he showed his love by the things he did, expressing his love through his actions, gifts, and generosity. Frank felt loved by Susan's positive reactions to and appreciation of his loving actions and thoughtful concern. It never occurred to Frank that Susan would doubt his love because he wasn't more verbally expressive. She wanted more communication.

In therapy, Frank began to learn that everyone has different needs with regard to what makes the person feel loved and cared for. He knew that he wasn't verbally gifted or comfortable being a talker in an intimate relationship. As the owner of several car dealerships, he talks every day to employees, customers, and auto executives on a professional level, not an intimate emotional level. In therapy Susan explained to Frank that she needed loving affirmations more than loving actions. Susan believed that Frank couldn't understand her need for him to show love through verbal expression. She felt loved when Frank articulated his feelings and emotions and provided empathy.

Ultimately, Susan chose not to reconcile with Frank and stopped coming to therapy. She believed that Frank lacked the ability to understand what she needed, and that it wasn't something he could ever give her. Frank accepted that he couldn't be as verbal as Susan wanted and needed him to be. He knew that his way of expressing love was through action. Susan and Frank are still friends but are no longer in a romantic relationship. They simply had different styles and ways of showing love. After his relationship with Susan ended, Frank better understood his way of expressing love and knew that his romantic future would include a partner who valued and accepted his style of loving.

Presence—Compatibility

Compatibility is the "chemistry" issue that everyone hopes to have in a romantic relationship. The element of compatibility in feeling loved is to enjoy your partner's companionship, conversation, and time spent together, whether just living life, running errands, or having sex. This encompasses all aspects of a relationship, ranging from sexual activity to taking out the trash. Most adults want a partner who is present for them emotionally as well as physically, so they can build a life together. People know within the first few minutes after they meet someone whether there is any romantic chemistry between them. Yet chemistry can develop over time. Eventually the element of chemistry has to be a factor in the relationship. The unspoken/spoken, subconscious/conscious, and intangible attraction to a potential partner is the first acknowledgment of compatibility in the romantic bond. When you meet someone you want to get to know and spend time with and be there for, you are *being present* for that person. The companionship element is different from the other four elements because it is more specific and general at the same time.

Being in your partner's presence and spending time with him or her is as critical as any of the other four elements of loving actions. Having a partner with whom you are compatible creates the foundation for building a intimate relationship. *The elements of building a life together include but are not limited to: your core ethical values, spirituality, parenting/stepparenting, the decision to have children, motivation, communication, career aspirations, money, sexuality, and developing an intimate bond.* All these intangible facets of your life create a backdrop for your ability to love and be loved. It can feel like a breath of fresh air when you are in the presence of someone who really understands, loves, and accepts you. Your ability to return that person's love and demonstrate your loving qualities starts and stops with you. The more you understand what values, desires, cravings, wishes, and hopes you have for your romantic life, the easier it will be to develop a strong relationship. A good understanding of your companionship needs is essential in order to bond with your intimate partner.

Many adults recovering from a divorce or breakup tend not to value or consciously want an intimate partner or companionship. The thought of having to someday separate from another partner seems too painful and psychologically exhausting. The companion/compatibility element of expressing and experiencing love is always a factor in relationships. It is terrifying to reopen your heart and soul to another person who might turn out to be another huge romantic disappointment. It is much safer—or so it seems—to develop an intimate relationship with a person who might not get inside of your inner "courtyard" of love and attachment—a very private place inside you that is not freely accessible to others. If you want your partner to be present for you, then you need to know and want to share your personal courtyard.

A partner who wants to share your life and values is a potentially worthy partner to allow into your romantic courtyard. Many people feel loved, cared for, and nurtured when their partners spend time with and expend energy on them. Companionship is vitally important to all of us. We all need a companion and we all know how and what that feels and looks like to us, our emotional comfort level. Many times our partner doesn't know the extent to which we need his or her companionship and emotional presence. The companionship element isn't based on entertainment or activities, but rather on being together and sharing the moments of life.

Companionship Questions

The questions below will help you to solidify, focus, and better understand the companionship element in your life. You must become acutely aware of your companionship needs in order to properly build a solid intimate relationship in the future. Your expanded understanding of how you feel loved with your companion is critical to developing a supportive, fulfilling relationship.

- Do you miss sleeping next to someone at night?
- Do you enjoy sharing your life and living space with a partner?
- Do you ever wonder why you aren't sharing your romantic life with someone?
- Do you crave a friend, partner, playmate, lover, and/or companion?
- What do you feel like when you imagine having a companion?
- What would your ideal companion's inner and outer qualities be?
- Do you consider yourself lonely?
- How would you cope with having older children and a companion?
- How important is companionship to you on your mental list of having an intimate partner?

- What have you used to replace romantic companionship in your life (i.e., animals, exercise, work, children, food, drugs, friends, making money)?
- How do you experience love when you have a partner?
- How do you show your loving feelings and thoughts to your partner?
- How important is your partner's presence in your life?
- When do you most miss having a companion?
- When did you last have a companion you liked and enjoyed?

Acceptance—Conflict Resolution

This is another misunderstood, nonnegotiable element in all types of relationships, especially romantic ones. Many adults minimize the importance of feeling accepted by their partners and being able to work out life's challenges together, but it is imperative that you be able to handle and address emotional tension, conflict, and disagreements with your partner. The ability to tolerate misunderstandings and not to personalize them is critical for your intimate partnership. It goes without saying that your emotional, mental, and psychological aptitude to handle and not to use conflict as a tool in all areas of your life is critical. *Romantic partners tend not to use the same executive skills to resolve their relationship conflicts that they use in dealing with the outside world.* This is because many people believe that their intimate relationships should have a different set of rules and unconditional understanding. These beliefs are erroneous and are based on the unresolved problematic parent-child relationship issues.[9]

An excellent example of this common misunderstanding is Mark, who believed that his wife should never question his judgment at home or in his career. Mark's subconscious rationale was that his mother never accepted or approved of anything he ever did or said apart/independent from her. He had never resolved his anger at his mother's demands for his complete submission to her wishes and desires. Mark's inability to be flexible, tolerant, and accepting of the differing opinions and thoughts of his wife, Nancy, ended their eighteen-year marriage in a bitter divorce. Before the marriage ended, Nancy had an affair with Mark's business partner, who, it turns out, felt the same way she did about Mark. The pair's anger over Mark's inflexibility was the emotional glue that held them together. Mark never felt loved or accepted by Nancy because she always questioned him. Nancy loved Mark, but his irrational need for her unquestioning acceptance of his behavior and beliefs wasn't a formula for intimate relationship success.

The desire for acceptance is a primary emotional drive from childhood into adulthood. We all want our parents to accept and understand our individuality. If we don't feel accepted—and thus have difficulty developing a sense of self—then we will have trouble dealing with conflicts later in life. *The degree to which we resolve, achieve, and develop our sense of self is directly correlated to our ability to handle conflict.* And the degree to which we accept and love ourselves is the same degree that we can handle and tolerate conflict. If you feel insecure about yourself in your marriage, it is very difficult to make emotional room for disagreements. Your emotional need to feel loved and accepted becomes the subconscious drive behind all of your interactions and decisions, and your constant longing for your partner's residual approval and love will be an unyielding source of stress and tension.

What Are You Really Arguing About?

Couples who constantly argue are unconsciously attempting to force each other to accept and love them. Their arguments become so emotionally charged and powerful that these deep desires for acceptance are lost in the ongoing relationship conflict/arguing. *The reason so many contentious relationships end in divorce is because the real fight is over not feeling loved and accepted.* Conflict and acceptance are incompatible during an argument and in a tension-filled relationship. Creating conflict in your life may be one of the ways in which you try to make your partner or other people in your life notice you. Becoming aware of your need or desire for conflict and tension will help you resolve your basic need for negative acceptance and attention. Many times people out of their insecurity and fear of not being noticed believe this old adage, *"There is no such thing as negative attention, any attention is good attention."* There are very productive and empowering ways to have people notice you, especially your intimate partner.

The importance of understanding the role and value of acceptance of yourself and your partner and fair conflict resolution between the two of you cannot be overstated. In the next chapter, we will discuss the different styles of intimacy and how conflict resolution (or the lack of it) may be critical to your love life. Going forward and attempting to build a new intimate relationship without acknowledging your need to feel accepted, loved, and supported is like going to the moon without oxygen. Developing tolerance for differences and creating an atmosphere of acceptance with your partner starts with you. The ability, insight, and knowledge to know your own values and feelings about a particular issue or behavior are your sole responsibility. Moreover, giving your partner permission—verbally and nonverbally—to disagree with you creates a strong emotional relationship bond. Your acceptance of your partner's differences allows you to build on your similarities and differences, which naturally will expand your capacity for feeling loved. Differences don't automatically translate into a lack of love between partners but rather a lack of acceptance and insight toward each other.

You don't need to spend your limited supply of energy—and we all have a limit—and love on fighting, arguing, debating, and trying to convince your partner that your positions and thoughts are "the right ones" or are "good enough." Ongoing acceptance and a sense of approval should be already present in the relationship. When you feel accepted, understood, adored, and not under constant judgment, then you can spend your emotional energy elsewhere.

Developing an intimate relationship where you both agree on

how to disagree is another foundational act of love. Acceptance and understanding creates a reserve of goodwill and empathy in the relationship. Everyone needs a healthy amount of goodwill and empathy for an intimate relationship to thrive. There is no right or wrong issue or unnatural need for acceptance. The key is to know what you need from your partner in order to feel accepted, emotionally safe, and secure. It might be verbal affirmations and occasional statements of love and commitment. It might be regular sexual intimacy or spending time together. Building a new romantic life involves your expanded insight into how you handle and tolerate emotional tension. Every romantic relationship, regardless of its boundaries, has conflicts, misunderstandings, and tension. The questions are: How do you handle the tension and conflict? What emotional tolerance do you have for staying connected to your partner during a stressful time? It is important to discuss with your partner how you will, as a couple, handle conflict and disagreements before they arise. Fair fighting—sticking to the topic at hand—avoids unnecessary escalation of angry feelings. Don't wait to have this discussion during a challenging moment. That is not the right time to address your style of conflict resolution. It isn't a negative issue to prepare for and understand what you need during a conflict.

Lastly, consider some basic relationship questions and desires you might have in beginning a new romantic partnership. What makes you feel accepted? Do you know the underlying reason why you argued with your ex? What happens when you feel tension or conflict with your partner? What is important to you during a conflict? Think about these questions and your answers as insight into your healing and personal change.

SUMMARY

These five areas of expressing love are important in all relationships. All couples have particular ways of expressing their affection, empathy, and concern to each other. Most intimate communication is unspoken, even subconscious. Hopefully, over time more will become conscious and verbally expressed. The better you can explain to your partner what you need and desire in your love life, the more likely your partner will be able to meet those needs. It is a common misunderstanding that the sense of rejection or lack of concern between couples might be an issue of commitment rather than a love language barrier. It is imperative for your romantic future that you understand what makes you feel loved and cherished and express it. These five primary elements of human contact are part of every relationship. The roles they play in your love life are constant and invaluable to developing and expanding your romantic bonds.

Now that you have read this chapter, what would you say is your primary way, element, action, gesture, and belief for feeling loved? Did your answer change after going through the five acts of love, or is it the same and clearer than before? In the next chapter, we will discuss how these acts of love interact with different styles of intimacy. Your style of intimacy will help explain which elements of love are the most important to you and why.

Chapter 8

YOUR RELATIONSHIP STYLE

Five Styles of Intimacy— Building a New House

I always get overly involved way too fast. I end up sleeping with my date and the relationship never goes anywhere. I don't mean to be physical so fast, but it has been a pattern since my divorce.
—Ann, age forty-one, mother of one, married for nine years, divorced for three years

When I get involved with someone, I always rush forward and sometimes move things too fast emotionally and physically. I really want to get remarried, but I am really scared about opening myself up again. My relationship history has been painful since my divorce. I just don't seem to meet anyone who I really bond with or like.
—Allen, age thirty-seven, married for three years, divorced for two years

WHY WE NEED INTIMATE RELATIONSHIPS

Each of us has our own particular pattern of, approach to, and style of bonding with a partner. Our individual way of forming an emotional connection with our intimate partner is our special style of creating intimacy. Numerous psychological volumes have been written on the value, importance, and necessity of emotionally bonding and forming secure attachments.[1] No one would argue about the value of forming and maintaining emotionally healthy and empowering relationships. For the purposes of our discussion, it is assumed that we all know and appreciate the psychological merits of attachment. Our discussion focuses on some common ways people form and develop emotional bonds in their love relationships. This process can be equated to the process of building a house. Building a house is a very detailed, time-consuming venture that requires a huge emotional investment. If you have ever bought a house, built one, or gone apartment shopping, you know the energy that it requires. Finding a proper home can be a very arduous process. The process of building an intimate relationship is no different.

If you take a closer look at your previous patterns of attachment, you will notice a special way that you attempt to form a safe and secure emotional bond. What feels secure and familiar to you in attaching might not seem that way to someone else. The goal in forming significant emotional bonds and attachments is to share our deepest needs, wants, and desires with another person. We all need to have our deepest longings addressed in our love relationships to feel alive and thriving. *It is only in the context of this very private, personal, and significant connection that we can experience our true and authentic selves.* We will never know our deeper selves without opening our hearts, minds, and souls to another person. Throughout time, literature has always encouraged the relentless pursuit of love and developing that connection, regardless of the outcome (i.e., fulfillment, heartbreak, personal growth).[2]

It is this natural drive to connect with another human being that pushes us forward in the pursuit of developing a significant love relationship. *We can and will learn a tremendous amount about ourselves through the experience of being connected to another person in a safe and secure relationship.* The purpose of rebuilding your life is to further your experience of your genuine feeling and knowledge about yourself. Your metaphorical private emotional courtyard particularly thrives through the bond of intimacy with another person. Emotional disappointment and heartbreak can naturally cause us to withdraw and make our intimate life smaller (unwilling to engage or develop another relationship). The fear of opening up to another person can be overwhelming. The key to enlarging your capacity for love, empathy, and emotional security starts with exploring your style of intimacy.

The bond you form with your intimate partner is how you experience love and how you can return it. It is crucial to remember that our old familiar ways of attaching to a partner can be redesigned in the future for a different experience. Many times our family history, our childhood, and our individuation—the way we formed our own identity separate from our parents—all play major roles in the way we make lifelong attachments and connections.

Our family emotional history is no different than our family medical history. The information is available to us to use and to redirect for our future intimate relationships. Murray Bowen, a family research psychiatrist, has developed a family systems theory that contends that our family legacy perpetuates our finest qualities as well as our essential flaws and predispositions.[3] *You can move to a foreign country to put as many miles as you can between yourself and your family, but you can't run away from yourself.* Rather than throwing yourself into despair about your familial past, your intimate relationship history, and your prior romantic connections, you can use this information to reframe (change your perspective) and to create a different future and a new sense of self.

FIVE STYLES OF INTIMACY

Your History Gathering

Before we discuss the five styles of intimacy, take a moment to reflect on the information, insight, and knowledge you have about your prior styles of attachment, based on your personal experience. You have done all of this before, and regardless of your past overall experience, you have a lot of information to draw from. You are more familiar than you might think with your past forms of attachment. For instance, what type of emotional bond did you have with your ex-partner? What was the emotional atmosphere surrounding your relationship? Did you find yourself wondering why you couldn't have a closer, more meaningful emotional connection? Over time, did your emotional connection begin to fade, weaken, and become increasingly distant? How did you address your feelings about this? When you think back to how you met and fell in love with your ex-partner, do you remember how you felt? Did you feel like you had met your soul mate and that your future was limitless? How did you handle or manage the feelings and emotions you had about your partner? Did you become overly involved, or did you stay aloof and distant and allow him or her to approach you? If you got married, how was your wedding day? What were you thinking prior to your wedding ceremony? Would you like to get married again to someone new?

Building the House

When you think back to first meeting your ex-partner, what is the one thing that stands out the most in your memory about him or her? Recalling the positive things about an ex-partner isn't for the purpose of reminiscing or reopening your old wounds. You may discover a great deal of personal information about yourself in relation to your ex-partner. It is important for you to process and understand how the bond between you and your ex-partner was developed and maintained. Your emotional bond to him or her is the baseline foundation (your particular style) that you are now redesigning and re-creating.

Driving Past the House

We are now going to metaphorically drive past the old house that you built with your ex-partner. Every relationship has a context or an emotional house that the relationship functioned in and around every day. When you recall your emotional house with your ex-partner, what is the mental picture you get? The goal is to look at that relationship and remember how it was held together emotionally, mentally, sexually, physically, and spiritually. The infrastructure of your relationship was held together by your emotional interaction. How that process worked every day became the atmosphere of the relationship. If you and your ex-partner were emotionally distant or ambivalent, the intimate relationship at home was probably cold and lacking a warm, nurturing bond. Did the emotional bond between you and your partner change over the course of the relationship?

Another completely different line of questioning—and one that is equally important to explore—involves your sexual intimacy. What role did sexual contact play in your initial bond? How did your sexuality develop with your ex-partner? What role did sexual intimacy have in your relationship after the initial stage? How positive was your sexual connection and chemistry? Was your sexual contact a form of open communication and nurturing? Was the sexual relationship strained? Was your sexual connection with your ex-partner satisfying? Did you have a sexual partner outside of the relationship? How important was the role of sex for you in your relationship? Did you have a particular frequency of sexual contact with a partner (e.g., three times a week, once a month)?

These questions are important to answer since you want to explore the old, familiar ways in which you formed your past intimate relationships. Regardless of how your relationship ended, there were strengths and weaknesses in the way you bonded with your ex-partner. Exploring your style of intimacy with your ex-partner is meaningful because it allows you to get away from the narrow perspective of it having been all bad, having been a waste of your time. An investigation of your style of intimacy allows you to look with some objectivity at your relationship, so you can learn from it and psychologically move forward.

Remodeling the House

The five styles of intimacy are:

1. Attached at the hip/intense/addictive
2. Ambivalent/distant/cool
3. Overly needy/desperate/perfectionist
4. Trusting/no trust (push away and bring closer)
5. Secure/flowing/organic

Four of these styles sound negative, but they are really just patterns that have to change over time rather than being "bad," wrong, or dysfunctional styles. Each style of intimacy has its strengths, and nearly all of them have some inherent weaknesses. The goal is for you to examine your prior style of attaching and consider what kind of emotional house you want to build for your romantic future.

Attached at the Hip/Intense/Addictive

"Fused" and "enmeshed" are other words that could be used to describe this intense style of attachment. In this attachment style, the couple cannot be apart—emotionally, physically, or mentally. There is no psychological room for either person to be separated from the other. The two people act as one emotional being and unit. They might talk ten times a day on the phone, text each other constantly, and never be out of touch for long periods of time. They immediately merge into one identity when they are together. The emotional bonding is consistent with enmeshment of the two people into one person, and it feels magical and surreal to both partners. The couple becomes one unit that is stronger, psychologically bigger, and more courageous than when the two are separate. The reality of the couple's becoming stronger and more stable as a unit is a legitimate strength and truth. But the fusion, enmeshment, and intensity can become elements of a relationship that evolve into addictive attachment. Addiction to each other is the undercurrent of this attachment style.

This intimacy bond is based on childhood fears of abandonment and rejection. These painful feelings and deep psychological fears are avoided when the two partners become enmeshed with each other. The couple don't allow room for any doubt about their emotional connection and commitment to each other. All doubt has vanished to allow the emotional glue of enmeshment to take hold. There is no psychological "room" or tolerance for individual differences.

A euphoria occurs during the initial phase of this developing intimate bond. The emotional rush can last anywhere from four weeks to two years. During this time both partners feel a sense of exhilaration because of the emotional fusion of energy and support in their lives. The intense and psychological process of becoming bonded is the primary strength of this style. But people can become addicted to the emotional high, rush, and pure excitement of becoming fused with another person. The addictive nature of this intimacy style is serious and very problematic. Addictions never allow the people involved to grow and evolve into emotionally functional adults. The addictive behavior is the eclipsing of the two people into one being. *The balance of emotion, cognition, and adrenaline has to be kept in check.* The couple must learn to tolerate time apart in order for the relationship to remain balanced and functional. Otherwise, this intimacy style becomes an addiction and potentially fatal for the relationship. No relationship can survive when two people are trying to function with only one emotional heart.

Many people rush into an instant relationship, becoming emotionally, sexually, and mentally overinvolved. This style is often referred to as "having a crush," "moving too fast," and "connecting to my soul mate." The couple meet and immediately spend all of their time and energy together. There is an unspoken urgency by both to be together at all times, and at any cost. Natural separation (e.g., living in different homes, having different friends, participation in different activities) is considered an impairment or hindrance to the relationship. Regardless of the age of the participants, this intense intimate connection can feel like a grade-school crush. All of the individuals' time, energy, and thoughts are directed toward the new relationship. For each partner, the other often becomes the means of retrieving the perpetual lost love from the past.

The key is for the couple to move beyond this initial over-whelming connection and develop a less addictive, more emotionally balanced connection. This intimacy style has no tolerance for any emotional gaps or misses in the relationship. Misses by one partner are viewed as a failure—a lack of commitment and sensitivity to the intimate bond—by the other. The reality is that the intensity, fast tempo, adrenaline rush, and rapid pace of the relationship simply can't be maintained over a period of years. No one is capable of being fused, enmeshed, and emotionally bonded for years without eventually resenting the other person. Like all addictive behaviors, the adrenaline high will run out and the couple will be faced with getting to know each other without the excitement or emotional charge.

Ambivalent/Emotionally Distant Intimacy

This style of intimacy is at the opposite end of the spectrum from the addictive bond. Instead of the fast-moving, supercharged style of enmeshment, this style involves a methodical, almost perfunctory approach to life, relationships, and emotional expression. This is a couple in which the partners rarely share any strong emotion or vulnerability with each other. There is a clear demarcation of where each person starts and ends in this relationship. Emotional boundaries are very strict, clearly marked, and nonnegotiable. Instead of the adrenaline rush of emotional enmeshment, there is a cool, levelheaded approach to intimacy. The couple initially go very slowly in getting to know each other. Their communication is infrequent and without any particular pattern or obvious interest on the part of either.

Over time, the relationship always has a very sober feel and low energy to it. There is no urgency or need to make things happen. Initially, both partners are satisfied with the natural pace of developing an intimate relationship. After a period of time, however, one of the partners will want to deepen the relationship commitment and the other typically will want to keep the status quo. The partner who wants to deepen the commitment will often give the other partner an ultimatum. These types of "acts" to move the relationship forward are usually met with mixed results.

The problem with this attachment style is the built-in reluctance to be more involved or committed—say, through marriage. *Many women have dated, loved, and left men who refuse to move forward in the relationship.* This attachment style also applies to women as well as men. Nearly every attachment style within a relationship has a natural timetable during which a deeper emotional bond develops, but the ambivalent style doesn't view the natural timetable as a relevant or necessary element. The classic unspoken belief is: *Why change anything? Everything is working fine!* The problem is all potted plants eventually have to be transplanted into the ground. The same holds true for intimate relationships: Intimacy is an ongoing dynamic, and all relationships need to move forward within the intimate bond. Relationships can be likened to the flow of energy; it is never stagnant or frozen, but always moving. The question is what direction is the relationship moving: forward or backward? For the individual in an emotionally distant relationship, commitment isn't a priority or even the main focus. In fact, the relationship is deemed not that important or all-encompassing. The emotional connection, verbal communication, and sharing of intimate secrets are very subdued. Neither partner is overly emotional, intense, or in need of becoming attached to the other. The sexual component is minimal and not at the center of the relationship. Sex with this distant emotional bond is viewed as unnecessary, or, at best, only a physical release. This is in contrast to most relationships, in which sexual chemistry and sexual attraction create a stronger attachment between the partners.

From the outset, the couple's attachment is very cognitive, well thought out, and peripheral. The relationship takes a backseat to career advancement and other personal activities. There is a low emotional energy (lack of excitement) exchange between the partners. Their expression of excitement and discussion of future plans in the relationship are very limited. Both partners are very guarded about personal issues and disclosures. The potential for the relationship to take a significant turn upward is rarely considered and discussion of the matter tends to be avoided. This is a couple in which the partners love each other and could date for many years and never question the direction of the relationship, but there is a clear lack of emotional vulnerability, exposure, and genuine expression of affection between them.

The attachment for this couple could very easily be an arranged marriage or a functional union with no passion or empathy between the partners. The bond is very distant and doesn't include any degree of personal loving disclosures or insights about the value and importance of the relationship. Though the partners usually know that they love each other, they rarely verbally express it. Either partner—or both—may be recovering from a traumatic divorce or breakup, and thus very reluctant to be overly involved with another partner again. The degree and level of guardedness is very high and very purposeful. The couple has a nonverbal agreement about keeping the level of vulnerability, loving expression, and sexual chemistry very subdued and removed. The style of intimacy is very safe and tends to be unfulfilling for both partners. There is a lack of nurturing and passion. Only a distant and reserved emotional bond holds the relationship together.

Overly Needy/Desperate/Perfectionist

This type of connection is motivated by a sense of deprivation. In these relationships, emotional deprivation is a long-standing personality pattern for each person in the relationship. Each partner has a deep sense of inadequacy and feels unworthy of being loved and accepted. *The intimate bond is based on the fear of not being good enough or having the confidence that someone would ever love them.* These shame-based beliefs—feeling defective, damaged, or flawed—aren't often readily present when the couple first meets, but during the process of getting to know each other, their underlying emotional insecurities begin to control the relationship. Neither partner wants the other to know about these awful feelings, so they hide their unresolved feelings of shame from each other. The partners share an irrational belief that if the other partner found out about the true nature and character, he or she would think the other was a fraud, a phony, or a "loser."

Unrealistic fears and irrational personal beliefs are common in all of us, but in this type of relationship bond, the partners have a very high degree of shame and overwhelming feelings of inadequacy. Their goal is to become emotionally, mentally, physically, and sexually attached as quickly as possible. The sooner the emotional bond is formed, the sooner the fear of being discovered as a fraud is assuaged—though only temporarily. The problem with this style of bonding is that the individuals' core issues of shame and insecurity don't go away with the new love relationship. In fact, the tension of these irrational beliefs begins to surface in the relationship as both partners spend a great deal of time suppressing their fears through exaggerated actions and signs of affection. The loving feelings are genuine, but not to the degree and magnitude that they are expressed and communicated. Both partners are constantly fearful that their "secret" will come out and they will thus be exposed and humiliated as someone other than what was originally presented. The amount of emotional energy that is expended ends up being greater than the amount of energy spent developing the intimate connection. The concealing of the underlying fear and shame is an impediment to the couple's bonding in a secure fashion.

These couples have the potential to develop very positive relationships if the unresolved feelings of shame, inadequacy, and insecure personal beliefs can be left in the past. But getting there is difficult, as the emotional bond is overshadowed by the need to keep each partner's "public self" from ever being seen as less than perfect.[4] Each partner feels his or her private self must never be exposed or fully seen by the other. If that private self is revealed, the exposed partner will usually terminate the relationship or completely devaluate the other partner. If the illusion of "perfection" of the other partner is gone, that will terminate the romantic relationship. The emotional experience of having the hidden, "defective," and extremely sensitive pieces of the personality exposed must be avoided at all costs. If the pattern of emotional devaluation—which is an emotional defense mechanism against feeling powerless—and emotional abuse (i.e., verbally demeaning, criticizing, anger, hostile communication, passive-aggressive behavior) becomes acceptable in the relationship, both partners will experience extreme rage and tension with each other. The pattern of verbal abuse often starts with one partner projecting his or her unresolved shameful feelings onto the other. The intimate bond in this style of attachment is simultaneously fragile and very strong.

The couple's emotional fragility requires that they avoid any actions, discussions, or perceptions that expose either partner to be less than perfect. The attachment is held together with the rage and anger of the one partner's shame-based emotions being expressed. Both partners will attempt to avoid these types of emotional lapses, painful disclosures, and misunderstandings.

The need to remain "perfect" within the relationship requires that when negative feelings arise, they are immediately projected onto the other partner. The cycle of devaluation, overvaluation, and deprivation becomes a very strong bonding experience and emotional connection. The couple finds its equilibrium by reflecting back to each other their "perfect" public selves. If that internal picture or emotional status of perfection is disturbed, the other partner will fight to regain equilibrium. This subconscious agreement of unconditional acceptance of the perfection of each partner offsets the deep sense of emotional deprivation and shame. Keeping any and all negative feelings submerged becomes a full-time occupation and a burden on the relationship. Many times when the weight of personal shame, emotional deprivation, self-loathing, and personal insecurity becomes overwhelming, the couple either separates or resolves to avoid the issue. The nonverbal agreement of avoidance between the couple forms an airtight bond, a rigid connection that isn't open to any other input or outside feedback.

Trusting/No Trust (Pushing Away and Pulling Back)

To better understand this style of attachment, think of a spinning roulette wheel. If you stop the wheel at a certain point, you might get an even number; the next three times, you might get an odd number. There is no constant, consistent reason, or logical pattern to the number selection. It is similar with this type of bonding: One day, one partner will attach with the other and make a very strong verbal, physical, mental, and emotional connection; the next morning, the same partner might do exactly the opposite, changing the attachment bond to being distant, cool, and aloof. The other partner has no idea why this sudden change has occurred, and the explanation given has nothing to do with the real underlying reason for the emotional distance. The partner creating the distance might blame it on a random event or peripheral excuse, but the pattern of merging and withdrawing is an ongoing cycle that doesn't allow for an intimate, stable, and secure bond to be established.

The partner who pulls away feels completely justified in his or her behavior and need for emotional protection, with no acknowledgment of or consideration for what this detachment and reattachment cycle does to the other partner. The unpredictability and irrational reasoning for the "push-pull" of the emotional bond is always random. There is no stability to this style of bonding; the detaching behavior has nothing to do with the degree of love, commitment, or sincere concern the detaching partner has for the other person. People who bond in this way can tolerate only so much positive feeling. The secondary reason for this distancing behavior is the emotional defense mechanism against feeling or experiencing strong emotions, feelings, and experiences with an intimate partner. The irrationality of this push-pull behavior is rooted in early childhood trauma issues that now translate into the fear of intimacy in adult romantic connections.

Over time, the relationship becomes an intermittent connection that is subject to sudden unpredictable change. The negative effect of this inconsistent connection is that neither partner can sincerely trust that the other will be emotionally available in moments of personal crisis or vulnerability. The emotional joining and leaving of the one partner keeps the deeper personal issues and loving feelings of both partners from being expressed or experienced. The "craziness" of the detaching is that it interrupts the growing and developing bond of love and empathy. The disconnections cause the partner who gets the brunt of this behavior to feel insane because he or she has an entirely different bond and understanding of the intimate relationship. He or she doesn't understand the other partner's need for emotional distance within the relationship and creation of this type of instablity.

The couple begins to develop and maintain a relationship that is based on how far one partner will detach and how closely he or she will reattach. Over a period of months, years, and decades, a pattern of random intermittent connection reveals a cycle of distance. The problem is that the beginning of the relationship didn't set the limits of the distance and closeness of the relationship that could be tolerated by either partner, so there is no consistent pattern or tangible reason for this behavior. The superficial argument for the partner's withdrawing behavior is based on his lack of trust for his partner. The issue for the partner who withdraws and returns isn't psychologically about trust but rather about emotional enmeshment and the fear of being emotionally "swallowed" up by the other partner. The person being rejected or pushed away has no clear understanding of the subconscious motivation for this difficult behavior. The couple over time will subconsciously agree that the pushing-and-pulling bond is appropriate and acceptable within a certain distance.

For instance, during the dating phase, the partner pushing away initially will become emotionally bonded for the first three months and then will suddenly not call or speak with the other partner for a week. When the detaching partner does call, he says he has no idea or any understanding of how his behavior has adversely affected the other person. The next two months of dating can be very smooth, and a strong emotional bond will redevelop again. Then at a later point, when the partner feels that the connection is too intense, uncomfortably close, or emotionally overwhelming, he will arbitrarily create a break in the attachment. These breaks are never discussed or communicated, they are simply acted out.

The reason behind the behavior by the detaching partner is the unspoken fear of being emotionally engulfed, swallowed up, and/or completely submerged by the other partner. These subconscious fears of emotional engulfment are based on the unresolved individuation separation process of the parent-child relationship.[5] The partner as a young child was overwhelmed by his/her parent emotionally, psychologically, and many times physically. The sense of self in the now adult is very fragile and can only tolerate so much closeness before he/she has to pull away as a defensive measure against emotional engulfment.

The partner leaving will only go as emotionally far as the other partner will tolerate and/or allow. There is an unspoken distance and closeness that the couple can manage and stay connected within. Many times this emotional "push-pull," "intimacy dance," or "trust versus no trust" is all in service of preserving the emotional attachment between the couple.

Secure/Organic/Consistent Bonding

Each attachment style already discussed has some of the elements of a stable, consistent, and loving style of bonding. One of the strongest features of this style is the absence of emotional interruptions, unresolved childhood trauma, and the need to act out old psychological issues. Both partners have a sense of their own individuality and have sufficiently separated and individuated from their family of origin. The emotional development of each partner allows for the natural progression of an intimate romantic bond. Each partner is allowed to have his or her own needs, desires, and wants, and to express them without judgment. The atmosphere of safety and security are the boundaries of this attachment. The unspoken agreement between these adults is respect. All the actions, feelings, experiences, and emotions are within the context of mutual respect and understanding. Neither partner behaves in a way that is intentionally motivated to devalue, disrespect, or diminish the other partner. Though these types of things occasionally happen, they generally result from a misunderstanding rather than an emotional defense mechanism. When there is an emotional miscommunication, the couple use it as an opportunity to deepen the relationship, not to create distance and conflict.

The couple resolve and address conflicts without any residual effect or avoidance of the problem. But even under the best of circumstances, relationships take effort and commitment to the process of growing and bonding. The primary difference here is that when conflicts arise, couples with this type of attachment deal with them fairly and their bond is strengthened, not weakened, by them. There isn't an artificial glass ceiling on the depth, width, and distance that this relationship can go (i.e., the trust/no trust attachment has a glass ceiling). The attachment is based on mutual respect and love. Each partner in this type of relationship has experienced one of the other four styles of attachment before. Each knows the value and importance of being two separate individuals in an intimate bond. Each has learned what the other needs in terms of acts of love and gives it gladly. Both know that feeling loved starts with accepting and giving it. The need to be understood beyond verbal expression (i.e., emotional insight into the other person) is the something that the attachment breeds and develops in each person.

The natural emotional flow, the understanding of each other, and the security in knowing that the relationship is a safe place feels reassuring. The lack of terror, fear, and anger between the partners allows room for positive emotional expression, empathetic experiences, and loving gestures to be the norm, not the exception. Each partner feels a deep sense of completeness with the other and can tolerate the other's differences and ignore the other's human flaws. Their unspoken and spoken approval of each other is an ongoing emotional bond and connection that is timeless and transformational for each partner. *Regardless of their familial part, their stepchildren, their children together, and their ex-partners, the couple is committed to fostering a loving atmosphere for each other that is drama free.* The custody of the children from a previous relationship or the residual impact of a traumatic breakup doesn't interfere with the secure attachment between the partners. The absence of self-defeating relationship behaviors allows for a safe emotional bond to evolve and take hold. This style of attachment is what the movie industry historically depicts and portrays as magical, but these couples know that the magic is a result of emotional growth, resolution of painful issues together, and a commitment to heal and grow—something we can all strive for and attain.

SUMMARY

Ultimately, the development of a healthier, stronger, more durable and functional bond must include the resolution and expanded understanding of each partner's need for acceptance and love. *All intimate relationships have the potential to heal the ageless repressed wounds of the inner self and past rejections.* Survivors of divorce, heartbreak, and emotionally shattering breakups all have the potential to find a healing pathway out of their despair, and that is through understanding their attachment needs and psychological wants. The primary purpose and timeless value of all intimate romantic bonds is to provide a safe and secure atmosphere for healing and the expanding of an individual's potential. The timeless truth of the "curative" nature of a good intimate relationship provides the strongest argument for loving again and opening our hearts to others. The most tragic part of separating and ending a love relationship is that it can become an excuse to stifle future opportunities to develop a new life with a significant other. *The ex-partner becomes a lifelong altering event.* No one who has gone through the experience of romantic disappointment and dissolution will ever debate the emotional pain that can only be triggered by a former lover. As the songs say: *Love hurts.* Forming and developing intimate bonds and attachments is always risky and scary—but it is also worth every ounce of effort we put into it. We feel alive when we are connected to and thriving with our intimate partner within the context of that supportive connection.

The merits and value of dating again and rebuilding your entire life from the inside out will always reap huge personal profits. Learning to form loving secure attachments again is necessary for your mental, emotional, and psychological health and well-being. Don't forget that part of our natural drive for growth and expansion always includes the desire for an intimate bond of love and security with another person. No one heals and reexperiences the power of love in a vacuum, or in a prolonged emotional rage, or by blaming one's ex totally, or by living in isolation. We heal, grow, change, and become new people through our subsequent love relationships. This truth can't be repeated enough. Now, we will shift our focus to pursuing your future love interests and fostering greater relationship healing.

SECTION III

CHANGING YOUR "EX-FACTOR"

What lies behind us and what lies before us are tiny matters, compared to what lies within us.
—Ralph Waldo Emerson

Chapter 9

DATING AND PICKING YOUR LIFE PARTNER

Your Nonnegotiable Factors

The prospect of dating and trying to meet men feels like sticking a fork in my eye—very unnatural. I didn't like dating in my twenties and I really don't like the idea any better now, at forty-nine. Yet I believe in relationships and want a partner and to build a new life with someone. I liked being married, just not to my ex-husband. I have been divorced for four years. I need to stop hiding and start dating appropriate men for me.

—Laura, age forty-nine, married for eighteen years, divorced for four years

I have discovered, after my girlfriend left me for my best friend, that I didn't ever believe I could have the kind of woman who I really wanted. After Melissa left I realized that deep down we really weren't a good match, but I didn't want to lose her even though we were about 70 percent a match and 30 percent a mismatch. Now I want a 90 percent match and 10 percent difference.

—Brent, age thirty-five, currently engaged for five years

THREE STORIES OF LOVE AND DATING

The Bra Story

Mike, age fifty-two, is a client who is getting back on his feet emotionally, mentally, and relationally after a very traumatizing divorce during which his ex-wife accused him of child sexual abuse. The allegations were later revealed to be unfounded, motivated by the prospect of more child/spousal monetary support. Mike forgave his ex-wife for her vindictive action, and the courts gave Mike full legal and physical custody of his seven-year-old son and ten-year-old daughter. This process took approximately three years and more than two hundred thousand dollars in legal fees. He knew that he needed to move forward with his life and start dating since things with his children (son now age twelve, daughter now fourteen years old) were stabilizing. Both his kids wanted him to meet someone and "get a life." Mike felt internal, family, and social pressure to date and move beyond his divorce. He knew that part of healing his ex-factor was developing an intimate relationship.

Mike related the following story to me after a very embarrassing father-son dating moment:

> I met this wonderful woman in my building at work three months ago. We decided to have dinner after our first coffee date, [which] lasted over three hours, plus several great phone conversations. We went to dinner and talked for hours. The verbal and emotional foreplay was incredible. While we were driving home, she reached inside of her dress and took off her bra and handed it to me. I took it and threw it in the backseat and told her I was keeping it. We didn't have sex, decid[ing] to get to know each other better first. We both laughed and she warned me not to forget the bra tomorrow morning when I had the kids in the car.
> *Well, I forgot it.*
> The next day after baseball practice, my son and two of his baseball teammates found a Victoria's Secret black lace bra on the

backseat. When they got out of the car, my son turned to me and said, "Dad, that is really gross; whose bra is it?" I stared ahead and couldn't remember a more embarrassing moment and wanted to jump out of the car. I told my son a lie that my date's bra had fallen out of her gym bag. My son looked at me with a high degree of doubt and said, "OK." I explained that a lot of things fall out of his gym bag, and my date's bra fell out of hers. I could feel myself melting inside as I explained this horribly awkward story.

The next day at the Whole Foods store, my son and I ran into an old girlfriend from several years ago. My son had never met her because she wanted to get married at the time and have babies. I already had two of my own and wasn't ready for marriage at the time, but nonetheless, Andrea was a beautiful woman. We all chatted for a few minutes, [and] as we were walking away, he asked me, "Dad, does the bra belong to her?" I said no, and then he asked about the date I had on Valentine's Day—the one who broke up with me at dinner—if it was her bra. At this point I wanted to burn the bra and pretend that the entire incident never happened. I can't believe my son's insistence on finding out who the bra belongs to.

I continued to explain to my son in the produce section of the store that I may meet a lot of women and that he will meet someone someday who will be a very special person and a possible marriage partner. My son looked at me again and said, "OK, Dad— but whose bra is it?" I told him it doesn't matter. We went home and he told his sister that the bra belonged to no one.

The Baseball Coach

Laura, who was introduced at the beginning of the chapter, met a wonderful man two years earlier at a friend's dinner party for newly single parents. At the time, Laura didn't feel comfortable dating or pursuing this very nice man, whom everyone thought was perfect for her. Laura recalls thinking when she saw him that she could really like him if she allowed herself to. Laura, the divorced mother of two boys, ages fourteen and nine, wanted to keep her love life separate from her boys. Two years later and still hating the idea of dating, she enrolled her youngest son, Luke, in Little League baseball. Luke was drafted by a coach named Ed. Laura didn't think anything of it until she took Luke to his first practice.

Laura related the following story to me:

I drove up to the field and I saw this athletic guy, handsome, forty-something guy playing catch and I almost drove my car into the fence. My mouth dropped because this is the guy I met two years ago and who dated a girlfriend of mine for about a year after that dinner party. Well, I dropped Luke off at practice. I didn't get out of the car and drove like a mad woman. I called [Nancy,] my girlfriend who knew Ed[,] immediately and asked her about his relationship status. She told me that her friend had broken up with him because they didn't have enough chemistry for a long-term relationship. Nancy told me not to date him. I asked why. She didn't think we were a good "match" and that he was too boring for me. Well, I have spent the entire spring obsessing about him and trying not to act like a high school girl with a crush on the jock at school. I waited after games to ask about my son and couldn't wait to see Ed.

Unbeknownst to me, my cupid son Luke invited Coach Ed over to the house after the game last Saturday to work with him on his pitching. Ed showed up at 3:00 o'clock in the afternoon and didn't leave until 2:00 a.m. This was after we drank a bottle of wine on the couch. We didn't make out or fool around. Ed confessed to me that he deliberately picked my son to be on his team so we could meet and get to know each other. My mouth fell to the floor, because this is the only man I had found interesting since my divorce. Then I acted like an idiot and asked him if we could have an "adult date"—dinner at a restaurant—sometime in the next week or two. I haven't asked a man out since I was in college. I have been avoiding Ed for two years. I have been miserable because this is the only guy I wanted to date and get to know. I knew the first time we met that we had a strong emotional/physical attraction, great chemistry, and I wanted to get to know him. He has two boys and everyone knows everyone, it feels very natural and good.

I asked my son the next day why he had Coach Ed come over to our house without asking me first? Luke said, "Mom, get a grip, everyone knows you like him and I wanted him to see our house." I almost cried because I didn't think my kids had any idea about my feelings and struggles about being a single mother. I didn't dare ask Luke if he had any other ideas about my life.

The Rose Bowl Game

This story takes place on New Year's Day, after the Rose Bowl football game, while walking out of the stadium. It is necessary to give a brief background that led up to the moment of truth in this situation—and, for that matter, all dating relationships. Julie, age thirty-four, had gone to a wedding in Boston for a long weekend seven months earlier. She met a lot of people from Los Angeles who had also come out for the wedding. Julie couldn't keep from wanting to talk to Evan, her best friend's boyfriend. Julie avoided talking to him, looking at him, or even standing near Evan because the chemistry and attraction was unnerving and very powerful for her. Julie also didn't want to be "that girl"—the one who "steals" her friend's boyfriend.

The weekend came and went, but Evan never left Julie's thoughts. In fact, she found out shortly after the wedding that Evan and her best friend, Mary, had broken up. Mary had lost interest in Evan and was now interested in another guy. When Julie heard this her heart dropped, because she knew she wanted to find Evan and talk to him. Julie never told Mary about her intentions or her possible romantic interest in Evan.

Julie got her chance several months later when she was out to dinner with a few girlfriends and ran into Evan and his friends. The two groups got together and had some drinks. Julie and Evan stayed up all night talking and getting to know each other. Over the next three months, they spent more and more time together. Julie didn't want to tell Mary because she was afraid Mary would be angry and it would affect their friendship.

The holidays came and Evan and Julie decided they wanted to date each other exclusively. The entire time, Julie was emotionally conflicted about developing a significant romantic relationship behind Mary's back. Evan didn't think it was a problem, but Julie was never completely comfortable with the relationship progressing while Mary had no idea of it.

Julie relates the following story:

> Evan and I were walking out of the Rose Bowl game holding hands, and we walked right into Mary and her new boyfriend. Mary's face turned pale white and she had this look of complete shock in her eyes. I wanted to die right there on the spot. Mary looked at both of us and said, pointing her finger at Evan, "I expected this from you, but I never expected this from you. Julie, you are one of my closest girlfriends. How could you?" I couldn't say a word. I have never felt so bad and awful. After that horrendous encounter, we walked out of the stadium and Mary immediately called me and told me to never talk to her again and that I was the biggest slut in town. We have never spoken since that day. I have called Mary many times, and she never calls back. I avoided the potential conflict and ultimately made it ten times worse when it all came out. I love Evan, but I wish I hadn't been so scared of Mary.

Evan and Julie got engaged six months after that encounter and married the following New Year's Eve. Mary and Julie have never spoken since, though they still have many friends in common. Julie wrote Mary a letter on her honeymoon apologizing for not confiding in her about her attraction to Evan.

GOING FORWARD—YOUR DESIRES

The three stories above point to the natural struggles of meeting a suitable partner and beginning a romantic/intimate relationship. In each case, the dater had certain emotional disappointments and challenges to overcome in order to establish a dating relationship. No single adult I know among the people I see in therapy or know socially ever feels 100 percent confident in his or her ability to meet someone, attract a soul mate, and build a fulfilling intimate relationship. Anyone who doesn't feel somewhat vulnerable about opening his or her heart and life to a new partner isn't seriously invested in or genuinely pursuing an intimate relationship. He or she is doing something, but it isn't moving toward healing prior relationship issues or concerns. Developing an intimate relationship is one of the most defining, challenging, and rewarding processes of one's life. There is no argument that dating and meeting potential partners can be very complicated. No one lives life in a vacuum, and introducing someone new into your life can be met with many unforeseen challenges. The problem isn't in joining two lives together but the challenges that appear along the way. The more you understand, resolve, and expand your insight into your emotional and romantic needs, the easier it is to navigate the new partnership. The three stories above all point to romantic relationships that have the potential to grow and develop regardless of the person's past "heartbreaking" circumstances.

Inherent in the intimate relationship process is a sense of feeling incredibly vulnerable and insecure, but also loved and empowered, all at the same time. *As has been said repeatedly throughout this discussion: We all need to be fully understood, loved, and admired.* These natural longings are what drive us to establish intimate emotional connections that support and nurture our basic human needs. Our deep emotional longing for a safe, nurturing, and supportive relationship is the motivation and drive to overcome our fears and enjoy this wonderful privilege and gift. Feeling loved and understood is one of the most empowering forces in a person's life. If you didn't know this, you wouldn't be reading this book.

Whether you are coming out of a contentious divorce; dealing with heartbreak, disappointment, or a major breakup; or just starting to seriously consider the prospect of having a life partner, the process can be overwhelming, depressing, and exciting. No one wants to feel rejected or dismissed by someone he or she finds attractive. Mark and Laura in the above stories had to resolve their emotional resistance to being open to the potential of an intimate relationship. Julie had to forgive herself for her mishandling of the situation with her friend. All three typify the genuine struggles of their place in life, whether divorced or never married, with or without children.

The couples in all three dating stories developed exclusive relationships that led to marriage, but none of the relationships followed the usual courtship pattern of meeting, dating, and going toward a permanent union. Each followed its own style of connecting, growing, and continuing to build an intimate bond. One variable that all three vignettes had in common was that the individuals involved were very clear about the chemistry they felt, their individual styles of communication, and the kind of relationship they wanted and needed. They also knew what actions, gestures, and emotional contact made them feel loved. Mark struggled with a chronic feeling of being "damaged goods" and couldn't tolerate anyone being verbally aggressive toward him or his actions. Laura believed she would die alone and couldn't stand random emotional contact or sexual encounters. Julie was convinced that she would never have a husband or children and needed someone who shared the high priority she placed on marriage and family. Yet these competent adults, like so many of us, did not allow their old emotional fears to direct their relationship futures. They understood their own personal intimate needs for a safe, supportive, and stable relationship.

These individuals' emotional clarity and sincere interest in finding a new partner and creating the kind of lives they wanted was nonnegotiable and not in doubt. This natural drive became the impetus for the courage to try to undertake the personal growth necessary to make a new type of commitment to a partner. None of these adults allowed age, prior relationship disasters, disappointments with the opposite sex, frustrating and painful breakups, or desperation to control their new relationship choices and partner selection. The fear of growing old alone, being isolated, and never realizing their dreams of a fulfilling relationship weren't part of their personal belief systems. They had resolved the negative residual effects of prior breakups, and their relationship belief systems had expanded as a result of their own healing process. All three had to overcome their past emotional disappointments and understand their roles in how their significant love relationships ended and why those relationships needed to end.

It is important to remember that nearly all relationships, regardless of the emotional pain their endings might cause, have value as building blocks for your life and your capacity to be emotionally intimate. When you are involved in a traumatic breakup, it is difficult to remember this truth. Your relationship history is important to explore for your past blind spots of self-defeating patterns, your past problematic personal themes, and your past negative beliefs about yourself and your worthiness.

YOUR LIST—YOUR SOUL MATE

Where is my soul mate? This is the right question to ask about your intimate future. The answer to this very popular question is rooted in a different question: *What makes you feel loved, adored, and supported?* No one can answer this question for you, nor should you allow anyone else to. Many well-meaning current partners, past lovers, family members, friends, and online dating services will attempt to tell you how love should work in your life. But the truth is, only you know the answer to this important question. If you can't recall what makes you feel loved, review chapter 7, and think about these questions:

- What does "feeling loved" look like to you?
- How does it work in your day-to-day life?
- Have you ever told your partner what little things make you feel loved and appreciated?

- What is one thing that always makes you happy when you are in a relationship?
- What is something that always makes you smile?
- Do you like to kiss your partner or have other physical contact every morning before getting out of bed?
- Can you expect your new partner to know how difficult it is for you to have necessary conversations (i.e., discussing coparenting issues) with your ex? Can you express that your need for "extra" emotional support varies given the level of contact with your "ex"?
- For instance, does feeling loved mean to you that your partner gives you a hug prior to your going to a family meeting with your "ex" in-laws (sign of affection and understanding your romantic past)? Does feeling loved mean watching your favorite TV show with your partner once a week (intimacy)?

Your emotional sense and need for feeling loved, nurtured, and adored has been developing since your childhood and is the central key to your current and future intimate relationship fulfillment. It is important to remember that when you feel loved, you are feeling understood, appreciated, and emotionally supported. All of these actions, feelings, emotions, and behaviors on the part of a partner help create an internal support within you that is life changing. Feeling loved is the foundation that will help you accomplish or attempt anything you want in your life. Children who feel loved thrive emotionally and have high achievement scores because they feel confident about their abilities and desires.[1] Adults are absolutely no different, although we may have never before truly allowed ourselves the chance to feel loved by our intimate partner.

Your insight into your own feelings and wishes reveals a great deal about your soul mate. For most adults, the list of basic relationship needs isn't exhaustive or complicated, but still it can be misunderstood by both you and your lover. Many relationships end prematurely because there is a lack of understanding—on both parts—about unmet emotional needs. Creating your new life starts with gaining a fuller and deeper understanding of your emotional needs, wants, and romantic longings. *To find your soul mate, you first must understand what you need from a partner to feel loved, adored, and intimately supported.* When your spoken and unspoken emotional needs and desires are satisfied by a partner, you have both a lover and mate in one person. This connection is transforming and forms the substance and fabric of your entire life.

There is a mainstream psychological relationship theory that we all have our own individual sense of what "feeling" loved, adored, and supported is. The problem is that everyone has his or her own set of feelings about intimate love that might be unknown to both the giver and the receiver. Your personal desires for an intimate partner can be usually narrowed down to four or five key qualities that might very quickly be expanded into forty to fifty nonnegotiable qualities. Fundamentally, your list will consist of some combination of the following five qualities, which can be fully expanded and better understood by you. Once you know what makes you feel loved, developing an intimate relationship becomes a very clear and exciting future. Some of your old patterns that resulted in getting emotionally involved with the wrong partner can now be more easily addressed and resolved, for now you know better that *what makes you feel "loved" is more important than how you are actually loved.* How you feel loved is strictly an individual process and that isn't transferable to other partners, only you. If eating ice cream is important to you, then you need to eat ice cream with your romantic partner. Your intimate relationships will reflect your new insight, and will thus be more fulfilling and deeply satisfying.

A list of what makes many of us feel loved includes:

Affection—emotional understanding, eye contact, kissing, being protective (physically and emotionally), providing empathy, physical touch (hugging, hand holding, back rubs), and loving approval. These behaviors tend to be nonverbal actions that lead to emotional closeness and a sense of feeling loved. This can be the unspoken glue between you and your lover.

Communication—how you discuss sensitive issues, fears, wishes, and desires (emotional and sexual). How much is too much or too little "talking"? When do you like to talk (morning, night, in person, by phone, e-mailing, cell phone, texting)? What are your favorite topics of interest in conversations? How do you know when someone is listening to you?

Intimacy—what makes you feel intimately connected with your partner? What are your emotional, mental, and physical expectations for your lover? How important is sexual chemistry to you? How would you prioritize your time with your partner, vacations, daily, weekly dates, and free time?

Compatibility—your personal values and what is truly important to you about the following areas: sexuality—frequency, emotional expression; spirituality—beliefs about god/universe; physical appearance/attractiveness; financial issues/spending, intellectual interests/education; recreational activities; hobbies/sports; family goals (children, stepchildren, coparenting, parents, relatives).

Stress/conflict resolution—what you need from your partner when you are upset, stressed, and/or anxious. Do you forgive easily or at all when you are hurt or misunderstood? Do you like to talk things out or do you tend to avoid conflict or difficult issues?

Reread this list and ask yourself on a scale from 0 to 10 how important these five qualities are to you, with 0 as "not important" and 10 as "extremely important/deal breaker." Going with your first "gut" instinct, write a number next to each category. This list is extremely important for you to ponder and to fully explore so you can understand how romantic love works in your life. You have emotionally survived and healed from your relationship endings, and now you can address your love life from a much wider perspective. Let's discuss in detail each of the five qualities so you can start to consciously create your own list of nonnegotiable needs in an intimate relationship.

YOUR NONNEGOTIABLE NEEDS

Affection is listed first because it is the most misunderstood element in intimate relationships. For instance, many women complain that their partners aren't affectionate or caring. Their partners, on the other hand, think their behavior is fine because they have never discussed what "affection" means to each of them. Many men complain that they don't like public displays of affection such as kissing, hugging, hand holding, or back rubs. Many men like affectionate gestures in private and only at certain times. Their female partners then think they are doing something wrong because their well-intended acts of kindness are experienced as irritating. Affection can be defined as the "soft" unspoken gestures between a couple that communicate love, support, and adoration. These gestures and acts help to create feelings of being cherished, special, and cared for. All of us emotionally thrive when we have the particular amount of physical and emotional contact we desire. It builds a secure relationship bond between us and our partner.

The problem with long-distance relationships is that partners are unable to touch and see each other every day. The mere act of giving and receiving a kiss before leaving the house is a comforting gesture that might not be consciously recognized until it is missing. Affection is the collection of smiles, supportive eye gestures, and positive body language and touches that pass between partners in a loving relationship. Of course, talking and communication are of paramount importance in a relationship, but a solid relationship can sustain itself during quiet times, when each reads or does a crossword puzzle, knowing that the other is there for him or her.

Affection Desires

Consider how you feel, think, value, and want the following things in your romantic relationship:

- Do you like hugging, holding hands, and back rubs?
- Do you enjoy public displays of affection, or do you prefer affection only in private?
- How important is eye contact to you?
- How important is receiving a phone call, e-mail, or text message saying your partner is thinking of you?
- Do you like receiving unexpected gifts from your partner?
- Do you enjoy physical closeness such as holding each other and cuddling together?
- Do you like walking next to your partner?
- Do you like having your body touched (not including sexual contact)?
- Do you like being greeted by your partner when leaving or coming back home?
- For instance, do you like it when your partner makes you a cup of coffee, buys your favorite perfume, makes you a cocktail before dinner, takes your kids out for dinner, or calls you after a minor misunderstanding?

Communication Desires

Ask yourself and how your emotional sense of connection is strengthened through your communication:

- Do you enjoy discussing everything—personal, professional, familial, and private matters—with your partner?
- When is it most important for you to have a verbal connection with your partner—during the day or at night?
- What are you afraid to share with or tell your partner?

- How do you communicate when you are upset or angry with your partner (e.g., yelling, silence, avoidance)?
- Can you ask your partner to meet your personal needs—sexually, emotionally, as well as affection?
- Do you need an emotional connection through conversation and in-depth discussions?
- How important is it to talk out your feelings when you are angry, depressed, anxious, or elated?
- What is one type of communication (i.e., full disclosure of your thoughts, expressing a particular fear, and/or your honest unedited response regardless of your partner's response) that you normally didn't have in your past relationships, but want in future relationships?
- When you are "upset," how do you want your partner to communicate with you (i.e., listen, problem solve)?
- How difficult has communication in the past been between you and your partner over emotionally charged issues or topics?

Intimacy Desires

Ask yourself what your true desires, wishes, and hopes are for a deeper sense of emotional intimacy and bond:

- What activities, gestures, and discussions make you feel emotionally connected to your partner?
- How often do you desire sex?
- Do you enjoy sexual activity/connection (i.e., foreplay, kissing, hand holding, foot rubs, hugs)?
- Do you like to pursue or be pursued sexually?
- Do you value spending free time with your partner?
- Do you enjoy doing couples activities with your partner?
- What are your expectations for your partner, sexually, emotionally, and mentally?
- Does your partner know from your direct communication what you need and want from him or her in terms of intimacy?

- Do you expect him or her to fully understand your wishes and desires for certain activities as a result of directly expressing them?
- Do you like your partner to do things with you that are more of interest to you than to him or her?
- How often do you do things that are more of an interest to your partner than you?
- What activities, gestures, conversations, and/or actions make you feel emotionally bonded to your partner?
- After spending large amounts of time with your partner, do you desire more time together or do you want a break?

Compatibility Desires

Ask yourself what things, values, activities, and overall beliefs make you feel compatible and emotionally bonded:

- How important is your partner's physical attractiveness to you?
- Does your partner ever suggest cosmetic elective surgery for you or him- or herself? How do you feel about that?
- Do you want a partnership where you both enjoy exercise and a physically active lifestyle?
- What are your spiritual beliefs and practices? Are they important to your relationship?
- What are your feelings about money—spending, savings, investments?
- How important to you is personal wealth in a partner?
- Do you understand your sexual appetite?
- How important is your partner's sexual appetite to you? Does it matter if you are in sync? If not, does or would it matter to either of you that much?
- Do you enjoy emotional expressions, signs of affection, communication, and recreational and family time with your partner?
- How much attention do you need in order to feel loved?
- Do you view yourself as a social person or as a more shy, withdrawn type? How would your partner fit into your personality

style? Is one of you outgoing and the other quiet? Does this work for you both?

- What is the most important character trait you want in a partner?
- What is the most significant nonnegotiable/deal breaker for you in a partner? This can be anything—don't dismiss your desire and need for it.
- How do you like your partner to express his or her feelings to you—verbally, sexually, emotionally, in writing?

Stress/Conflict Resolution Desires

Ask yourself how you and your partner would like to handle the "stressors" of everyday life:

- What do you need from your partner when you are upset, anxious, or scared?
- When you have a misunderstanding or a minor conflict with your partner, are you quick to forgive or do you hold a grudge?
- Do you like to resolve conflicts or do you prefer to avoid hot issues?
- Do you yell, argue, or get very demonstrative when you are angry?
- How frequently do you or your partner's strong expressions of anger scare you?
- How would you like your partner to handle relationship conflicts?
- How do honesty, openness, and full personal/relationship disclosures (i.e., personal secrets or shame issues you might have) operate in your intimate relationships?
- What is one quality, action, or habit that you won't tolerate in an argument—a deal breaker other than dishonesty?
- What is your tolerance level for emotionally charged arguments, disagreements, and/or angry outbursts?
- Do you like your partner to be more direct or passive when you are upset with each other?

These five sections with probing self-examination questions are designed to help you to focus on what is really important to you in a partner and in an intimate relationship. After reading these numerous questions, consider all of the different ideas, personal and intimate questions, and behaviors of how you would like your next intimate relationship to be for you. Which section above best addressed your most important needs and desires in an intimate partnership? Your desired intimate relationship will be based on your newly expanded personal insight into all the facets of your life. You don't need to become a serial dater in order to find your intimate partner; rather, you need to become more aware of your feelings and emotional needs regarding love and emotional attachment.

WHAT LOVE LOOKS LIKE TO YOU—NO RULES

Some of the most important questions that you need to ask yourself while reading this book include: *What is your primary sense of feeling loved? What actions by your partner make you feel loved? Can you accept loving gestures by your partner? Do you believe that you deserve to be loved the way you need and want? Who in your past showed you unconditional love?* The more conscious you are of your answers to these kinds of questions, the more your intimate relationship can reflect your new level of insight and emotional contentment. Your answers are the master key to unlocking your romantic future. Your deeper awareness allows you to move past your old emotional, mental, and physical relationship roadblocks and self-defeating choices. The more you are able to focus on the feelings and acts of love you need to feel fulfilled in a relationship, the less frustration, disappointment, and despair you will encounter.

The amount of time that you spend on painful relationship pursuits can be dramatically reduced. *One of the goals of moving past*

*your ex-factor is to greatly diminish the emotional pain and suf-
fering in your life and relationships.* Your understanding of your
own individual needs for affection, communication, intimacy, compatibility, and conflict/stress management enables you to create a
new, better romantic life for yourself. If you are going to make better
choices in your intimate relationships, we have to be better
acquainted with your needs pertaining to love. These five elements
are the foundation of all intimate and romantic partnerships. The
better able you are to communicate and allow your desires, wants,
and needs to be met by your partner, the more support, love, and
adoration you will experience. And the way you prioritize the five
intimate elements informs how and why you operate a particular
way in your intimate partnerships.

Acknowledging your unspoken and spoken desires, as well as
your longing for acceptance and love, is the pathway to a deeper and
more satisfying love life. It is your right to have your own needs for
emotional connection, communication, and physical affection
understood and met. You don't need to rationalize or apologize for
the things that make you feel loved, supported, and adored. You have
the maturity, life experience, and confidence to know what does and
doesn't work for you in a relationship. All of these basic human
needs for love and acceptance and all the other variables are the
foundation of your future romantic partnerships. The pursuit and
fulfillment of these natural adult human needs is the primary reason
why marital and other commitments can be both so positive, transforming, exciting, and powerful—as well as so troubling and painful.
People will always seek out intimate relationships in the hope of
having their fundamental needs for love and acceptance met and
understood. The more we know about our own love story, the better
able we are to get what we need and want in our relationships.

There is no other relationship in your life that will have a greater
impact on you than a long-term intimate bond. All of your prior relationships—with childhood friends, parents and siblings, girlfriends
or boyfriends, and colleagues—feed into the formation and creation

of your life with a significant partner. We are all wired genetically to develop these connections as a way of handling the challenges of adulthood. The following list of questions will help you better understand how to successfully meet eligible partners, date, and develop stable long-term relationships.

- **What is one thing you emotionally always wanted in your childhood?** It could be feeling loved and adored, consistent attention, or emotional support. The answer to this question is key to understanding what drives you to make certain connections in your intimate relationships. In other words, the thing you most wanted as a child is probably one of the most important things you want in your life today.

- **What is the most important thing to you in a relationship?** This is the one thing—be it an action, feeling, belief, or physical gesture—that makes you feel loved, cared for, and securely bound to your intimate partner. This might include trust, honesty, and security. Whatever it is, don't leave it out of your next intimate relationship.

- **What is the one thing that would get you to open up your heart again to an intimate relationship?** You would be fooling yourself to think that after a severe relationship disappointment and breakup, the prospect of a new love relationship isn't scary—and maybe even impossible to imagine at this time. You have already chosen to come out of your cave, to heal, and create a new type of intimate relationship in your life. Now is the time to apply what you've learned about yourself to a new situation. Your life is a collection of events, and you are going to enjoy some great events again, regardless of your past relationship history.

- **When you imagine yourself in a relationship, what does that mental picture look like?** It is very difficult to do anything if we can't first visualize ourselves doing it. Take a moment and close your eyes to consider what it would feel like to have an intimate partner in your everyday life. What needs to change in your life—emotionally, psychologically, and mentally—for this to occur? What are your automatic built-in roadblocks, barriers, and excuses for not moving forward in your life? Can you begin to let go of your disappointment and consider your romantic future? Your rejoining the world of dating and intimate relationships—using your new insights to develop better relationships—will be the proof of your healing.

- **What will the first month of your new relationship look like?** How would you like to start your dating? What, where, and how would you like to begin the process of meeting a partner and exploring the possibilities of a new intimate partnership? How much physical contact would you like? How many phone calls and dates? How much time spent together? Don't be surprised by your answers because you already know exactly how you want to start building a new relationship life.

- **Can you forget about dating and the "rules," and think about relationships?** Your goal isn't to have a string of meaningless first dates, which might happen, but rather a great first month with a potential partner. Don't lose sight of the fact that you want a relationship, not a revolving door of new dates every week. Relationships take time to develop and unfold. If you want to date and check out potential partners, that is normal and good. Obviously if someone is off-putting, it makes no sense to date him or her. When you find someone who sparks your interest, seems intriguing to you, and gets your full attention, then consider the ideas in this chapter. Aside from meeting people, dating is a way to better understand our mate selection process. Dating is also something to embrace and not to reject or avoid. Meeting people can be exciting and difficult, but it is about creating a future and fulfilling intimate emotional needs.

- **What would you like ultimately in your marriage/exclusive relationship?** Think about where you'd like to end up in your romantic life in the next twelve to twenty-four months. Start with where you want to be in twenty-four months and work back from there. It is useful to have a goal and be mindful of your objectives and purpose, and where you want your romantic life to be heading. It is difficult to date and become intimately involved if you don't know where you want to be in the future.

YOUR "A" LIST

There are numerous Web sites, online dating experts, life coaches, movies, classes, talk shows, and magazine articles and books specifically designed to help you date and find your perfect partner. Many of these different resources are valuable and often insightful. But before any these ideas will work, you need to become your own best friend and advocate for your own intimate partner selection. It all starts and stops with you. The more you incorporate your particular needs for love, acceptance, and support into your dating life, the more fulfilling your love life will be. It sounds simple, but the application can be challenging. No one is exempt from the frustrations of engaging in intimate relationships. Your goal is to first better understand your needs so that you are able to find a partner who is a good match for you. Your "A" list is your creation and your private matter. No one besides you needs to know what you think or want in your next intimate relationship. This isn't an exhaustive list, because if these four or five nonnegotiable qualities are present for you, then many lesser issues will be addressed. On this page, with a pen, write down your "A" list—five things that you consider absolutely necessary in a new intimate relationship.

1.

2.

3.

4.

5.

Now, close the book and reread this list again in a few days. Watch what happens in your life over the next four to eight weeks in your dealings with the opposite sex. Your goal is to get out of your own way. Go past your old roadblocks, move out of your old comfort zones, and allow your intimate life to unfold. Remember, your soul mate is a person who loves, adores, and understands you. Your innermost feelings and desires are all the personal information you need to create, build, and develop your new intimate relationship.

Chapter 10

PERSONAL RESPONSIBILITY

Your New Choices

The ultimate measure of a man is not where he stands in moments of comfort and convenience, but where he stands at times of challenge and controversy.
— Martin Luther King Jr.

When we choose to hold onto our grievances, we will fill our minds with pain, conflict, and suffering. When we choose to forgive, we immediately feel lighter, as if tons have been lifted from our backs.
— Gerald G. Jampolsky, MD

MOVING FORWARD

The only thing worse than going through a life-shattering divorce or relationship breakup is continuing to relive it. Many adults—some of whom have been divorced numerous times—know full well the pain of divorce and romantic breakups. These men and women always comment that one of their exes was the most difficult to "get over" and leave in the past. In the quotes above, both Martin Luther King Jr. and Gerald G. Jampolsky point all of us in the right direction for our own healing and peace of mind. The direction you are moving toward in the next chapter of your life is one of detachment-forgiveness, and courage to open your heart again to a romantic partner. The agony of betrayal, disappointment, lost love, and abandonment are all very significant emotions that can turn into personal life-changing events (i.e., divorce, breakup, canceled wedding, no engagement, child custody visitation issues). Many adults unintentionally allow their unresolved emotional pain to become a brick wall that they can never surmount. The key is to go beyond your pain—romantically and emotionally—toward healing and personal empowerment. There are critical times in your life when you will be faced with a very big decision to move forward and address the crisis or simply avoid it.

The path of avoidance will always lead back to the crossroads of decision making in your life. Some people spend years avoiding, psychologically running from, and hiding their internal fears and old parent-child issues. But those who avoid the issues always find themselves grappling with the same unresolved issue at the next fork in their lives. Life has a funny way of bringing our problems back to us again and again until we resolve them.[1] Ask yourself this: What are you avoiding dealing with in terms of your ex-factor? Take a minute and think about your answer because it is a glimpse into your past. *By healing it in the present, you create a new potential and possibility for the future.*

Your divorce, relationship ending, and heartbreak are all made up of these real moments (disappointment, emotional mood swings, reality of your dreams ending) of truth and courage in your life. Your ability to detach, forgive, resolve, reconnect to a new romantic partner, and to rebuild your life, love again, and reinvent yourself is a tremendous undertaking. M. Scott Peck's popular book *The Road Less Traveled* (1980) was the first mainstream summation of the value of undertaking the painful personal journey that we all must start when our lives feel "broken."[2] Your pathway leading to the "road less traveled" is all your past emotional pain and present suffering. *Your entire life—your future potential, family, career, and mental and physical health—all depends on your moving forward and let-*

ting go of past negative experiences and embracing the new. The new may seem even more frightening and scary than the old, but it isn't.

Fear always looks and feels like an old familiar devil, when it is really just the old face of your despair. Your old issues of unfulfilled love, incomplete romantic connections, and repetitive patterns of sadness and frustration are very familiar and emotionally seductive. The seduction is not questioning the old patterns and experiences in your romantic encounters. The unresolved pattern of unsatisfactory romantic bonding/connections, residual resentment toward your ex-partner, blaming the world for your failed relationship, and your anger are very safe and recurring emotions and fill up your life every day. This painfully avoidant style of behavior may be no more apparent than when one observes a highly intelligent couple divorcing or breaking up. They get entrenched and emotionally invested in arguing about every issue, dollar, frequent flyer mile, and minute spent with or without the kids. All the fighting is subconsciously designed to keep them from having to deal with the issues of detachment and forgiveness.

But avoidance, residual anger, and resentment as daily emotional choices only serve to reinforce a deep sense of personal failure on your part. The nonstop self-loathing and critical self-judgment work to prevent the opportunity to receive or give love and to start a new chapter in your life. The way out of this maze is through the doorway of self-forgiveness.

> "The most beautiful and romantic relationship
> has to begin with you!"[3]

The time has come for you to release your disappointment, resentment, and anger toward yourself and your ex-partner. The quote above summarizes this entire book: *Your entire romantic relationship future starts with you.* Your new life, your next chapter with your new intimate relationship, all start with you moving forward on your pathway of healing and enlightenment. All psychological, spiritual, and emotional enlightenment always involves self-acceptance, self-love, and the absence of tension with regard to your past.

Your Responsibility

The pathway to self-acceptance is really the same as the road to self-forgiveness. Both require that you find the timeless secret of many religions and philosophical teachings: *personal responsibility*.[4] Taking responsibility for your role—your half of the relationship, your "crazy" behavior and anger—is the fastest way to release yourself from your ex and move forward.

In California, the freeways have special lanes called "diamond lanes." These lanes are designated for vehicles traveling with two or more passengers. It is the fastest lane during rush-hour traffic; the other cars, each carrying one passenger, sit in traffic watching the diamond lane vehicles freely flow. Get in the diamond lane of life and invite personal responsibility and self-acceptance as permanent guests to join you on your journey. Consider the following statements as to how you can acquire this life-changing insight and the key to your new life. These soul-searching thoughts are designed to help you move beyond your wall of resistance and unconscious fears.

The Self-Forgiveness List

- I willfully picked my ex as a partner.
- I am fully responsible for my role in the relationship from the beginning to the end.
- I did and said things that contributed to the ending of our romantic bond.
- I accept my faults, shortcomings, and lack of insight during my relationship.
- I am fully responsible and liable for all of my words and actions taken in moments of anger and rage.

- I am resolved not to engage in anger, tension, and scary emotional outbursts toward my ex-partner or in front of our children.
- It doesn't matter who was right or wrong in the marriage; my life is in front of me.
- Perfection and the need to be right are ways to minimize my responsibility and continue to be angry toward my ex-partner.
- I forgive and accept myself for doing the best I could with my ex-partner, given my own abilities, wounds, and unresolved emotional pain.
- It is important that my ex-partner finds love and fulfillment in his or her future.
- Blaming my ex-partner for the ending of our relationship is pointless. We each had a role in the relationship, regardless of the ending.

The Self-Acceptance List

- I will allow my future to be different than my past.
- The only opinion of me that matters is mine.
- I know that choosing love starts with me.
- I am not perfect, nor will I ever be.
- Perfection and the pursuit of it is a powerful source of self-loathing.
- One of my greatest gifts is my ability to be honest and empathetic toward others.
- I have more insight into choosing and receiving love today than I did six months ago.
- I can forgive myself for how my relationship ended.
- My life will always be a series of beginnings and endings.
- Personal acceptance and success derives from my ability to be courageous and to allow others to be themselves.
- Harsh judgments, criticism, and anger are all masks for my fear that I will not be loved and accepted.

- I am developing more insight and compassion, as well as the ability to forgive.

The Personal Responsibility List

- My love life is a collection of all my choices and decisions.
- I will no longer blame my ex-partner for the ending of our relationship. It takes two people to have a relationship, and I am part of the beginning, middle, and end of the relationship.
- I am fully accepting of my role in my relationship and my behavior toward my ex-partner.
- Our relationship needed to end so that we could both grow separately.
- The timetable for our marriage/romance is over, and that relationship is no longer an option.
- My ex will find a new partner, and it isn't my concern.
- I am deeply appreciative of our children and the gift they are to me and my ex-partner.
- I willingly fell in love with and married my ex-partner.
- My unresolved issues, emotional pain and suffering, and the reactivation of my anger and disappointment are not my ex-partner's responsibility.
- My psychological wounds and emotional pain predate my relationship with my ex-partner.
- I've chosen to change the course of my romantic life.
- In the past, I have said and done things in moments of anger that aren't acceptable in my life, today or in the future.
- I am aware of my emotional "hot buttons" and issues that I allow to control me.
- Bad choices or mistakes can best be seen as valuable life lessons.
- I sincerely wish my ex-partner the best in his or her romantic future.

LOVE IS COMPLETELY RESPONSIBLE FOR ITS ACTIONS

These lists are designed to help you move forward onto the diamond lane on whatever highway you'd like to be on. It might take a while before you can fully accept and emotionally digest all these statements and your own truth about your ex, but your personal growth hinges on your ability to release yourself and your ex-partner from your anger and resentment. Don't worry or concern yourself about your ex's anger issues or residual resentment toward you. (Please note that here I am not referring to extreme cases of violence— sound judgment must always be your guide.) It doesn't matter if your ex-partner ever extends the same graciousness or forgiveness toward you. *Your healing process is completely about you, not about your ex-partner.* Don't spend any more of your energy on your ex— on whether he or she ever acknowledges his or her role in the breakup.

Your healing process is strictly about your rebuilding and re-creating your own life. If writing your own statements of personal responsibility, self-acceptance, and self-forgiveness will help you, then you should do it. No matter how you feel or what you want everyone to know about your marriage—the injustice, unfairness of it, your ex-partner's continuing spiteful behavior—it simply doesn't matter. The fight is over; you have nothing to prove and you require nothing from your ex-partner. Regardless of whatever valid points you might have regarding mistreatment and insensitivity by your ex, at the end of the day you need to forgive two people: *yourself and your ex-partner*.

Many adults find the latter easier than the former. I strongly encourage you to wholeheartedly do both and never question or doubt the merit of your loving. Your life will directly benefit from your intention of forgiveness and your attempt to create peace for yourself and your ex-partner. Even if your ex-partner continues to behave badly toward you, you still need to find the emotional capacity and self-respect to move on.

I should note here that the intention of forgiving and going beyond your anger, resentment, and bitterness is a rare process. Those who attempt to move forward with a forgiving heart will always benefit and are very successful in their future romantic life. *Most people don't want to take the steps necessary to emancipate themselves from the past.* Releasing your anger and self-righteousness is a very hard thing to do. The tragedy is that many well-meaning adults allow these negative emotions to become the substance of their future relationships and, in some cases, their entire lives. You wouldn't be reading this book if you weren't committed to healing and changing the course of your life. It is now time to take different action.

FORGIVENESS AND DETACHMENT ALLOWS FOR YOUR CHANGES AND YOUR EXPANSION OF LOVE

Change Is in Your Future

You are in complete control of your romantic destiny. You are also in charge of what intimate partners come into your life. Not allowing yourself to bring your ex-partner with you on the next part of your journey is wise and will benefit all parties concerned. It might sound ridiculous, but most adults continue to carry their ex-partners along with them well after their divorce or breakup. Just like an airplane, you have a baggage limit, and you don't have room in your life for old baggage anymore.

As you head into the next chapter of your life, you will most likely encounter and have to cope with several critical challenges and issues to consider:

- The first challenge is one you have already faced—forgiving and detaching yourself from your ex-partner. This is an ongoing process when there are children involved.

- Second, you and your children are a package deal. You can't divorce your children. You are a parent for life. You will need to take their best interests into consideration when selecting a new partner.
- Third, your ex-partner might meet someone who has children and/or bring yours into their new relationship. The time your children don't spend with you, they are with your ex-partner, who might be living with a partner with his or her own children—another man or woman will also be a parental influence on your children.
- Fourth, your new relationship might include having children of your own. Do you want more children?
- Fifth, your new partner might have children from his or her prior marriage and you will be a stepparent to a new set of children.

The changes that come with remarriage, stepchildren, and all the possible family configurations require you to be—to the best of your ability—emotionally neutral with your ex-partner. You need his or her cooperation, or at least his or her silence, about your new life. Your life is in front of you, not in the past, so keep looking forward.

The ideas above are about some of your new personal responsibility in action in the next chapter of your life. Your understanding of each challenge will be a significant factor in making your future as painless and drama free as possible. Hating your ex-partner and/or talking to your kids about how "awful" their mother or father is only makes things worse for everyone—especially you. Likewise, speaking negatively about your new partner's ex to their children is a fatal mistake and a formula for endless conflict and tension. We will discuss later in the chapter some very practical do's and don'ts for parents, stepparents, children, stepchildren, in-laws, new family members, and you.

BLENDED FAMILIES—TRUE STORIES

Whether you have children or not, this section is very important to understand, since there is more than an 85 percent chance that you will be involved in a relationship that does include children.[5] Up to this point, we have discussed the process of finding an intimate partner who is an accurate reflection of your new emotional development. Now is the time to look closely at the next frontier in your life. In this future, you will be building and expanding your immediate family circle and introducing new members into it. The new members might be stepchildren, new children, in-laws, cousins, siblings, and longtime family friends. Your family circle will only expand as you develop the insight and flexibility in your relationship future about this huge phenomenon that is specific to our current time in history: the blended family.

One of my main motivations for writing this book was the multitude of struggles created by the brand-new learning curve that comes with the blended family. Theoretically, a blended family is one created by combining the members of your family—including children from prior relationships—and your new partner's family into your new union. This is a very delicate process involving nearly everyone in your current and past lives. Before we go into the discussion of sharing bedrooms in the new house, let's discuss the remarriage process. How the new partner enters the picture will greatly affect how he or she is accepted by your children and extended family.

The Brady Bunch—Remarriage

I remember as a teenager watching *The Brady Bunch* and wondering where the other parents were. I was the same age as Marcia Brady and always found her to be an interesting and attractive possible stepsister. Some thirty-five years later, my own children explained to me one day while I was driving them to school that the other parents were never part of the show because both Mike and Carol Brady were widowed. Having the ex-partners vaporize and disappear is a very convenient way to join two preexisting families but a very unrealistic wish and denial of the inherent challenges of joining two families. Some of you may think that not everyone can be so lucky and have his or her ex-partner vanish from the future, certainly, not something very likely or good for you or your children. But if your ex-partner did disappear, it would cause a whole other set of problems for your children, so I'm certainly not recommending it.

The question my clients frequently ask is: *How do I remarry and join our two families?* Let's answer this question in two parts, the first being the remarriage element and the second being the actual blending of the families. How well the first element is handled is a great predictor of how the second will turn out.

The concept of remarriage in this time in our social history almost always includes the concept of blended families. The figures discussed in chapter 1 are very telling: 70 percent of all families are some type of blended family. First-time marriages and all the different combinations of having children (common-law marriages, unmarried couples having children, single adults having children) and marriages in which one partner is divorced and the other is married for the first time are now very common situations that existed only rarely thirty-five years ago. Blended families are now the norm rather than the exception to family life today.

Meeting, dating, and building a future with a new partner is an exciting process. The actual joining of all the different parts of your life with your new spouse is where conflict, tension, and misunderstanding can erupt and become deal breakers. Before we launch into a full-blown discussion on the value of blended families, it is important to discuss the remarriage process when there are children involved. Even if you don't have children, there is a better than 50 percent chance that your new partner will, so it is important to understand all the issues involved.

The New Partners

Your New Partner

Let's face the most common mistake parents with children make when introducing their kids to their new partners. The famous parental belief *"My kids will love you"* is a great launching point for our discussion. This statement might be completely true, or completely false, or something in between. The fact is, your children will have their own opinions about your divorce, postdivorce life, and new romantic life—and make no mistake: your children, regardless of their ages, will have very strong opinions about your new partner. Don't incorrectly presume that your children are without opinions, thoughts, and feelings about your selection of a new partner. Remember that your children don't want a mother or a father replacement. They already have two parents. It is the divorced parent who wants a new mother or father for his or her children; for your children to love your new partner and embrace him or her, regardless of age, is based on the lingering negative divorce issues. How well the divorce/breakup was managed is an excellent indicator of how well the process of introduction and acceptance of the new partner will go.

It is important to be mindful that your children will always want you to participate in their lives. This fact may escape you, perhaps because of prior custody tension or because of "parent alienation"— your ex-partner's interfering with you and your children. *The number one concern in all remarriage cases and new romantic arrangements is that the preexisting children may feel displaced.* The sense of loss, regret, and fear of losing their father or mother is very real for young children, teenagers, and even adult children. Your children's age doesn't diminish their feelings about your romantic status or partner selection. Your custody agreement or informal custody time with your children needs to be reinforced and discussed with them. Your young children, teenagers, or adult children need to be reassured of their place in your life with your new spouse. The number two concern in all remarriages with your children is the underlying fear and unspoken threat that your children will "lose" you emotionally and physically (less time with you) when you remarry and have a new family. Your children fear being left in the backwash of your life. Even if your children live with you full-time, this fear is *always* present to some degree.

We could discuss particular steps you should take for introducing and bringing your new partner and your children together, but it is the emotional process that is primary. One thing that must be paramount is understanding the psychology of remarriage (your ex-factor) and your children. If you don't force, push, or demand that your children share your excitement about your new partner, the transition will go much easier for them. Your children might love your partner, or they might think he or she has horns growing out of his or her head. *It doesn't matter how your children respond; what is important is how you handle their reactions.* All your actions, intentions, and desires must be guided by your patience and parental insight into your children's need to understand how their family unit is expanding. There is no prescribed timetable for when, how, or if they should meet a new someone special in your life. Your prevailing mission is to remain emotionally connected with your children while all the potential changes are occurring. It is imperative that you not underestimate the powerful impact your new partner will have on your existing family unit.

There are a few minor things that you can do to minimize conflicts, reduce the tension, and help blend your spouse and your children into a new life. These can be the backboard to rebuilding your life and going forward into your next chapter of life. Above all, remember that your children will always be involved with you and need to be part of your future. Sometimes the excitement of creating a new family, remarriage, getting a new house, and all the things that go with this process will always include your patience and understanding of how "hard" all these changes are for your children.

- Your children need to be reassured of their place, position, and value in your life. This is more than decorating a bedroom, although even that helps. It is all about your emotional bond and conscious attention to them as they experience the many changes caused first by your divorce and then by your new relationship.
- Whether their parents are married or divorced, children always worry on some subconscious level about losing their mother or father. This fear is particularly active when there is a new romantic relationship developing for one of their parents. Your awareness will go a long way in reducing this fear of loss and abandonment. If you have been absent from your kids' lives, it is never too late to get involved.
- Allow your children to have their own responses and opinions about the new marriage and blended family. Your reaction is more important than your children's rejection or acceptance of the new family. Most times their refusal to accept the changes is about finding a "safe" place with you.
- Boundaries, boundaries, boundaries. If there is any question about your need to develop, maintain, and keep emotional, psychological, and physical boundaries, let's answer it now: Yes. Knowing where you start and stop with your children allows them to reconnect and develop more emotional safety and security with you. There are issues between you and your kids that need to be confidential. You and your new partner also need boundaries from the children. Lastly, your ex-partner's role in your new family needs to be clearly defined.

Love Is Action.

Love in Action Only Produces Happiness.

Fear in Action Only Produces Suffering.[6]

Your Ex's New Partner

Your ex's remarriage has the potential to reactivate all the dormant, unresolved issues between you and your ex-partner. It is a reminder that the relationship between the two of you is completely over and done. The relationship is permanently changed, and there is now someone else in the place that you once had with your ex. Even if you welcome and celebrate the remarriage of your ex-partner, it changes the existing balance of your family.

Another cold glass of water to the face is the realization that someone other than you will have a substantial impact on your children. This issue becomes a major sticking point for many ex-partners. You have no control over who meets and marries your ex-partner, and neither do your children. Your children will be exposed to different parenting and communication styles, and will be expected to bond to some degree with your ex's new partner. *Under no circumstances should you become critical or overly negative about your ex's new partner.* Your children will do much better if you remain as neutral as possible about the changes in your ex's life. It is important that, regardless of your personal feelings, thoughts, and concerns, you remain in the role of the supportive parent with your children. Keeping your opinions to yourself is always a wise and prudent choice. Your children will have their own opinions and thoughts about the new partner, just as they will regarding new people in your life. All of your lives will be undergoing changes. Don't allow your anger and sense of disappointment to be the guiding force in your life and hinder your ability to navigate your family.

The New Family

Stacy's Story

I met Stacy at a school event that our children attended. Stacy, who is thirty-nine years old, is married and has two children, ages seven and eleven. She knew that I was writing this book and offered me her personal story about meeting her stepfather for the first time when she was thirteen years old.

> I immediately didn't like him. I didn't speak to my stepfather for four years. I would ask my mother in front of him about why she couldn't do better and marry a richer, smarter husband. I ignored him as if he didn't exist. I was awful to Herbert. He never spoke to me either. My behavior had nothing to do with my stepfather. He was a whipping board for me toward my mother. My mother could have married anyone and I was going to give them a hard time. Now, twenty-five years later, my mother is still married to Herbert and he really is a good guy. It just took me about ten years to finally accept and like him. I literally went out of my way to make his life miserable. I didn't give him an emotional break until after college. I met Herbert when I was in the sixth grade, and I was convinced that I could ruin his life. I was awful to him beyond description. I am surprised we all survived those first ten years together. In fact, I would tell my mother that my father was a better man than Herbert and make sure he heard me. I have a lot of empathy for children with stepparents. I feel bad for the stepparents. Herbert never did any wrong other than be in my life as a teenager.

Matthew's Story

Matthew is a single, never-married film director who is thirty-six years old. He has had several significant romantic relationships. He admits that he has a difficult time emotionally separating his disdain for his stepmother from his girlfriends in how he treats them and feels about them. Intimacy with women brings up all his unresolved issues with his stepmother. His biological mother was uninvolved in his life after the age of ten. During his parents' divorce, his father got full legal custody of him. His mother moved from California to New York, and he never saw her again until after he graduated from college. Matthew told me:

My father remarried when I was thirteen. It was a nightmare. My mother, who was the sweetest woman I ever met, left California after the divorce, and I didn't see her for twelve years. My father forbade me to see my mother. He did this because of my evil step-mother. I am telling you the truth; my stepmother had horns on her head. I spent the next five years of my life—until I left for col-lege—torturing Kathy [my stepmother]. I would call her a maid, our housekeeper, my father's prostitute, and a gold digger. I was ruthless, because she attempted after our first meeting to tell me that she was my new mother and I had to listen to her. I told Kathy I already had a mother; she said, "No, you don't; she is gone." I immediately hated that bitch. I now feel bad for my father. He tried to keep the peace between us all the time. Nothing worked because I was always after my stepmother's temper and getting her to blow up. Unfortunately, I usually was able to upset my stepmother and create a huge mess at home. I one time threw a tennis racket at her from the backyard and hit her. I knocked her out. My father never knew what happened. Everyone thought she fell down. Now Kathy and I barely talk to each other. My feelings from high school have never gone away. I still don't like her, and she doesn't like me. It is a shame. My father still tries to bridge over our conflict, but it is useless. On holidays I go to my father's and now I see my mother also. We wasted so much energy fighting with each other.

These two stories point to an underlying issue that often arises in the blending of families: setting boundaries. The burden of responsi-bility for making a new family blend and grow together starts with the biological parent and the new partner respecting the preexisting parent-child relationship. In other words, it is the new partner learning to respect the parent-child relationship and their history together. Herbert didn't personalize Stacy's provocative behavior. In fact, he went out of his way to avoid any conflict with Stacy. His actions allowed her to eventually come around to accepting her par-ents' divorce and her mother's remarriage to him.

Neither Stacy nor Matthew wanted to lose their relationship with their primary parent—the parent they lived with the majority of the time. In truth, Stacy didn't mind her stepfather; she was angry with her mother for forcing him into her life. Matthew had the same issue because his father forbade him from speaking to his biological mother and allowed Kathy to force herself into the middle of a very messy divorce. Matthew, a preteen at the time, was clearly grieving for the loss of the mother-son relationship with his biological mother. He was suddenly faced with a stranger, Kathy, telling him that she was the new mother in his life. Both of these blended family situations are common, toxic, and very avoidable.

The outcomes of the long-term relationships between Stacy and Herbert and Matthew and Kathy point to the truth about the slow and sensitive initial approach by the primary parent with the child and toward the new partner. Kathy's insistence on replacing Matthew's mother was a fatal mistake that is still being felt twenty-five years later. His father's insistence on setting up an unfair boundary—forbidding contact between Matthew and his mother—only exacerbated an already tense situation. In contrast, Stacy and Herbert today have a secure relationship and a healthy respect for each other. The early tension became a very strong bond between them. In this case, Herbert allowed Stacy to eventually come around and accept him. Herbert kept Stacy's mother out of their relationship, and it was a brilliant move.

DO'S AND DON'TS FOR BLENDING FAMILIES

The time spent trying to win over the children in developing a blended family is usually a wasted effort. Children, teenagers, and adult children are like cats. If you allow them to come to you, they will—in their own time, at their own pace and desire. When you allow your children to approach, accept, and emotionally join your expanding family, it works much better. *You can't force or pressure your children to be excited about the changes in your life. Just allow it to naturally evolve.* Your new partners must trust and be patient with the process of developing a loving relationship and building a new family. If the intentions of the adults involved (you and your new partner) are good and the motives genuine, the children involved will come to love and emotionally join their expanding family—but remember, it will take time. The list of do's and don'ts below will help you facilitate the process of growing, building, and having the kind of family that you have always wanted for you and your kids. Don't be attached to a timetable or to the "should" syndrome. There isn't a mandate or requirement about how your children or stepchildren must assimilate into your new blended family. Allow your children to follow your lead and they will.

- Don't criticize your ex-partner's new partner. Your children will know your unspoken feelings and judgment. It is important to not only watch what you say to your children about their new parental figure but also how you feel about it. Many times we communicate nonverbally our disapproval of something without saying a word.
- Practice taking time out periodically to ask your children how they feel about your new partner/new family/new children. Whatever anger or frustration your children might express initially, these feelings can change over time.
- Expect difficulty in combining two families. All families have their challenges. It is important to remain patient when the family is having a difficult moment.
- Don't *ever* give your negative opinion of your new partner's family and their changes to their children or your own children. Being neutral is always a positive position to maintain with all the members of your new and preexisting family.
- Always avoid confrontations with your ex in front of your new family and children.
- Your children want you in their lives. It is your responsibility to figure out how to do it.

- Your stepchildren need your support and understanding of their new relationship.
- Don't be the disciplinarian with your new partner's children. Take the position as the supporter for your partner with their children. It is always very important not to become the "doormat" for their children. These "parent-child" matters have to be worked out with you and your partner.
- When in doubt about your role, choose to respond, not to react.
- Your children live in two homes; you don't. Don't forget the effort it takes to do that. Traveling between two houses is never easy regardless of the close physical proximity.
- Remember that your ex-partner made up half of your children.
- You can't divorce your children. The same holds true for children. They can't divorce their parents. You are a family for life.
- Saying no sometimes is a very loving action.
- You can't be a best friend and a parent to your children at the same time.
- "Stepparent" and "stepchild" are legal terms, not emotional or family terms.
- Be patient when joining two preexisting families. Rome wasn't built in a day, and neither is a new family.
- You can't force your stepchildren to like you. Be yourself and be fair, and they will eventually come to appreciate and love you.
- Always discuss with your partner what each of you "expects" and wants with the new family. Unmet or unrealistic expectations can become a major source of conflict and strife with all the new family members.

SUMMARY

If you haven't already let go of your ex, there is nothing more I can say to make you let go of him or her and of all the attachments of that relationship. It is solely your decision and choice to move forward. It is that simple and clear: You either bury the hatchet or carry it to your grave. Obviously, our entire discussion is intended to illuminate the value of moving forward with your life and throwing away your "hatchet." Meeting a new partner and building a new family unit is valuable, meaningful, and healing. All of the discussions, growth points, emotional processing, and personal inventories of your emotional and psychological status, they all point to this moment: *of detachment and self-forgiveness.*

Couples who spend another three to five years fighting and attempting to separate by arguing (i.e., legal divorce proceedings, lawsuits against each other, prolonged child custody battles) are only postponing the inevitable. The only relationship roadblocks in your life are the ones you put there. You can go beyond all of the drama, disappointments, shattered dreams, and empty promises of your former relationship. Your future is yours to embrace. Let go of your anger, fear, and disappointment; your entire life hangs in the balance. Resolution with your past is the pathway to a more fulfilling future.

If you believe healing your broken heart is a waste of time, reread chapter 1 and this chapter. My office waiting room is full of divorced couples arguing—years after their breakup, separation, or divorce—about money, custody, real estate, holiday gatherings, and unresolved anger. *The fight can last as long as you want it to.* The only question you have to ask yourself is: *Am I done fighting with my ex-partner?* Your answer will determine the direction of your life. Consider the options. You can either continue damaging yourself or choose to heal. You can choose to have a new love life or choose to continue to be disappointed and sad. The choice is solely yours. I want to leave you with this classic quote about the power of making choices, which I recently heard on ESPN.

> *You were not born a winner, and you were not born a loser. You are what you make yourself to be.*
> —Lou Holtz

I completely agree with Lou Holtz's philosophy of life and our opportunity to make good choices. The last few pertinent questions you should ask yourself now are: *What choices have I made to make my romantic life a new reality?*

How do I want to view myself?

What choices am I avoiding?

What is the one thing I am the most fearful about regarding romantic relationships?

These are the kinds of questions that you should be asking yourself. Your future might seem very bleak today but it will change. Your persistence to resolve your ex-factor and move forward with the new changes that are necessary for a different outcome in your life are possible. Continue to choose the pathway of insight and understanding of your hopes, desires, and dreams. Those core feelings will always point you in the right direction and are an excellent compass for your journey forward.

Chapter 11

YOUR JOURNEY INTO YOUR NEW LIFE

I didn't believe this day would ever come. I didn't think I would ever—I mean ever—get married [again]. This is the scariest thing I have ever done or will do. I knew I needed to marry Steven and if I didn't, my life would be very lost and empty. Marriage doesn't scare me anymore.
—Anne, age thirty-three, married for the second time

The idea that the sun would shine again in my life was lost for me during my divorce. I didn't think the pain would ever stop. My heart felt like a piece of clay and lifeless. When I got over my divorce, I met Nancy. I can't believe I had the courage to marry her, and six years later, we are closer now than when we married.
—Tom, age fifty-six, father of two adult children, married for the second time

CHANGE IS CONSTANT

It is in the context of our intimate relationships that our entire life will be impacted, exposed, affected, changed, turned upside down, and healed. Intimate relationships are the "crucible" in

265

which every area of our adult life is touched, impacted, and influenced. There is no other kind or type of relationship setting that has the degree of emotional tension (both positive and negative), inherent energy, and potential to shape our lives than the intimate bond of love. Nothing else in your life—with the exception of a child—will cause you such a great amount of pain while potentially giving you the greatest fulfillment of love and acceptance. Your family shaped your personality from your childhood through your teenage years. Your adult intimate relationships are the continuation of your lifelong process of growing, evolving, and changing. Your life is always in the process of changing, discarding what is old and no longer useful and embracing what is new and better. It is a continuous process in which we all participate, willingly or not. And the most active arena of change in many adults' lives is that of intimate relationships.

We tend to forget that the process of love is never static—it is always evolving. *Regardless of your spiritual, religious, or psychological orientation, the truth is that change is a constant.* One of the foundational truths of applied physical science is that change is a constant factor and force in our universe.[1] It is for this very reason that it is tragic when we allow our heartbreak, disappointment, and despair to become an insurmountable roadblock to our current and future happiness. Emotional wounds, childhood traumas, unresolved parent-child issues, vindictive ex-partner(s), coparenting issues, stepchildren, and new partners make up the raw material of our overall transformation. Divorce, breakups, endings, and new relationships are all pieces of the ongoing changes in our lives. These highly charged events become the very learning tools for our greater overall development. It is for this reason alone that our intimate relationships, marriages, live-in lovers, and romantic partners are our future experiences of change.

Our romantic bonds become catalysts for changing our lives in ways we didn't even know we needed changing. Many times our deepest issues are as hard to see as the back of our head. Though we can't see it, we would know if the back of our head was missing. The analogy is we don't always fully understand our issues, fears, disappointments, or heartbreaks until we are fully confronted by the reality of the romantic situation. This could be a divorce summons, finding out your partner is having an affair, or being told your marriage is over. It is from these moments of painful awaking that we realize our heart and soul are broken. Then we just don't know how to reach these emotional wounds, clean them out, and heal the past for the good of our present and our future. The analogy of our head, our heart, and pain can be addressed in the context of our lost love. The keys to re-creating your romantic future are in your ability to maneuver through the maze of your heartbreak and despair.

Becoming more insightful at managing your own personal hell and moving toward a more peaceful place is a worthwhile task. When a relationship ends, it is understandable when we tend to react in a defensive psychological manner. We often become enraged, defensive, revengeful, and aggressive. It could be said that, symbolically, the back of our head has been blown off and our deepest wounds have been fully exposed by our former lover. We pick and choose, consciously or unconsciously, the people in our lives who understand, love, hurt, wound, and heal us. Unfortunately, it often isn't until our emotional pain and suffering exceed our comfort level that we make the necessary and significant changes in our lives. In this life, *pain is our greatest motivator for change and for the pursuit of happiness and fulfillment.* If you completely removed, avoided, or ignored all the emotional pain in your life, you would never consider changing or gain any personal insight or personal growth. It is simply impossible to avoid any and all degrees of emotional pain and discomfort. Emotional pain is the leverage that moves us toward change. Still, the residual unresolved issues that cause your great emotional pain from your past will always find a pathway into your present-day love relationships. When the old familiar issues of fear, anger, abandonment, and abuse appear, it is time to resolve them and move forward.

The part can never be well unless the whole is well.
—Plato

Plato was one of the greatest philosophers in human history. He knew that we need to heal our emotional wounds before we can become fully healed. Plato lived thousands of years ago, yet this truth is as relevant today as it was in his lifetime. Your divorce or breakup is a valuable opportunity for you to bring about change that will help you achieve deeper intimacy, stronger attachments, and more fulfilling relationships. If you choose to mend, restore, and rebuild your inner self, your intimate relationships will reflect these changes.[2] The whole of your life can't be fully functional and healthy without the sum of the parts being healed and repaired.

Plato encourages us thousands of years later to address all the parts of our lives and to not ignore those that are wounded. Two of the pieces of your life that you can actively heal and restore are your love life and your personal belief system. The six faces of love discussed in chapter 5 are among the primary building blocks that will help you move beyond your tragic breakup and resulting sense of betrayal. The six faces of love are designed to create new insight and expand your capacity to experience love, empathy, understanding, acceptance, and forgiving/detachment. These six aspects of self-love will enable you to change your perspective and open up your heart to a new intimate bond.

*The most powerful agent of growth and transformation
is something much more basic than any technique:
A change of Heart.*
—John Welwood, author

All of the changes in your love life must come from within you. Your rebuilding a new romantic relationship—a symbolic new home—hinges on your ability to make the necessary changes. The things you desire in life can all transpire from your ability to do a few things differently and understand them more fully. The following list of the six faces of love is designed to help change your heart, romantic approach, and belief system in your intimate life. *Internal changes are the most powerful changes that any woman or man will ever make in his or her adult life. A change of heart is changing the control center of your entire life: your belief system.* How you view yourself, your love life, and the greater world is always amenable to change. Regardless of how sad, depressed, or despairing you might feel about your ability to change your heart and the course of your life, it is always possible. Changing your heart is worthwhile work that will stand the test of time. In reviewing the essentials for change, remember the following:

- *Believe you deserve more.* Your intimate relationships start and end with your subconscious beliefs and choices. Your expanded understanding of your past parent-child relationship and those types of childhood issues are the keys to allowing your hidden desires to surface and become reality. Allowing your sincere desires and wishes to become conscious is instrumental to bringing about the life you want and deserve.
- *Expand your emotional comfort zone.* You can allow someone to become attached/bonded to you, and you can do the same. Making your emotional attachments to be more secure and fluid enables your comfort zone to expand and grow. The more you understand your personal need for the acts and gestures of love, the more you can allow someone to become close to you.
- *Rebuilding trust* starts with trusting you and the more-informed choices you make. Understanding your old patterns of love and intimacy allows you to trust yourself in making different choices. Trusting a new partner begins with developing a secure and stable type of emotional bond and attachment. This is especially a challenge when you have been betrayed in the past by an affair or chronic infidelity. Trust can always be developed by you for your romantic connections.

- *Stop blaming.* You are solely responsible for your past, present, and future. Your ex-partner isn't the reason for your continuing to be a victim rather than an active participant in your present and future. Your unresolved issues around intimacy predate your ex, and they are yours to face. Your relationship story belongs to you and only you. Your ex might be a major player, but you own the team. You control how little or how much your past relationships will continue to impact your life. It's your choice. Blaming is avoiding your responsibility and action taken or avoided in the marriage or love relationship.

- *No more self-defeating choices.* Your capacity for love starts with new choices for intimacy and emotional connection. You know what type of personality, attitude, and relationship behavior are and are not good for your future. Self-acceptance, self-forgiveness, and personal responsibility are the elements necessary for changing old patterns of self-loathing and self-defeating behavior.

- *Let go of the ex.* Your life starts to move forward with less impairment, tension, and fear once you've removed your emotional hook from your ex-partner. You are the only one who can detach yourself from your pain, depression, and despair. This phase is necessary for any of the other five to occur so you can become an active part of your life. Focusing on your ex-partner can be a convenient way to avoid having to move forward with your love life. You can make your ex-partner the very reason (legitimate or not) for never trusting or loving again, but don't do it. You don't want that to be your romantic story or love relationship legacy. Your life doesn't have to stop evolving because your intimate relationship status has changed or ended abruptly.

These six faces of love all come together through different applications to redesign your love life and to heal your ex-factor. There is a truism in psychology: *There is no substitute for action.* Insight, understanding, and rethinking your prior choices of partners are important, but only if they lead to new action. Your love life is all about building a new life and taking action. Your future hinges on your ability to take new action and to be emotionally clear about your motivations and intentions. One of the critical areas in which your new perspective will be apparent is in how you approach the meeting and selection of a new partner, and the development of a new love relationship.

One of the ways to change how you see love is expanding your capacity and tolerance for being loved. Many adults complain to me that they feel very uncomfortable with their new partners loving affection, empathy, and secure emotional bonding. These new loving gestures feel very foreign and unfamiliar to many adults recovering from their ex-factor. Developing a wider spectrum of accepting a new partner is never limited to anyone's past or chronic failures. *Regardless of your sexual orientation, love is love, relationships are relationships, and everyone has the same challenges.* Don't allow arbitrary social restrictions to hold you back from pursuing your romantic intentions and desires. Your acceptance of empathy and compassion from your significant other is evidence that your capacity for love is expanding. If you want a different outcome in your love life, you no longer have the luxury of rejecting a worthy sender of love to you. As we have discussed before, many times it seems much easier to reject a new love rather than allowing your heart to be vulnerable again. Your ex-partner's lack of interest in you, loss of love, abuse in all forms, infidelity, rejection, and/or a spiteful divorce/breakup were devastating and heartbreaking for you. These types of disappointments often cause us to narrow our emotional comfort zone to a point of isolation. It is important that we not allow our past to dictate our present and future choices.

It is worth remembering that your goal of creating a new life will require you to go beyond your old comfort zone and your old style of attachment. You will need to let go of your anger so you can begin taking the practical steps necessary to redesign and rebuild your life from the inside out. We have discussed that the first step to building your new house begins with being able to see it, believe it, and allow it to happen. The old feelings of rejection, shame, anger, abandonment, and fear that you aren't lovable are all subject to change. The six faces of love directly address the need for you to expand and further develop your personal foundation of intimacy. Your fears of getting hurt will only hold you captive to a very solitary and lonely life of emotional seclusion.

> *To truly understand, all men must be willing to psy-chologically die in order to live.*
> —George Morales, personal friend of mine

THE NEAR-DEATH EXPERIENCE

The actual process of your transformation was discussed and explored in chapter 1; this is the foundation of your ex-factor recovery. People going through a relationship loss know that nothing quite compares to those feelings of devastation and despair. Your life seems to go on hold while you are engaged in a war with the person you used to sleep next to every night. *The paradigm shift from love to detachment to a new life can feel like a journey of a million miles.* The problem is, you may feel like you are crawling on your knees on the road to despair at mile one. Your life may look like a bomb was dropped into the middle of your emotional home, and you never saw it coming. What is even worse is that you didn't believe it would ever happen—and it did. No one is ever prepared—emotionally or mentally—for all the changes and challenges that come with a divorce or breakup.

The five stages of recovery from a divorce/relationship ending launched you on the path to your personal revolution. These phases and experiences of piecing your life back together encompass all the different aspects of love, attachment, healing, and personal responsibility, blended families, self-accept, and giving and receiving empathy. It is a complicated process to re-create your life but worth every ounce of effort you put into it. All the different elements of your inner life, parent-child relationship, your parents' marriage, your prior love life, your children, and the thousand other factors that make up your life are all connected to your ex-factor. There is nothing in your life currently that isn't impacted by your life-changing transition and renovation.

The five stages can all occur at the same time or they can happen sequentially. The stages can even keep occurring for years after the initial relationship ends. The average divorce disillusionment in the state of California takes approximately three full years (thirty-six to thirty-eight months) to be completely resolved from the day of the first court filing.[3] It isn't unusual for a residual wave of anger and resentment to impact your life for many years. Your healing and recovery is a continuous, ongoing process. To reiterate, the five stages of recovery from a divorce or breakup are:

- *Whiplash*—"What in the hell just happened? My life is over."
- *Denial*—"I just never thought it would happen. We can work this out, things aren't that bad."
- *Anger*—This stage usually replaces the first two with the force of a Category 5 hurricane.
- *Resolution*—This is where the emotional tension has dramatically dropped. Your life is beginning to feel a new sense of normalcy and stability. The fight is over.
- *Hope, Insight, and Creativity*—You are feeling psychologically, mentally, physically, and emotionally empowered with hope and love.

Many times, the first step in developing insight, resolving your divorce, and mending your heartbreak is to admit that the death-rebirth process has happened. Your journey out of the valley of despair is more than a theory or a nice concept to think about. Your entire life is an ongoing series of deaths and rebirths. One of the quickest ways to move through this very powerful process is to understand your need to detach from your emotional pain, from your ex-partner, and from your old emotional behavior. Being able to detach yourself from your old baggage is imperative if you are going to find your way out of your valley of despair and panic. A sense of resolution and hope will always accompany your ability to detach, as you remain in a neutral, nonblaming state toward your ex and overall life. Detachment is symbolic of pouring water on a raging fire; it might not completely extinguish the fire in your soul, but it will cool it down and reduce the tension and drama. All aspects of your life will benefit from a reduction in your feelings of anger, hatred, or blame. Common sense will always dictate that reducing any degree of anger or tension in your life toward your significant other (past, present, or future) is prudent and wise.

THE SUN DOES SHINE AGAIN

Tom and Anne

In the brief anecdotes at the beginning of this chapter, Anne and Tom acknowledged their surprise, pleasure, and happiness at being able to re-create and rebuild their romantic lives and their futures. These two adults lived through the five stages and didn't believe that they would ever survive their debilitating disappointment and despair. They both spent most of their emotional rebuilding period in the anger stage, blaming their exes for all their problems and misfortunes. It wasn't until they stopped pointing the finger at their exes that their lives started to change and become more like what they wanted. Anne allowed herself to see that there was another side to her divorce. She knew that if she remained bitter, she would miss out on the best man she had ever met. For Anne, marrying Tim took more courage than her first marriage did because she was terrified of repeating the cycle of disappointment and despair. Anne had worked at resolving her mother-daughter issues and her need to always be "right" in her romantic relationships. Tim and Anne have been happily married for almost two years.

Tom's divorce was a shattering, life-changing experience. He lost his job, his daughter went to live with his ex-wife, and he had to fight to keep his ex from moving out of the country with her. Tom grieved over the loss of his family dream of bliss and happiness. Much like life itself, Tom realized that the process of marriage and love is always changing and creating new opportunities for growth and expansion. Since his marriage to Nancy, Tom has created a secure emotional bond with his wife. They have a very strong and very close emotional attachment with each other. Tom knew that if he allowed himself to work through all the stages of his ex-factor (see chapter 1), he would prevail and see his life become better than he ever expected or imagined. The most difficult part for Tom was the sadness and disappointment of losing his child and his hope for a happy home. Ironically, Tom now has a better relationship with his daughter, with his ex-wife, and with himself than ever before.

> *The greatest revolution in our generation is that of human beings, who by changing the inner attitudes of their minds, can change the outer aspects of their lives.*
>
> —Marilyn Ferguson, psychologist

CONCLUSION

An Ongoing Process

The most telling ongoing aspect of your ex-factor reconstruction process, project, and desire is your ability to refrain from entering into the familiar war or the old emotional fight with your ex-partner.

The argument might be tempting, providing a chance to get even with a great sarcastic dig. But acting aggressively toward your ex-partner in any way is always a lose-lose situation for you. This is a particularly important task when you have children with your former partner. Your children are 50 percent from your ex-partner. All of our discussions about detachment directly benefit your children; they should not witness you bashing your ex-partner. Detachment implies not getting into a verbal sparring match with your ex-partner when your children are within hearing distance. In my professional experience, this is one of the biggest issues and a pervasive problem among ex-partners with children.

Detachment Is Self-Acceptance

Your Ongoing Goal: This is the expanded version of how detachment can ultimately lead you to self-forgiveness, self-acceptance, personal responsibility, and emotionally letting "go" of your ex-partner and all your romantic history. It is always a process of gaining increasing amounts of emotional insight as you move forward in your future. Your ability to expand and tolerate more affection, love, and acceptance all starts with your ability to remain detached from old habits, old relationship patterns, and outdated beliefs about yourself.

The New Home

We have discussed at great length the goal of symbolically finding, designing, and building the home/the relationship of your dreams. That emotional home is the loving relationship that is or will be in your life. There is nothing in your adult life that will measure up to the importance of a loving, supportive intimate relationship. The most important relationship—outside of the one with yourself—is your intimate connection and attachment. Your parent-child relationship set the stage for your romantic relationships, and you set the stage for how your life will evolve from this point forward. You have all the tools, insight, courage, and priceless experience gained through your emotional pain to create the romantic story you want and deserve. *It isn't a lack of available partners or eligible lovers that holds you back—it is you.* You control who will or will not come into your intimate life. Take your foot off the brake and allow yourself the chance to move forward. You have enough information, experience, and directions to build and design any type of emotional home relationship you want. What will your new home look like and who is living in it with you? Your new home will be a reflection of all the things you want and desire.

I know from watching my parents, my friends, and my clients struggle with their relationships—and from my own heartbreak—that the dynamics of love between two adults is a life-changing experience. There are very few things that will move you to tears or joy like a past or new lover. No one is prepared for the surprises, gifts, excitement, fulfillment, and agony that come into your life in the name of love. It is our natural quest to pursue a loving, secure, and safe bond that gets us moving out of the valley of despair. *Love will always be the motivation that gets us to pick ourselves up out of despair and replace it with hope.* Developing hope, compassion, and love is the greatest formula for a successful and powerful life. Now that you have the tools to transform your life, the power is in your hands to bring about the future you desire and deserve.

I want to personally thank you for taking the time to read this book. I know it will transform your entire life and that of everyone in your world.

> *Create an act of power and forgive yourself for everything you have done in your whole life. Then accept everything you are going to do in this life. Forgiveness and self-acceptance is the only way to heal your emotional wounds.*
>
> Miguel Ruiz

ENDNOTES

CHAPTER 1

1. "Special Report: America by the Numbers," *Time*, November 26, 2007, pp. 38–44.

2. Ibid.

3. David Richo, *When the Past Is Present: Healing the Emotional Wounds That Sabotage Our Relationships* (Boston: Shambhala, 2008), pp. 2–7.

4. Judith S. Wallerstein and Sandra Blakeslee, *Second Chances: Men, Women, and Children a Decade after Divorce* (Boston: Houghton Mifflin, 1996), pp. 3–6, 277–80.

5. Jeannette Lofas, *Family Rules: Helping Stepfamilies and Single Parents Build Happy Homes* (New York: Kensington Books, 1998), pp. 13–22.

CHAPTER 2

1. American Psychiatric Association, "Life Stressors," in *Diagnostic Statistical Manual of Mental Disorders*, 4th ed. (Washington, DC: American Psychiatric Association, 1995), pp. 25–31.

2. Judith S. Wallerstein and Sandra Blakeslee, *Second Chances: Men, Women, and Children a Decade after Divorce* (Boston: Houghton Mifflin, 1996), pp. 21–28.

CHAPTER 3

1. Leslie Bennetts, "The Truth about American Marriages," *Parade*, September 21, 2008, pp. 3–6.

2. Harville Hendrix, *Getting the Love You Want: A Guide for Couples* (New York: Owl Books, 2001), pp. 3–15.

3. American Psychiatric Association, "Personality Disorders," in *Diagnostic Statistical Manual of Mental Disorders*, 4th ed. (Washington, DC: American Psychiatric Association, 1995), pp. 629–74.

CHAPTER 4

1. Harriet Goldhor Lerner, *The Dance of Anger: A Woman's Guide to Changing the Patterns of Intimate Relationships* (New York: Harper & Row, 1986), pp. 1–5.

2. Leslie Bennetts, "The Truth about American Marriages," *Parade*, September 21, 2008, pp. 3–6.

3. Ibid.

4. Gerald G. Jampolsky and Diane V. Cirincione, *Love Is the Answer: Creating Positive Relationships* (New York: Bantam Books, 1991), pp. 3–9.

4. John E. Sarno, *The Mindbody Prescription: Healing the Body, Healing the Pain* (New York: Warner Books, 1998), pp. 127–38.

6. Fred Luskin, *Forgive for Love: The Missing Ingredient for a Healthy and Lasting Relationship* (New York: HarperOne, 2008), pp. 51–78.

7. Lerner, *The Dance of Anger*, pp. 24–40.

CHAPTER 5

1. Mark Bryan, *Codes of Love: How to Rethink Your Family and Remake Your Life* (New York: Pocket Books, 1999), pp. 5–25.

2. M. Scott Peck, *The Road Less Traveled: A New Psychology of Love, Traditional Values and Spiritual Growth* (New York: Simon & Schuster, 1980), pp. 15–18.

3. American Psychiatric Association, "Psychotic Disorders," in *Diagnostic and Statistical Manual of Mental Disorders (DSM-IV-R)* (Washington, DC: American Psychiatric Association, 1995), p. 273.

4. Miguel Ruiz, *The Mastery of Love: A Practical Guide to the Art of Relationship* (San Rafael, CA: Amber-Allen, 1999), pp. 18.

CHAPTER 6

1. Salvador Minuchin, *Families & Family Therapy* (Cambridge, MA: Harvard University Press, 1974), pp. 28–52.

2. Murray Bowen, *The Family Life Cycle* (New York: Gardner, 1988), pp. 18–45.

3. Stephan B. Poulter, *The Mother Factor: How Your Mother's Emotional Legacy Impacts Your Life* (Amherst, NY: Prometheus Books, 2008), pp. 19–49.

4. W. Robert Beavers, *Psychotherapy and Growth: A Family Systems Perspective* (New York: Brunner/Mazel, 1977), pp. 58–78.

5. Stephan B. Poulter, *The Father Factor: How Your Father's Legacy Impacts Your Career* (Amherst, NY: Prometheus Books, 2006), pp. 20–39.

CHAPTER 7

1. Phillip C. McGraw, *Life Strategies: Doing What Works, Doing What Matters* (New York: Hyperion, 1999), pp. 56–87.

2. M. F. Mahler, *The Psychological Birth of the Human Infant* (New York: Basic Books, 1975), pp. 22–36.

3. T. Berry Brazelton, *Working & Caring* (Reading, MA: Addison-Wesley, 1992), pp. 24–38.

4. Mary Ainsworth, *Effects on Infant-Mother Attachment: Attachment across the Life Cycle* (London: Routledge, 1991), pp. 38–62.

5. Eve A. Wood, *There's Always Help, There's Always Hope: An Award-Winning Psychiatrist Shows You How to Heal Your Body, Mind, and Spirit* (Carlsbad, CA: Hay House, 2004), pp. 167–89.

6. John Gray, *Mars and Venus in the Bedroom: A Guide to Lasting Romance and Passion* (New York: HarperCollins, 1995), pp. 23–34.

7. William Pollack, *Real Boys: Rescuing Our Sons from the Myths of Boyhood* (New York: Owl Books, 1999), pp. 3–19.

8. Stephan B. Poulter, *Father Your Son: Becoming the Father You've Always Wanted to Be* (New York: McGraw-Hill, 2004), pp. 2–15.

9. Mark Bryan, *Codes of Love: How to Rethink Your Family and Remake Your Life* (New York: Pocket Books, 1999), pp. 28–53.

CHAPTER 8

1. John Bowlby, *A Secure Base: Parent-Child Attachment and Healthy Human Development* (New York: Basic Books, 1988), pp. 56–78.

2. Patricia Allen and Sandra Harmon, *Getting to "I Do": The Secret to Doing Relationships Right* (New York: HarperCollins, 2002), pp. 21–29.

3. Murray Bowen, *The Use of Family Theory in Clinical Practice* (Northvale, NJ: Jason Aronson Books, 1988), pp. 122–34.

4. American Psychiatric Association, "Narcissistic Personality Disorder," in *Diagnostic and Statistical Manual of Mental Disorders*, 4th ed. (Washington, DC: American Psychiatric Association, 1995), p. 629.

5. Stephan B. Poulter, *The Mother Factor: How Your Mother's Emotional Legacy Impacts Your Life* (Amherst, NY: Prometheus Books, 2008), pp. 305–31.

CHAPTER 9

1. Samuel Slipp, *Object Relations: A Dynamic Bridge between Individual and Family Treatment* (Northvale, NJ: Jason Aronson Books, 1992), pp. 24–44.

CHAPTER 10

1. Miguel Ruiz, *The Voice of Knowledge: A Practical Guide to Inner Peace* (San Rafael, CA: Amber-Allen, 2004), pp. 178–80.

2. M. Scott Peck, *The Road Less Traveled: A New Psychology of Love, Traditional Values and Spiritual Growth* (New York: Simon & Schuster, 1980), pp. 15–17.

3. Ibid., pp. 181–84.

4. Helen Schucman, *A Course in Miracles*, 2nd ed. (Mill Valley, CA: New Age Publishers, 1992), pp. 4–6.

5. US Census Bureau, *Summary of Findings of Blended Families* 2004. Introduction.

6. Miguel Ruiz, *The Mastery of Love: A Practical Guide to the Art of Relationship* (San Rafael, CA: Amber-Allen, 1999), p. 71.

CHAPTER 11

1. Deepak Chopra, *The Seven Spiritual Laws of Success* (San Rafael, CA: Amber-Allen, 1994). Newton's law of constant change (pg. 7).

2. David Richo, *When the Past Is Present: Healing the Emotional Wounds That Sabotage Our Relationships* (Boston: Shambhala, 2008), pp. 160–71.

3. *L.A. Magazine*, January 2008. The Los Angeles Bar association says average divorce takes three years (pg. 8).

BIBLIOGRAPHY

Ainsworth, Mary. *Effects on Infant-Mother Attachment: Attachment across the Life Cycle*. London: Routledge, 1991.

Allen, Patricia, and Sandra Harmon. *Getting to "I Do": The Secret to Doing Relationships Right*. New York: Quill, 2002.

American Psychiatric Association. *Diagnostic and Statistical Manual of Mental Disorders*, 4th ed. Washington, DC: American Psychiatric Association, 1995.

Beavers, W. Robert. *Psychotherapy and Growth: A Family Systems Perspective*. New York: Brunner/Mazel, 1977.

Bourne, Edmund J. *The Anxiety & Phobia Workbook*, 4th ed. Oakland, CA: New Harbinger, 2005.

Bourne, Edmund J., Arlen Brownstein, and Lorna Garano. *Natural Relief for Anxiety*. Oakland, CA: New Harbinger, 2004.

Bowen, Murray. *The Family Life Cycle*. New York: Gardner, 1988.

———. *The Use of Family Theory in Clinical Practice*. Northvale, NJ: Jason Aronson Books, 1988.

Bowlby, John. *A Secure Base: Parent-Child Attachment and Healthy Human Development*. New York: Basic Books, 1988.

Brazelton, T. Berry. *Working & Caring*. Reading, MA: Addison-Wesley, 1992.

Brown, Byron. *Soul without Shame: A Guide to Liberating Yourself from the Judge Within*. Boston: Shambhala, 1999.

Bryan, Mark. *Codes of Love: How to Rethink Your Family and Remake Your Life*. New York: Pocket Books, 1999.

Byrne, Rhonda. *The Secret*. New York: Beyond Words, 2006.

Chapman, Gary. *The Five Love Languages: How to Express Heartfelt Commitment to Your Mate*. Chicago: Northfield, 2004.

Dacey, John S., and Lisa B. Fiore. *Your Anxious Child: How Parents & Teachers Can Relieve Anxiety in Children*. San Francisco: Jossey-Bass, 2002.

Davidson, Jonathan, and Henry Dreher. *The Anxiety Book: Developing Strength in the Face of Fear*. New York: Riverhead Books, 2003.

Dyer, Wayne W. *The Power of Intention: Learning to Co-create Your World Your Way.* Carlsbad, CA: Hay House, 2004.

Eliot, John. *Overachievement: The New Model for Exceptional Performance.* New York: Penguin, 2004.

Estes, Clarissa P. *Women Who Run with the Wolves.* New York: Random House, 1992.

Freedman, Rory, and Kim Barnouin. *Skinny Bitch: A No-Nonsense, Tough-Love Guide for Savvy Girls Who Want to Stop Eating Crap and Start Looking Fabulous!* Philadelphia: Running Press, 2005.

Gottman, John. *Raising an Emotionally Intelligent Child.* New York: Simon & Schuster, 1997.

Gray, John. *Mars and Venus in the Bedroom: A Guide to Lasting Romance and Passion.* New York: HarperCollins, 1995.

Grotke, Abigail. *Miss Abigail's Guide to Dating, Mating & Marriage: Classic Advice for Contemporary Dilemmas.* New York: Thunder's Mouth Press, 2006.

Harrison, Harry H., Jr. *Father to Daughter: Life Lessons on Raising a Girl.* New York: Workman Publishing, 2003.

Hart, Archibald D. *Children & Divorce: What to Expect, How to Help.* Waco, TX: Word Books, 1982.

Hay, Louise L. *Heart Thoughts: A Treasury of Inner Wisdom.* Carlsbad, CA: Hay House, 1990.

Helgoe, Laurie A., Laura R. Wilhelm, and Martin J. Kommor. *Anxiety Answer Book.* Naperville, IL: Sourcebooks, 2005.

Hendrix, Harville. *Getting the Love You Want: A Guide for Couples.* New York: Owl Books, 2001.

Hetherington, E. Mavis, and John Kelly. *For Better or for Worse: Divorce Reconsidered.* New York: Norton, 2003.

hooks, bell. *All about Love: New Visions.* New York: Harper Perennial, 2001.

Jampolsky, Gerald G., and Diane V. Cirincione. *Love Is the Answer: Creating Positive Relationships.* New York: Bantam Books, 1991.

Jordan, Marian. *Sex and the City Uncovered: Exposing the Emptiness and Healing the Hurt.* Nashville, TN: B&H Books, 2007.

Kelly, Joe. *Dads and Daughters: How to Inspire, Understand, and Support Your Daughter.* New York: Broadway Books, 2005.

Kindlon, Dan. *Too Much of a Good Thing: Raising Children of Character in an Indulgent Age.* New York: Hyperion, 2001.

Kushner, Harold S. *When Bad Things Happen to Good People*. New York: Schocken Books, 1981.

Lerner, Harriet Goldhor. *The Dance of Anger: A Woman's Guide to Changing the Patterns of Intimate Relationships*. New York: Harper & Row, 1989.

Levine, Mel. *Ready or Not, Here Life Comes*. New York: Simon & Schuster, 2005.

Lofas, Jeannette. *Family Rules: Helping Stepfamilies and Single Parents Build Happy Homes*. New York: Kensington Books, 1998.

Lofas, Jeannette, and Dawn B. Sova. *Stepparenting: The Family Challenge of the Nineties*. New York: Kensington Books, 1985.

Luskin, Fred. *Forgive for Love: The Missing Ingredient for a Healthy and Lasting Relationship*. New York: HarperOne, 2007.

MacKenzie, Robert J. *Setting Limits: How to Raise Responsible, Independent Children by Providing Reasonable Boundaries*. Rocklin, CA: Prima, 1993.

Magids, Debbie, and Nancy Peske. *All the Good Ones AREN'T Taken: Change the Way You Date and Find Lasting Love*. New York: St. Martin's, 2006.

Mahler, M. F. *The Psychological Birth of the Human Infant*. New York: Basic Books, 1975.

Maxwell, John C. *Winning with People: Discover the People Principles That Work for You Every Time*. Nashville, TN: Nelson Books, 2004.

McGraw, Phillip C. *Life Strategies: Doing What Works, Doing What Matters*. New York: Hyperion, 1999.

Minuchin, Salvador. *Families & Family Therapy*. Cambridge, MA: Harvard University Press, 1974.

Mittenthal, Sue. *Still Hot: The Uncensored Guide to Divorce, Dating, Sex, Spite and Happily Ever After*. Philadelphia: Running Press, 2008.

Moore, John D. *Confusing Love with Obsession*, 3rd ed. Center City, MN: Hazelden, 2006.

Osherson, Samuel. *Wrestling with Love: How Men Struggle with Intimacy, with Women, Children, Parents, and Each Other*. New York: Random House, 1992.

Peck, M. Scott. *The Road Less Traveled: A New Psychology of Love, Traditional Values and Spiritual Growth*. New York: Simon & Schuster, 1980.

Peurifoy, Reneau Z. *Overcoming Anxiety: From Short-Term Fixes to Long-Term Recovery*. New York: Henry Holt, 1997.

Pollack, William. *Real Boys: Rescuing Our Sons from the Myths of Boyhood*. New York: Owl Books, 1999.

Poulter, Stephan B. *The Father Factor: How Your Father's Legacy Impacts Your Career*. Amherst, NY: Prometheus Books, 2006.

———. *Father Your Son: Becoming the Father You've Always Wanted to Be*. New York: McGraw-Hill, 2004.

———. *The Mother Factor: How Your Mother's Emotional Legacy Impacts Your Life*. Amherst, NY: Prometheus Books, 2008.

Poulter, Stephan B., and Barbara Zax. *Mending the Broken Bough: Restoring the Promise of the Mother-Daughter Relationship*. New York: Berkley Books, 1998.

Real, T. *I Don't Want to Talk about It: Overcoming the Secret Legacy of Male Depression*. New York: Scribner, 1997.

Richo, David. *When the Past Is Present: Healing the Emotional Wounds That Sabotage Our Relationships*. Boston: Shambhala, 2008.

Roth, Geneen. *Feeding the Hungry Heart: The Experience of Emotional Eating*. New York: Macmillan, 2002.

Ruiz, Miguel. *The Mastery of Love: A Practical Guide to the Art of Relationship*. San Rafael, CA: Amber-Allen, 1999.

———. *The Voice of Knowledge: A Practical Guide to Inner Peace*. San Rafael, CA: Amber-Allen, 2004.

Sarno, John E. *The Mindbody Prescription: Healing the Body, Healing the Pain*. New York: Warner Books, 1998.

Shaffer, Susan M., and Linda P. Gordon. *Why Girls Talk and What They're Really Saying: A Parent's Survival Guide to Connecting with Your Teen*. New York: McGraw-Hill, 2005.

Slipp, Samuel. *Object Relations: A Dynamic Bridge between Individual and Family Treatment*. Northvale, NJ: Jason Aronson Books, 1992.

Spindel, Janis. *How to Date Men: Dating Secrets from America's Top Matchmakers*. New York: Penguin, 2007.

Spring, Janis Abrahms. *After the Affair: Healing the Pain and Rebuilding Trust When a Partner Has Been Unfaithful*. New York: HarperCollins, 1996.

Steadman, Lisa. *It's a Breakup Not a Breakdown: Get Over the Big One and Change Your Life*. Avon, MA: Polka Dot Press, 2007.

Thomas, Katherine Woodward. *Calling in "the One": 7 Weeks to Attract the Love of Your Life*. New York: Three Rivers, 2004.

Twerski, Abraham J. *Addictive Thinking: Understanding Self-Deception*, 2nd ed. Center City, MN: Hazelden, 1999.

Wallerstein, Judith, and Sandra Blakeslee. *The Good Marriage: How and Why Love Lasts*. Boston: Houghton Mifflin, 1984.

———. *Second Chances: Men, Women, and Children a Decade after Divorce*. Boston: Houghton Mifflin, 1996.

Walsch, Neale Donald. *Tomorrow's God: Our Greatest Spiritual Challenge*. New York: Atria Books, 2004.

Weiss, Brian L. *Same Soul, Many Bodies: Discover the Healing Power of Future Lives through Progression Therapy*. New York: Free Press, 2004.

Wood, Eve. *There's Always Help, There's Always Hope: An Award-Winning Psychiatrist Shows You How to Heal Your Body, Mind, and Spirit*. Carlsbad, CA: Hay House, 2004.

Zieghan, Suzen J. *The Stepparent's Survival Guide: A Workbook for Creating a Happy Blended Family*. Oakland, CA: New Harbinger, 2002.

INDEX